DEFINING RELEVANCY

DEFINING RELEVANCY

Managing the New Academic Library

Edited by Janet McNeil Hurlbert

LIBRARIES UNLIMITED LIBRARY MANAGEMENT COLLECTION

Gerard B. McCabe, Series Editor

LIBRARIES
U N L I M I T E D
A Member of the Greenwood Publishing Group

Westport, Connecticut • London

Library of Congress Cataloging-in-Publication Data

Defining relevancy : managing the new academic library / edited by
Janet McNeil Hurlbert.
     p. cm. — (Libraries Unlimited library management collection,
ISSN 1557–0320)
  Includes bibliographical references and index.
  ISBN 978–1–59158–419–3 (alk. paper)
  1. Academic libraries—Administration. 2. Academic libraries—United
States. I. Hurlbert, Janet McNeil.
  Z675.U5D368 2008
  025.1'977—dc22   2007039210

British Library Cataloguing in Publication Data is available.

Library of Congress Catalog Card Number: 2007039210
ISBN: 978–1–59158–419–3
ISSN: 1557–0320

First published in 2008

Libraries Unlimited, 88 Post Road West, Westport, CT 06881
A Member of the Greenwood Publishing Group, Inc.
www.lu.com

Printed in the United States of America

The paper used in this book complies with the
Permanent Paper Standard issued by the National
Information Standards Organization (Z39.48–1984).

10 9 8 7 6 5 4 3 2 1

CONTENTS

III. Collaboration for Learning: Managing Information Literacy

IV. Promoting the Library: Competition and Collaboration

V. Integration of Staff, Services, and Assessment: What Is Needed? How Will We Know? Who Will Do It?

CONTENTS

VI. Connections for College Archives: Taking on New Missions

VII. Issues and Challenges for the Future: A Bibliographic Essay

INTRODUCTION

Janet McNeil Hurlbert

Connection. Competition. Collaboration. These three words define management of college libraries today and in the future. They also describe the contents of the chapters in this book, which focus on planning for the multiple directions that must be considered and effectively acted on by college library managers.

Academic libraries, especially in a smaller college setting, changed little over the decades. The early history of American college libraries tells us that in 1876 the most pressing issue was whether students should have access to the shelves (Holley 1977, 15). For many years the answer to usage problems within the library emphasized organization—cataloging and classification. Providing persons assistance was seen as impractical by the profession (McElderry 1977, 62) and unneeded if you could just get the arrangement right. Humorous as these observations may be now, it really has not been so long since technical services staff outnumbered public services; the fundamental purpose of library instruction was designed to tell 30 (or more) students something at the same time rather than individually at the reference desk; the chief features of new buildings emphasized housing the ever-increasing collection; and college libraries felt totally secure in their role on campus. As technology became a central focus for libraries, it was specialized technology—reserved for providing or processing research information. The pace was increasingly frantic and consuming. Librarians at smaller colleges bemoaned that they couldn't afford more technology, but their role was still secure.

With the full incorporation of the Web on college campuses and in the daily lives of our students, suddenly whether students had open access to the shelves or to the most recent issue of a particularly popular periodical was no longer a quandary. Despite the information literacy movement that is tied very closely to the curriculum (or should be), we find ourselves in a world where we, as managers, can go many days without feeling that we are educators. We have had to take on new roles and concerns that resemble the business world, and we have begun to think like our public library counterparts who, for years, have had to adopt business models if they wished to be successful within their communities.

O'Connor (2007) discusses the characteristics of the new library manager. He asserts that we will need to plan for futures that we may not completely understand, serving and working with people who are very unlike us in outlooks and habits. The managers of today and the future must be effective in gathering evidence and making informed judgments. "They will have to work confidently with uncertainty" (16).

The Association of College and Research Libraries issued a report on the top 10 assumptions that will have a significant impact on library planning for the next 10 years (Mullins, Allen, and Hufford 2007, 240). While some of these assumptions acknowledge the logical extensions of much of what we have always done by emphasizing changing materials formats, intellectual property rights, and privacy issues, they also highlight the growing business nature of the institutions we serve. The sensible conclusion on our part is that we, too, must run more of a business operation, especially since another assumption is that "students will increasingly view themselves as customers and consumers" (Mullines et al. 2007, 241). The corporate model is very much a part of an Online Computer Library Center (OCLC) study on college libraries in which the question is asked, "What is the 'Library' brand?" (2006, 6-5), and the report concludes with a call for rejuvenation.

Competition is a major concern in the business world and in ours as well. The good news about our "customers" is that college students use libraries more than the average population (OCLC 2006, 6-5). The bad news is that it is no longer the first place they look for information, and they are a confident lot. For example, surveys administered at my small college used to show incoming freshmen overwhelmed by our 180,000-volume library. Now confidence abounds because of search engines and Web sites that students have used in high school research. Even with faculty dedicated to undergraduate teaching, librarians compete as we try to push our information literacy agenda amidst the other across-the-curriculum programs in writing, speaking, critical thinking, and technology. There is only so much time and attention that faculty wish to take from the core of their existence—their disciplines. We also compete with ourselves. Will students prefer our buildings with helpful, instructive staff over well-designed library Web sites, especially when smaller college libraries can offer a wide range of resources with unlimited access?

For the first time, library buildings compete with profit-making corporations, and creature comforts are considered the norm. A recent project on my campus involved a marketing class. Each student was asked to write an essay about the positive and negative aspects of the library, then to make suggestions as to how the library could have a bigger impact on our student population. The preponderance of responses, both good and bad, had to do with such things as furniture, lighting, and study rooms. Likewise, suggestions for a better library concentrated on more food options, better seating, and a punch card system that would offer prizes for the number of books checked out in a semester. Some students even made direct comparisons to Barnes & Noble. Libraries have always competed for resources on campuses, but as college administrators question the future role of the library and directors explain our mission as less of a repository for research materials (which libraries can do well) and more of an intellectual gathering place (that could possibly be replicated in other environments), the job of convincing becomes more difficult.

Academic librarians have always known about the importance of goodwill on campus, but collaboration became vital when technology forced our relationship with IT departments, and it has only increased. Having the kind of buildings we want often means inviting other operations to join us—counseling services, career centers, writing and tutoring facilities. Library managers may be the direct supervisors for only a percentage of the people employed within the building. Collaboration with faculty takes on new meaning when we consider the success of our information literacy goals. One or two library workshops won't do it. Information literacy has to penetrate a course and be guided by the classroom faculty member to accomplish the desired outcomes. Faculty should be willing to trust, partner, and share control with librarians, with faculty eventually taking a lead in believing that how students utilize and evaluate information is a key component of an education. We also look internally for collaboration. Staff must be aligned in different ways, with new job descriptions, to mount a centralized support system for twenty-first-century users.

As administrators, we were quite secure in our library's position on campus. Assessment was a small part of our job responsibilities because what students thought and how they benefited from our services and collections did not affect our operations in major ways. We knew that we marched to higher educational standards. All that has changed, and we need to connect to our users as never before and not just in the digital sense. The OCLC report "learned that respondents had much to say, when asked, about their libraries, the people who staff them and the services offered" (2006, 6–5). Librarians have become terribly concerned about relevancy and lifestyle fit. Rush Miller (2007, 1) poses questions about the future of research libraries—a future that will be fundamentally different from the past where collections will no longer be their legacy. If research libraries question the future, we, as smaller academic libraries, need to follow their lead. Miller states that "above all, it is time for us to stop criticizing alternatives to libraries and to begin to understand better why some of them are so appealing to our users" (1). We must examine the connections that users are making to information and technology, forget trying to change—or ignore—those aspects of use that we cannot change, and incorporate similar features and approaches to reach our goals—and our students—successfully.

The chapters within this volume serve as guides for strategic planning. They concentrate on understanding our users, new collaborative directions for information literacy, realignment of library staffing and resources, and the integration of physical building and function. Some chapters contain studies and models that can be replicated at similar institutions. Others offer documentation that can be used in reports or presentations to administrators and boards. All convey good ideas, and all illustrate the optimistic and enthusiastic approach that library managers are taking to meet the challenges of making our libraries relevant to the future of our academic institutions. Connection, competition, and collaboration—and revolution, too.

REFERENCES

Holley, Edward G. 1977. "Academic Libraries in 1876." In *Libraries for Teaching, Libraries for Research: Essays for a Century*, ed. Richard D. Johnson, 1–33. Chicago: American Library Association.

McElderry, Stanley. 1977. "Readers and Resources: Public Services in Academic and Research Libraries, 1876–1976." In *Libraries for Teaching, Libraries for Research: Essays for a Century*, ed. Richard D. Johnson, 58–70. Chicago: American Library Association.

Miller, Rush. 2007. "What Difference Do We Make?" *Journal of Academic Librarianship* 33 (1): 1–2.

Mullins, James L., Frank R. Allen, and Jon R. Hufford. 2007. "Top Ten Assumptions for the Future of Academic Libraries and Librarians." *College and Research Libraries News* 68 (4): 240–41, 246.

OCLC Online Computer Library Center, Inc. 2006. *College Students' Perceptions of Libraries and Information Resources*. Dublin, Ohio: OCLC Online Computer Library Center, Inc.

O'Connor, Steve. 2007. "The Heretical Library Manager for the Future." *Information Outlook* 11 (3): 11–16.

I

ANALYZING OUR USERS:
MAKING THE CONNECTION

1 CHANGING DEMOGRAPHICS: MEET THE STUDENTS AND FACULTY OF THE FUTURE

Christopher Cox

For years, libraries have existed in a constant state of flux. Innovative technologies have changed the way we deliver services, materials in new formats have appeared on our shelves, and competition from businesses like Borders, Amazon, and Google have forced us to reexamine how we serve students and faculty on our campuses. Our biggest future challenge, however, will come from our users. The next 10 years will bring about changes in the demographics of our students and our faculty. How will these changes impact libraries and the products and services we provide? What follows is a glimpse of the students and faculty of the future: what they'll look like and what they'll expect from us. By learning more about them, we can determine what we'll need to do and how we'll need to change to effectively meet their needs.

STUDENTS

If there is one word that best describes the coming generation of students, it is "diverse." The students of tomorrow will be more diverse racially and ethnically, more diverse in their background and current life situations, and more diverse in age, representing a number of generations, including Boomers and Gen Xers but more specifically the Millennial generation.

Howe and Strauss (2000, 14) define Millennials as being born between 1982 and 2002. At 76 million strong, they are the largest generation in history. While it's hard to precisely predict how many of this cohort will graduate high school and enter college, the Educational Testing Service's enrollment analysis suggests that the nation's undergraduate population will expand to more than 2.6 million students by 2015 (Swail 2002, 19). Colleges will need to increase their enrollments to compensate for more demand. In a time of reduced budgets and rising resource prices, libraries will be expected to offer additional resources, study space, and services to these students with little increase in support.

Their significant size offers them an equally sizable influence. Libraries today are staffed primarily by Boomers (U.S. Department of Labor 2006, 216). As Sweeney (2005) suggests, Millennials have vastly different needs and expectations than Boomers, and libraries will be forced "to rethink and redesign library resources, technologies and buildings" (165). In an effort to prepare for the onslaught, our conferences and literature are filled with attempts to characterize Millennials and better predict what their demands might be. Abram and Luther (2004), in "Born with the Chip," outline nine Millennial characteristics (Format Agnostic, Nomadic, Multitasking, Experiential, Collaborative, Integrated, Principled, Adaptive, and Direct). Sweeney (2005) further defines Millennials expectations, behaviors, values, and characteristics, then offers a list of steps libraries might take to reinvent themselves. What follows in this chapter is an amalgamation of what the author feels are the five primary Millennial characteristics that will most impact libraries.

They Are Ethnically Diverse and Celebrate Diversity

The populations using the library are becoming more diverse. By the beginning of the twenty-first century, non-Hispanic whites, now the majority population representing two-thirds of the total population, will become the minority, shrinking to less than half the total population (Swail 2002, 19). According to the 2000 U.S. census, 39 percent of people under18 are people of color (Asian, black, Hispanic, Native American), compared to 28 percent of people 18 or over (Broido 2004, 73). This increased diversity is thus likely to be reflected in the Millennial undergraduate population. The Educational Testing Service predicts that enrollment of both Asians and Hispanics will swell on campus and that students of color will represent approximately 2 million of the expected 2.6 million undergraduate population (Swail 2002, 19). More and more students will also be biracial or multiracial; 3.95 percent of those under 18 described themselves as multiethnic in the 2000 census, and the number continues to rise (Broido 2004, 74).

Immigration patterns are partly responsible for these changes. Today, approximately one out of every five children age 18 or younger is either an immigrant or the child of an immigrant (College Board 2005, 4). The children of immigrants face daunting educational challenges. We know that there are major "education gaps" among race/ethnic groups in terms of course preparation, grades, and test results, resulting in their being less prepared for college than their colleagues (College Board 2005, 5). Immigrants and the children of immigrants who go to college, often the first of their generation to receive postsecondary education, may have difficulty adjusting to college, which could translate into lower matriculation rates. Arriving from Latin America and Asia, many new students will be bilingual or come to college with less-than-stellar English-language skills.

4

Libraries have been struggling with increasing the diversity of our profession. In 1998, more than 86 percent of librarians were white, with Blacks, Hispanics, Asians, and American Indians each representing 5 percent or less of the total librarian population (Lynch 1998, 68). Despite the Spectrum Scholarship Program of the American Library Association (ALA) and the efforts of ALA affiliate groups such as the Black Caucus and the Asian Pacific American Librarians' Association, change has been slow. An ethnically diverse student body will expect to see themselves reflected in the staff, faculty, administration, and student workers of the library. Efforts to hire a racially diverse staff and student workforce will help libraries make students of color feel more welcome. Libraries in areas with high Hispanic populations may want to hire librarians fluent in Spanish. In the tradition of the learning commons, libraries that provide space for campus services like the language lab, writing center, or even the diversity office will be offering students of differing ethnic backgrounds additional reasons to enter the building.

Being diverse, Millennials celebrate their diversity, and they'll expect the library to do the same. Libraries will want to partner with campus organizations to offer programs that promote diversity and educate about cultural diversity. They should strive to display diversity in their collections, including collecting materials in different languages. Libraries can be foreboding places for those undergraduates who find themselves struggling to meet new academic expectations. The services offered by the library should meet the needs of all members of the student population and exhibit openness, acceptance and support. Overall, libraries should examine their products and services thoroughly, both in person and on the Web, to ensure that they accommodate all genders and ethnicities.

Another trend that is both comforting and disconcerting is the increasing number of women attending college. Women now represent 57 percent and 59 percent of undergraduate and graduate enrollment, respectively (U.S. Department of Education 2006, n.p.). Women are also earning degrees in fields such as medicine, law, and business, fields that were once dominated by men. The downside of all this is that an alarming number of men are dropping out or not attending college. This inequality is particularly pronounced for African Americans, among whom only 26 percent between the ages of 18 and 24 are enrolled in higher education (College Board 2005, 6). Libraries may need to work harder to recruit men for student employment and may need to consider the role of gender in the library instruction classroom.

They Are Nontraditional

Scholars are still unsure how higher education will be affected by increased diversity. Institutions on the West Coast may be more heavily impacted by this trend than those on the East Coast. Economic factors may cause increased enrollments in community colleges, followed by a "transfer bubble" at many public, four-year institutions, while private college and universities could find their enrollment numbers unchanged (College Board 2005, 8).

The National Center for Education Statistics reports that three-quarters of all undergraduates are nontraditional (U.S. Department of Education 2002, 37). Nontraditional students are defined as having one or more of the following characteristics: delaying enrollment, not entering college directly after graduating high school, attending part time, working full time (35 hours a week or more), being financially independent (as defined by financial aid), having dependents, being single parents, or lacking a high school diploma. The more nontraditional characteristics students possess, the less likely they are to persist in college after the first year.

Nontraditional students could be Millennials or could be from previous generations. They may take classes in person or may take advantage in the increasing number of distance education opportunities offered by today's universities. Changes in the nature of work, the economy, and the job market have resulted in many adults returning to college to gain additional skills, degrees, or certificates. Boomers retiring earlier may also return to school in anticipation of a second career.

An increase in nontraditional students could provide libraries with a number of challenges. Nontraditional students may not be able to visit the physical library during normal hours, choosing to do their homework after work or after their children are in bed. They'll want the library open when it's convenient for them, perhaps 24/7, even when building and staffing issues make it inconvenient for us.

One solution is to beef up the library's virtual information gateway—its Web site. The library should offer both in-person and off-campus users equal access to information products, services, and specialists. Around-the-clock access to information resources like periodical databases and electronic journals is already the norm. Libraries need to expand these offerings, adding suites of electronic books and reference works. Traditional services like circulation, reserve, interlibrary loan, and reference should be reexamined. Can your users renew materials online? Are reserve and interlibrary loan materials electronically retrievable? Is a reference librarian available to them whenever and wherever they may need them?

Also familiar to nontraditional and traditional students on many college campuses is the course management system (CMS). Since the CMS is the delivery mechanism of course content and in some cases the nontraditional student's sole contact with the college, the library should work to be as integrated as possible into courses offered within it.

They Expect Choices and Instant Gratification

Millennials are tough customers. Since the generation itself encompasses so many diverse tastes and viewpoints, they expect the same from the places they frequent. There isn't just one Millennial style of music: they like all kinds of music (Sweeney 2005, 167). Millennials have diverse tastes, and libraries will be expected to display diversity in their collections and have what they want available when they want it, or they will go elsewhere. Millennials are also more willing to shop around for exactly what they want. They have more money than their parents at their age and have no brand or store allegiances. With so many choices, libraries will have to work hard to get Millennials to visit us physically and virtually again and again.

Unfortunately, libraries have done a bad job of marketing to and sharing our message with Millennials. The evidence is no clearer than in the Online Computer Library Center's survey (OCLC 2006) to determine high school and college students' perceptions of library and information sources. Millennials speak about our libraries in stereotypes. When asked to describe "the first thing you think of when you think of a library," books, quiet, and "outdated and lame" topped the list (OCLC 2006, 3–25, 3–26). As a result, they go to Borders, Starbucks, or the local cybercafe instead of visiting us. These places are seen as hip and trendy, and they frequent them as they once did the library. For them, "the days and hours of service, location, décor, food and drink, and other amenities all appeal and are much more convenient" (Sweeney 2005, 174). Their reaction to our Web presence is not much more favorable. While Millennials describe us as more trustworthy and accurate than search engines, they find search engines like Google easier to use, more convenient, and fast (OCLC 2006, 2–10). In fact, OCLC found that while 84 percent of college students were satisfied with the assistance we provide, 90 percent were satisfied with that of a search engine (2–13). Unless libraries work to dispel these stereotypes and solve the problems Millennials perceive, we will continue to see competition from businesses like Borders and Google.

Because of their diversity, Millennials are very interested in personalization. They download personalized ring tones, create playlists for their iPods, and have fast food their way. They expect the same level of personalization from their library services. Libraries have experimented with offering personalization—at least virtually. For a while, portal approaches like MyLibrary were the trend, allowing users to create their own home pages of frequently used resources. Lately, however, libraries have returned to the "one-size-fits-all approach" of virtual services, the only personalization coming from audience-specific pages for students and faculty that assume that all members want the same thing. Libraries need to revisit the MyLibrary approach. MySpace's success stems from its creation of a one-stop social access point, offering Millennials the ability to create personal profiles, update their blogs, and store their bookmarks all from one convenient location. With all these popular services in one place, why would Millennials go anywhere else? Amazon "remembers" previous searches and orders and suggests others that may be of interest. You can even look "inside the book" prior to purchase. As Sweeney (2005, 167) bemoans, our library catalogs just don't allow such customizability. Even our database vendors allow users to create accounts to save searches and citations, run alerts, and customize the search interface. How long will it take for academic libraries to treat their users like individuals?

Along with virtual personalization, Millennials will expect personalization of service and study space in the physical library. A diversity of needs demand a diversity of student spaces—comfy chairs, study tables, collaborative spaces, and quiet spaces. Libraries should offer not only a variety of study spaces but also spaces that allow personalization. We all note how chairs and tables get dragged around our libraries. Why not buy them with wheels so that students can spontaneously create the study spaces they desire? The newly constructed Minneapolis Public Library offers users the option of listening to music on their own iPods through a wireless audio system that pipes music directly to a particular space or study table.

Overall, the library buildings of tomorrow will be much more flexible spaces than the libraries of today. Today, libraries tend to prefer permanent space setups: anchored and braced stacks and hardwired information commons. Sweeney (2005) suggests that libraries "design library spaces that can continuously, easily, quickly, and cheaply adapt to new Millennial needs" (174). Libraries should consider stacks on wheels that can be moved out of the way when the library wants to convert stack space to open space for a program or community event. Another example of how libraries are anchored in their way of thinking is the service desk. The library may be six floors, but if you want help from a librarian, you have to go all the way down to the first floor to find the reference or information desk. Millennials want help where and when they need it. Give the librarian a cell phone, personal digital assistant, or laptop and let them roam the library—or, better yet, the campus—slipping the surly bonds of the desk to offer expertise where it is needed. Because of a lack of staff, the Minneapolis Public Library is experimenting with a Star Trek–like wireless communication device from Vocera that will allow librarians to communicate with each other and with users on different floors. Generations change, and libraries will need to change early and often to accommodate their space and service needs.

Finally, Millennials are impatient, self-sufficient, and nomadic, expecting anytime, anywhere access to the information they require. They are in constant communication with friends via their cell phones, instant messaging, and other technologies. They expect the same level of communication with us. Abram and Luther (2004, 35) point out the lack of services that libraries currently offered to these devices, specifically the inability to use them to search the library catalog or databases or even get the library's hours. Millennials won't want to wait in line at the circulation desk. Libraries are already experimenting with self-checkout stations and radio-frequency identification (RFID) tags to make checkout quicker and easier. Combining service points, like reference with circulation or reference with the technology help desk, will appeal to Millennials. Millennials also won't want to wait a half a day for an answer to their e-mail reference question. As was previously mentioned, libraries will want to further explore 24/7 virtual reference via instant messaging or other means to meet the needs and expectations of this cohort.

They Are Digital Natives

Each year, Beloit College publishes its mind-set list of new students entering college. One thing that you can't help but recognize is how embedded technology is in their lives. Millennials will expect libraries to have wireless networks and lots of network ports throughout the building. Although we'll never be able to meet the demand, they'll want computers—the more, the better. They'll want information to be available in electronic format and be easily accessible, or they will ignore it. They will have a high level of expectation for the library's Web page, especially because of their familiarity with Google. In response to Millennial preferences, many libraries are now purchasing and implementing federated search products, allowing students search box access to the plethora of digital collections the library provides (Abram and Luther 2004, 34). Another solution is to add library content to services like Google Scholar and other Millennial tools (Sweeney 2005, 173). Not only must libraries work to make their content easier to search, but they must make it accessible where the students are online.

Another locale where technology proliferates is the classroom. Many libraries have built cutting-edge labs to house their library instruction classes. Librarians test gimmicky technologies such as SmartBoards and personal response systems to spur interaction. While Millennials expect the convenience of technology—the Web or CMS page with lecture notes or PowerPoint lectures always at the ready, for example—they expect an effective application of technology to their learning environment. Instruction librarians should be careful not to employ technology for technology's sake and first determine the best delivery mechanism for the content (Oblinger and Oblinger 2005, 2.10).

Rapidly evolving technologies will require that librarians stay abreast of changes in order to remain viable and on the leading edge (Association of College and Research Libraries [ACRL] 2003, 12). Luckily, libraries have forever been in love with technology, and librarians have been more than willing to experiment with the latest software or gadget. Many libraries are responsible for maintaining and supporting the course management systems on their campuses. The University of Minnesota Libraries host software that enables anyone on campus to create his or her own blog. Many librarians are currently creating wikis and podcasts to test how these new technologies might be used to deliver library services. Millennial users who enter the library to see a plasma screen glowing with events and highlights will recognize the library for the technological playing field that it is. Libraries should continue to take the lead on campuses when it comes to applying the technologies that Millennials are and will be using.

They Enjoy Gaming and Media

Millennials grew up playing computer games, and such behavior has had a profound effect on how they learn and interact with one another. Sweeney (2005, 170) notes the parallels between information literacy skills and those skills students have acquired from gaming: games teach users by allowing them to make mistakes, offer instant feedback and interactivity, reward players for analytical reasoning, and stimulate collaboration. Many of these skills can easily be applied to the research process—searching, discovering, and acquiring knowledge.

Abram and Luther (2004, 36) suggest libraries build gaming characteristics into library systems. Librarians have already begun to integrate gaming with the advent of tutorials like the Texas Information Literacy Tutorial and other "research simulators." How about an integrated library system that works like a game, asking questions and then spitting out the exact item the user was seeking? Abram is fond of using the example of the University Health Network of Toronto, which applies a gaming interface to its leukemia database, helping medical researchers to better understand the disease (Abram and Luther 2004, 36). Alliance Library System's Second Life library project has taken this a step further, re-creating the library in a totally virtual environment. Placing research in an environment that Millennials are familiar with will help them learn and apply what they have learned.

With their penchant for video games, it is no surprise that Millennials are visual and auditory learners. They like all things media and will expect the media collections in the libraries they frequent to be top-notch. Regardless of the educational mission of the institution, libraries should collect DVDs, CDs, and audiobooks. How many academic libraries do you know that have video game collections? If Millennials learn best by playing them, why shouldn't libraries collect and circulate them? Imagine the popularity of the library that, in addition to media viewing rooms, has computer gaming rooms for students?

The essence of media is that its format is ever changing. Libraries will need to work hard to stay one step ahead, and many libraries are already behind. How many libraries already offer music in MP3 format instead of CD? The Virtual Library of Virginia (VIVA) recently penned a deal with PBS to offer streaming versions of popular PBS video titles like *NOVA* and *American Experience*. These videos can be downloaded by VIVA members and viewed on any PC with a network connection and adequate bandwidth. The videos can even be linked within an institution's CMS. What about pictures? Digital cameras have revolutionized how images are created and shared. Web sites like Flickr make this process even easier and also allow users to add metadata and "catalog" their images. How many special collections departments do you know that allow electronic access to every image in their archives? Millennials will expect this to be the case.

Another way in which this visual learning component is being explored is in database search interfaces. Of late, there has been a flurry of activity among vendors to offer graphical results lists, a visual map of associations, or overviews of interest. EBSCO has recently teamed up with AquaBrowser to offer such a list, and Stanford University is testing a Grokker-powered interface to its library catalog. The mind maps these represent are familiar to Millennials, who have used them in classes to explore and "define the domains, sources, and words that they might use to explore a problem or research area" (Abram and Luther 2004, 36). The visualization of search results is also currently manifesting itself in groups of tags called "tag clouds." Users are able to apply key words or individually generated subject headings to groups of photos, bookmarks, or other digital objects. Rather than search for them, users can determine which subjects have the most items by noting their font size.

Such lessons should be taken to heart by librarians. The majority of library Web pages and information handouts are text heavy, perhaps because the Boomers creating the handouts are primarily text learners. However, only 20 percent of Millennials are text-based learners. Both Web pages and handouts should be redesigned with the Millennial visual learner in mind. One of the most practical ways to do this is to have the Millennials themselves create them for you.

They Learn Best Experientially and Collaboratively

Not only has gaming made Millennials more visual and auditory learners, but it has also made them more experiential in their learning styles. Rather than reading about doing something, they'd rather learn by doing. This has particular implications for the library classroom. Millennials will not be content to sit passively and listen to a 50-minute lecture about how to perform research. Library teachers will need to integrate more active learning techniques into their lessons. For example, rather than demonstrating a series of databases, ask students to search them first and then report back to the class on their experiences and preferences for the assignment. Or, better yet, give students a practical research problem or scenario and ask them to solve it by using library resources and research techniques. Such problem-based learning is popular in science and business classes. Macklin (2001) has written extensively on how librarians can utilize this technique to actively engage Millennials. Because of the diversity of Millennials, a librarian's best bet is to offer a mix of classroom activities aimed to appeal to a variety of learning styles.

Such experiential and visual learning preferences have a downside. The National Endowment for the Arts (NEA) survey *Reading at Risk* (2004, ix) reports a dramatic 10 percent decline in literary reading from 1982 to 2002, representing a loss of 20 million potential readers. Particularly alarming is the decline in literary reading among Millennials, a decline 55 percent greater than that of the total adult population (–28% vs. –18%). We have anecdotally witnessed this in our libraries as circulation of the books in our stacks continues to plummet and we cancel more and more print newspapers and journals in favor of electronic alternatives. What does this decline in reading mean for the future of libraries? Will books and magazines cease to exist? The NEA (2004) suggests that the decline in literary reading could foreshadow an "erosion of cultural and civic participation" (xii). This seems highly unlikely when Howe and Strauss's research on Millennials is taken into account, but are there other consequences of this trend that we cannot yet predict?

For Millennials, "'collaborative learning' has become as popular as independent study was for Boomers or open classrooms for Gen Xers" (Howe and Strauss 2000, 155). Millennials are team players, working in groups in classes to complete projects, participating in team sports, collaborating in person and online. Millennials will expect to work in teams when they arrive in our classrooms. They will also expect libraries to include collaborative spaces. The University of Wisconsin—Eau Claire has a number of reservable meeting spaces, each containing a computer packed with software, a plasma screen, and tables accommodating from 5 to 10 people. These teams engender collaborative research as well. Sweeney (2005, 171) envisions groups of students collaboratively searching for information and discussing the results via instant messaging.

This need for collaboration is also reflected in recent technologies, including social networks like Facebook and the highly popular MySpace, which recently earned the honor of becoming the Internet's most popular Web site. If most of your users are in MySpace, shouldn't you be there as well? Libraries should experiment with virtual collaborative spaces like wikis and blogs, offering Millennials the option of communicating with others about their research or about library materials. OCLC has added wiki functionality to WorldCat so that users can review and comment on the books and media contained therein. Giving Millennials a voice is a surefire way of helping them to see the value of libraries and will give them reason to come back to our Web sites again and again.

FACULTY

The faculty at our institutions will change in similar ways to our students. First of all, our faculty is aging. The majority of faculty are 55 or older (31%), most of them hired in the sixties and seventies to educate the bumper crop of Boomers (Ma 2004, 13). With the end of mandatory retirement, many are continuing to work into their seventies. The year 1998 saw an increase of faculty over 70 from 2 to 1 percent (Ma 2004, 12). The same trend holds true in librarianship. The *Occupational Outlook Handbook* states that "3 in 5 librarians are 45 or older and will become eligible for retirement in the next 10 years" (U.S. Department of Labor 2006, 216). As a result, there is an ever-growing age gap between the faculty and the students they're being asked to educate. Faculty and librarians will have to continually inform themselves about the new students they will be teaching, updating themselves on new technologies and new teaching techniques.

As faculty retire, there is a growing vacuum of people to take their place. Because of an increase in tuition and a decrease in financial aid, there are already fewer graduate students at our institutions and fewer PhDs being awarded, particularly in science and engineering. New faculty are being hired, and they have different needs than their counterparts. They are intellectual omnivores, more interdisciplinary in their training and research (ACRL 2003, 36). They are also specialists and will expect us to carry specialized databases and journals in their disciplines. They will represent the majors that are hottest today: business administration and management, psychology, biology, education, and nursing. If the author's experiences are any indication, these faculty are more apt to value teaching as highly as they will research, will be more willing to experiment with new and innovative teaching methods, and will be more likely to give Millennials the personalized attention they seek. Since they care so much about their students' success, they will be more willing to collaborate with us to integrate information literacy into their courses. Their interests will transform our collections and services.

The faculty members who do retire will vary significantly in age. Some will retire in their fifties and sixties, and these graying Boomers will want to continue to be involved in their communities and institutions. They'll have money in their pockets and time on their hands. Libraries should work to find outlets for this faculty, whether it is offering them volunteer opportunities and continuing education programs or soliciting them for donations or for membership in friends organizations so that they continue to be active in the decisions and livelihood of the library.

Another trend in higher education is the transition from hiring tenure-track faculty to hiring full-time, nontenured faculty or part-time faculty. According to Ma (2004, 8), the proportion of tenure-track faculty dropped from 58 percent in 1987 to 53 percent in 1998, while the proportion of non–tenure-track faculty rose dramatically from 8 to 19 percent. In contrast, the number of part-time or adjunct faculty increased by a whopping 79 percent between 1981 and 1999 (ACRL 2003, 36). Budget constraints and rising enrollments are to blame. Libraries are not exempt from this trend. More part-time librarians are being hired on our campuses as well. These changes will have lasting effects on our libraries. More part-time librarians will mean a reduction in customer service and increased turnover of staff. Librarians will find it difficult to develop lasting relationships with adjunct faculty, relationships that result in library instruction sessions and other librarian–faculty collaborations. Curricular reform with information literacy as its focus could also suffer if this trend continues (ACRL 2003, 36).

The faculty at our institutions will also become more diverse, though at a far slower rate than that of our students. The proportion of full-time minority instructional faculty increased from 12 percent in 1991 to 15 percent in 2001 (Ma 2004, 2). The majority of this diversity is concentrated in the assistant professor rank, no doubt a product of recent minority hiring initiatives. The diversity of our students will dictate a diverse faculty and library staff. Universities will have to do a much better job of recruitment if Millennials are to see themselves reflected in the front of our classrooms.

The proportion of women full-time instructional faculty increased as well, from 32 percent in 1991 to 38 percent in 2001 (Ma 2004, 14). While this may appear encouraging, Ma points out that "there appears to be an inverse relationship between the proportion of women faculty and . . . rank" (14). There are more women at the assistant professor rank than at full professor. Women are also not as likely to be represented in the administration of our colleges and universities. This trend is unfortunately reflected in our profession as well.

Overall, the total number of employees at degree-granting institutions rose by 31 percent and the total number of faculty by 40 percent (Ma 2004, 4). This is significant growth, almost 22 percent higher than that experienced in other sectors. With the coming influx of Millennials, colleges and universities will need to hire more employees to serve them. It is yet to be determined whether library staffs will also grow. The author pessimistically believes otherwise. As librarians retire, there will be the need to reallocate positions to newer kinds of jobs, such as digital scholarship or open-source projects (OCLC 2003, 12). Staff reductions and realignments will further the need for collaboration—not just between libraries but between libraries, other institutions, and companies.

CONCLUSION

So how can academic libraries weather the significant demographic shifts previously predicted? Throughout this chapter a variety of product and service suggestions have been offered to assist librarians in better meeting the needs of our future students and faculty. These are only suggestions, however. We must remember that we need not make these decisions in a vacuum—we have hundreds of members of each stakeholder group ready and willing to assist us. Ask students and faculty to actively participate in library decisions. Employ surveys like LibQual or create your own and ask advice about current and possible future services. Ask students and faculty to help choose new products and get their assistance with usability testing. When it comes to promotion, who better to come up with campaigns that will appeal to Millennials than Millennials? Finally, form student and faculty advisory groups for a source of constant, frank feedback. If students and faculty are more fully invested in the decisions and daily life of the library, they will come to value it more and advocate for its continued existence. With their help, libraries will embrace change and evolve to successfully meet the needs of the students and faculty of the future.

REFERENCES

Abram, Stephen, and Judy Luther. 2004. "Born with the Chip." *Library Journal* 129 (8): 34–37.

Association of College and Research Libraries. 2003. *Environmental Scan*. Chicago: Association of College and Research Libraries.

Broido, Ellen M. 2004. "Understanding Diversity in Millennial Students." *New Directions in Student Services* 106 (Summer): 73–85.

College Board. 2005. *The Impact of Demographic Changes on Higher Education*. Available at: http://www.collegeboard.com/prod_downloads/highered/de/ed_summary.pdf. Accessed December 1, 2007.

Howe, Neil, and William Strauss. 2000. *Millennials Rising: The Next Great Generation*. New York: Random House.

Lynch, Mary Jo. 1998. "Librarians' Salaries: Smaller Increases This Year." *American Libraries* 29 (10): 66, 68–70.

Ma, Jennifer. 2004. *Trends and Issues: Recent Trends in Faculty Demographics and Employment Patterns*. New York: TIAA-CREF Institute. Available at: http://www.tiaa-crefinstitute.org/research/trends/docs/tr110104.pdf. Accessed December 1, 2007.

Macklin, Alexius S. 2001. "Integrating Information Literacy Using Problem-Based Learning." *Reference Services Review* 29 (4): 306–14.

National Endowment for the Arts. 2004. *Reading at Risk: A Survey of Literary Reading in America*. Washington, D.C.: National Endowment for the Arts. Available at: http://www.nea.gov/pub/ReadingAtRisk.pdf. Accessed December 1, 2007.

Oblinger, Diana, and James Oblinger. 2005. "Is It Age or IT: First Steps toward Understanding the Net Generation." *Educating the Net Generation.* EDUCAUSE, 2.1–2.20. Available at: http://www.educause.edu/ir/library/pdf/pub7101b.pdf. Accessed December 1, 2007.

OCLC Online Computer Library Center, Inc. 2003. *The 2003 OCLC Environmental Scan: Pattern Recognition Executive Summary.* Dublin, Ohio: OCLC Online Computer Library Center, Inc. Available at: http://www.oclc.org/reports/escan/downloads/escansummary_en.pdf. Accessed December 1, 2007.

———. 2006. *College Students' Perceptions of Libraries and Information Resources.* Dublin, Ohio: OCLC Online Computer Library Center, Inc. Available at: http://www.oclc.org/reports/pdfs/studentperceptions.pdf. Accessed December 1, 2007.

Swail, Watson Scott. 2002. "Higher Education and the New Demographics." *Change* 34 (4): 15–23.

Sweeney, Richard T. 2005. "Reinventing Library Buildings and Services for the Millennial Generation." *Library Administration and Management* 19 (4): 165–75.

U.S. Department of Education. 2002. "Special Analysis 2002: Nontraditional Undergraduates." *Condition of Education.* Washington D.C.: National Center for Education Statistics. Available at: http://nces.ed.gov/programs/coe/2002/analyses/nntraditional/index.asp. Accessed May 29, 2007.

———. 2006. *Condition of Education.* Washington D.C.: National Center for Education Statistics. Available at: http://nces.ed.gov/pubsearch/pubsinfo.asp?pubid=2006071. Accessed September 12, 2007.

U.S. Department of Labor. 2006. *Occupational Outlook Handbook.* Washington, D.C.: U.S. Government Printing Office. Available at: http://www.access.gpo.gov/su%5Fdocs/sale/sb-270.html. Accessed December 1, 2007.

2 SOCIAL SOFTWARE, WEB 2.0, AND LIBRARIES

Edward M. Corrado

Social software is all about sharing information. Scientists may use a blog to report findings to others in their field. Two or more colleagues may collaborate on a scholarly article using a wiki. Two professors may discuss a paper they are copresenting at a conference using instant messaging or Internet relay chat. Sharing, expanding, and creating information is what scholarship is all about. The traditional role of librarians in terms of scholarship is preserving, organizing, and making information available. In social software environments, where are the librarians? If we accept the premise that social software is a new medium for scholarship, then librarians need to be able to adapt to this environment and find ways to maintain their role in scholarship and cope with the new medium. Librarians must still maintain their traditional roles and competencies, and by expanding into online social environments and taking advantage of social software, librarians and libraries will be able to remain relevant for years to come.

Clay Shirky (2003) described social software as "software that supports group interaction" (n.p.). Social software is a genre of software applications, often Web based, designed for easy use and is often thought of as a means of fun and entertainment. Social software is also implemented by businesses, colleges, and other organizations. For example, a number of library automation vendors have blogs to share information about products and trends that affect the integrated library system world to their current customers and library community as a whole. Although social software has been gaining a foothold in the corporate world, this does not necessarily mean that it will or should gain a foothold in small academic libraries. Or does it? Our patrons, especially the Millennial generation and those who will come after them, have been born into a digital environment and frequently use social software and social networking sites. They expect other Web sites to have the same features. Librarians need to be aware of these expectations and how Millennials use social software applications in order to reach out to them where they live and play in the online world. Because Millennials were born digital, they have an advantage over previous generations who are digital immigrants. There is more to it than that, however; they are a young generation with a multimedia-oriented culture. As Sweeney (2005) points out, they "have acquired their own new lifelong culture" (166), and they soon will be able to affect local and national elections. They will also soon be professors and business leaders. Librarians, who are fighting for mind share in Millennials, must understand how they, too, can live and converse in online environments to better serve this new generation.

Social software applications have been growing rapidly since the advent of Web 2.0. It allows people to easily create and interact with online content, not just passively view it. This is why Tim O'Reilly (2004), who coined the term "Web 2.0," admiringly said "people are in fact a kind of killer app." (n.p.). O'Reilly (2005, n.p.) described seven concepts relating to Web 2.0: (1) the Web as a platform, (2) harnessing collective intelligence, (3) data as the next "Intel Inside," (4) end of the software release cycle, (5) lightweight programming models, (6) software above the level of a single device, and (7) rich user experiences. Social software like Web 2.0, which is possible in large part because of social software, takes advantage of people as an application to create, modify, integrate, and share content. One reason this is possible is because most social software is open and extensible in that it can be linked, expanded, and combined with other social software applications.

This chapter describes some common social software technologies and related concepts and looks at ways that small academic and other libraries may take advantage of them. It also points out some of the challenges that social software and Web 2.0 bring to libraries. Questions are raised that, because of the evolving nature of social software and Web 2.0, often are left open for the reader—and the future—to answer.

SOCIAL SOFTWARE

Instant Messaging and Internet Relay Chat

Instant messaging (IM) is a synchronous form of online communication in which two (or more) people communicate using typed text. It is similar to e-mail except that it allows conversations to take place in real time. In order to use IM, a user must have access to a piece of software known as an IM client. Clients connect to the IM server that acts as a go-between to other IM clients. Usually IM clients are downloaded and installed on the user's computer, but Web-based clients exist as well. While IM clients normally connect to an external service such as AOL Instant Messenger or Yahoo! Messenger to communicate, there are IM server programs available, such as Jabber, that can be installed on local servers.

One of the most popular uses of IM in college libraries is for virtual reference. While there are applications designed specifically for virtual reference, some libraries have found that IM is a better and less expensive alternative. Small college libraries with limited budgets may not be able to afford to purchase programs that are designed specifically for electronic reference. They also may not have the staff necessary to install and maintain this specialized software. IM offers a lower barrier of entry because many patrons (and librarians) are comfortable with the technology because they already use IM for social purposes. In addition, it is likely that patrons who would want to use virtual reference already have IM clients installed on their computers.

An older relative of IM is Internet relay chat (IRC). IRC differs from IM in that is designed primarily to be a many-to-many form of communication instead of a one-to-one form of communication. IRC requires each user to have an IRC client. Like IM clients, IRC clients are normally installed on the user's local computer; however, there are some Web-based clients available as well. Once a user has a client, he or she will need to connect to an IRC network in order to communicate with other people. There are hundreds of networks available, and some of the most popular ones are EFnet, Freenode, and Undernet. Once users connect to an IRC server, they will need to join a channel. Most channels are focused on a particular topic. If users cannot find a channel on a topic they want, often they can create a channel and invite others to join. A popular IRC channel among software developers who work in libraries is the #code4lib channel on Freenode.

Because of IRC's many-to-many nature of communication, it can be used for online meetings and conference planning. A significant part of the planning for the 2006 Code4lib conference happened on the #code4lib IRC channel and by using other social software such as wikis. This is explained later in this chapter. IRC can also be used to get help and support from colleagues when questions arise about how to address a specific problem. It can be helpful to get a perspective from experts around the world in real time using an IRC channel, especially when a person has a question about a specific issue. Because of their size, this may be an occurrence that happens more in smaller college libraries then in larger university libraries. Many people can "talk" at once, and a more interactive discussion replaces the e-mail list. IRC has also been used at conferences and in classrooms for back-channel commentary from members of the audience or students. Audiences can communicate in real time about what the speaker is saying and share further information about the topic without interrupting the speaker and distracting others.

One barrier to using IRC (and to a lesser extent IM) is that some Internet firewalls are configured to block the ports that IRC and IM use to communicate. This may be done because college administrators do not understand the potential value in allowing this form of communication and desire to limit secondary conversations. They may also wish to stop the spread of Internet worms and viruses that rely on these ports.

RSS

RSS is not social software per se, but it is an open XML file format standard used by social software to syndicate Web content. Depending on the version of

RSS in question, it can stand for really simple syndication, RDF site summary, or rich site summary. RSS files that are continually updated are called RSS feeds. RSS feeds typically consist of a headline (or title), a short summary, and a hyperlink that allows the user to access the full content using their Web browser. In order to subscribe to RSS feeds, a user needs an RSS aggregator or newsreader. RSS aggregators can either be installed on a local computer or be Web based. The RSS aggregator will automatically retrieve all the RSS feeds to which a user subscribes so that they are viewed from one convenient place. Social software and social networking sites make RSS feeds available to people, informing them of changes and updates. RSS is also used by many journal publishers to alert people to tables of contents for new issues. By creating a Web page that automatically includes updated RSS feeds of journal tables of contents, small academic libraries can keep faculty informed of the latest scholarship in their field with minimal staff time invested. Newspapers and other online news sites often generate RSS feeds consisting of headlines of new stories. RSS has also been used in libraries to inform people of library news and events. Another use of RSS in libraries is the subject-specific feeds of new acquisitions created by The College of New Jersey Library. This allows listings of recent acquired library print material to be automatically included in the college's course management system and subject guides (Corrado and Moulaison 2006, 62).

Web Logs (Blogs)

Web logs, or blogs for short, are often used as online diaries. Blogging software allows users to create entries as often as they like without needing to know Hypertext Markup Language (HTML). While people who write blogs (bloggers) often assign subjects or categories to individual entries, blogs are typically arranged in chronological order. Many blogs are comprised of random thoughts and entries similar to the way a personal diary may be used; however, there are blogs that are extremely focused on a specific topic of interest to the blogger. For example, Lorcan Dempsey, vice president and chief strategist of the Online Computer Library Center, has a blog that focuses on libraries and Web services. Some other popular personal blogs relating to librarianship include "Librarian in Black" by Sarah Houghton-Jan, "Information Wants to Be Free" by Meredith Farkas, and "The Shifted Librarian" by Jenny Levine. Blogging software can be installed on local servers, or bloggers can use one of the various Web sites that operate blog hosting services. Most blog hosting services offer free blogs and rely on advertising and selling added services for revenue.

Blogs support social interaction in a number of ways. When a blogger creates a new post, readers from around the world can leave comments to add to the discussion. Blogs may be linked together using TrackBacks. For example, blogger A can post a "comment" to blogger B's entry on his own blog. The "comment" automatically shows up on blogger B's blog as well. This weaving of TrackBacks and other links from blog to blog forms a loosely connected social network of blogs often referred to as the blogosphere.

Headlines or whole entries from blogs can be syndicated to other Web sites. In other words, they are syndicatable. There are some Web pages that syndicate blogs on a particular topic in order to allow for "one-stop shopping" for those who are interested. The Planet Debian Web site, for example, publishes entries from blogs written by people involved in the Debian GNU/Linux community. Blogs are also subscribable, allowing people who are interested in a particular blog to be notified by e-mail, RSS, or other means when a blog's content has been updated.

Libraries use blogs in many different ways. Librarians can use blogs for librarian to librarian communication and discussion on a particular topic of interest. In the summer of 2006, a number of librarian-bloggers interested in system librarianship raised awareness of various issues involving women in system librarianship. This important, albeit impromptu, discussion may not have happened without the blogosphere.

Professional associations, such as the Association of College and Research Libraries with its ACRLog, and many commercial integrated library system vendors use blogs to keep membership, customers, and the library community advised as to what is happening within their respective organizations. A common use of blogs in libraries is to use one to disseminate information about library events, services, and other library news. Because of their ease of use, a blog can be set up by a small academic library so that librarians can easily update news and events without the need for a Web developer or other information technology (IT) staff. Blogs can host virtual book clubs and disseminate information about conference sessions. Conference attendees can blog about presentations they attend for people who are interested in a session but for whatever reason could not attend.

Some scholarly journals and magazines have blogs with entries that complement articles in a recent issue or deal with hot topics in their scope. One such blog is Action Potential. The editors of *Nature Neuroscience* operate this blog as a forum for the editors to discuss new and exciting developments with their authors, readers, and the rest of the neuroscience community.

Blogs allow for new ways to disseminate information, and this has implications for libraries. If *Nature* has a blog, should this be reflected in the bibliographic record for the journal in the online catalog? If so, how should it be reflected? If a faculty member uses a blog to discuss scholarly work, who is preserving this work? Should librarians be involved in the archiving of this intellectual content, and, if so, how do they accomplish this?

Wikis

A wiki is a Web site that enables users to create, edit, and remove content in a manner that is similar to word processing, without needing to understand HTML. Wikis allow for easy group collaboration since they make it easy for people to edit Web sites with only a Web browser. Wikis, like Wikipedia, are often editable by anyone who goes to the page, but they do not need to be. The person administering a wiki can restrict who can edit or even view a wiki using a user name and password. Unlike blogs, wikis are not usually arranged in chronological order. Wikis, however, often allow readers to view previous revisions of the Web site and individual wiki pages.

Wikis that are configured to allow anyone to edit them have both pros and cons. A positive aspect to this is that it creates a low barrier for people to create and edit content. It also allows anyone to correct a mistake or omission instantly that they find in a wiki. Conversely, allowing anyone to edit a wiki can also lead to problems. One example is the highly publicized story about John Seigenthaler Sr.'s entry in Wikipedia, where he discovered that someone had falsely written that he was accused of being involved in the assassinations of John and Bobby Kennedy (Seigenthaler 2005, n.p.). Besides character assassination, another danger of wikis is that they can be anonymously edited and subject to Internet vandalism. Reports of incidents such as the Seigenthaler one are relatively rare because of community policing (an informal form of peer review) that wikis enable. A December 2005 special report published in the journal *Nature* found that despite the Wild West nature of Wikipedia, the difference in accuracy between Wikipedia and *Encyclopedia Britannica Online* "was not particularly great" (Giles 2005, 900). An advantage that an online wiki-based encyclopedia (or other reference resource) has is in its nature; it is much quicker to reflect recent news events, new terminology, and new subject areas.

Small academic libraries can utilize wikis in a number of ways. Librarians collaborating on a project can use a wiki. Policies and procedures can be placed on a wiki and easily updated. Wikis can also be used to share information between librarians. At The College of New Jersey, a wiki has been implemented in the library's Media Services Department that allows student workers and staff to communicate effectively on a daily basis, view and update policies and procedures quickly, and track projects such as shelf reading. Staff and student workers, including those who were wary of implementing new technology, quickly learned the wiki language and syntax. This wiki has proved so successful that the library is implementing wikis for staff and librarians in other areas of the library.

Wikis have the potential to significantly affect the nature of the scholarly communication process. For example, researchers can post preprints on a wiki and allow the scholarly community to collaborate and provide peer review and feedback directly to the researcher, thus bypassing the traditional peer review and scholarly journal editing process. Should libraries be involved in this process? Should libraries provide a place for researchers in their institutions to store this content, and how should this content be preserved? Should bibliographic records for wikis be included in the online catalog?

Social Tagging and Folksonomy

A concept shared between many different forms of social software and Web 2.0 sites is social tagging. Tagging is when someone assigns personal key words, or "tags," to an item. Tags can be applied to almost anything that can be categorized, including digital photographs, books, articles, and Web sites. Amazon's 43 Things is even designed for people to tag other people. Personal tagging has been available in various computers programs for a while, but now some Web sites are offering what is known as social tagging. Social tagging is when tags that are assigned by someone can be viewed by members of a group. This group can range from a couple of librarians to a class full of students to anyone who is able to access the Internet. While social tagging may appear to be anarchy or the Wild West of the classification world, when used in large enough communities, useful patterns emerge and a more democratic structure is apparent. The resulting patterns are called folksonomies. Folksonomy (folk taxonomy) is a classification schema that relies on people to create their own personal cataloging terms to categorize and arrange items. Folksonomies are not truly taxonomies since the terms have not been considered beforehand and no hierarchy of knowledge exists. This means that unlike Library of Congress subject headings, there is no controlled vocabulary or hierarchy that can be used to show relationships between terms.

While the lack of controlled vocabulary can be perceived as a weakness of folksonomies, it is also its strength. Folksonomies tend to be much more responsive to current jargon, terminology, and trends than taxonomies. They are more inclusive and are responsive to the long tail of knowledge and interests. Folksonomies also offer some advantages over Internet search engines that use Web crawlers to harvest metadata from Web sites. This is particularly apparent when dealing with photographs, videos, audio files, and other non–text-file formats. This is also true of dynamically changing content that may appear in blogs, wikis, and newsletters. While search engines do an amazing job of indexing the Web, because of the sheer volume of changes, they are unable to keep up with all of the continuously changing Web sites.

This is not to say that folksonomy does not have its distracters, however. As previously discussed, folksonomies lack any meaningful hierarchy. They can also be imprecise because there is no thesaurus to provide a preferred form of entry. Since there is no quality control, there are also problems caused by spelling errors. Folksonomy's lack of precision, thesaurus, and hierarchy can make it difficult or impossible to find a particular item. In this way taxonomies may be better suited for finding and searching, while folksonomies may be better suited for discovering and browsing. If you want to find a picture of *a specific breed of cat*, using a folksonomy may not be practical. However if you want a picture of *any cat*, including ones labeled *my_cat*, *the_cat*, and *happy_cat* by users, then a folksonomy may work better than a taxonomy.

The growing use of social tagging and the emergence of folksonomies bring challenges to the library world. While it is difficult to imagine that social tagging and folksonomies with all of their imprecision and lack of order will replace well-thought-out taxonomies anytime soon, it is just as difficult to imagine that they will go away. Will librarians embrace social tagging and allow it to live side by side with more traditional cataloging and classification methods?

In some libraries, social tagging is already incorporated into online catalogs and digital libraries. A small academic library could allow social tagging of an image or other collection that would otherwise go without indexing because of budget constraints. While this may not offer the best possible access, it offers some access when otherwise there might be none. If librarians do embrace social tagging and folksonomies, even on a small scale, what can they do to better educate users so that they will create better tags? Should libraries make users aware of common conventions, such as using the singular versus the plural and how to deal with compound words? Should librarians encourage users not to use tags like the name of your cat or *my_cat,* which have little or no meaning in the broader context, in an effort to improve the folksonomy? Or will these efforts be counterproductive and cause the resulting folksonomy to lose its folksiness, thus making it less effective and appealing?

Social Bookmarking

Almost all Web browsers have allowed users to "bookmark" Web pages since their early 1990s inception. Recently, social bookmarking has become very popular. Internet bookmarks are stored on the Web instead of on an individual's computer. These social bookmarks can be shared with colleagues or the world in general. Many people who enter the Internet from multiple computers even use social bookmarking to access their own persistent bookmarks when they access the Web. Although social bookmarking sites allow users to make bookmarks private, often people allow anyone to view their bookmarks. In this way, social bookmarking is reflecting the early days of the Web, when many, if not most, personal home pages included a list of Web sites that the home page owner visited frequently.

Social bookmarking sites allow users to assign tags and key words to sites they bookmark. They also allow the user to comment on, briefly describe, or create an abstract of the site they are bookmarking. Another feature offered by some social bookmarking sites is known as "cloud tags." These are used as a visual representation as to what tags are most often assigned to a site that has been bookmarked. Cloud tags have also become popular with other sites that allow social tagging, including retail sites. Some popular social bookmarking sites include del.icio.us and CiteUlike. While del.icio.us is pretty much a free-for-all in terms of the Web pages people socially bookmark, other sites are designed for people to tag specific types of items. CiteUlike is of particular interest to librarians and scholars because it is a free service intended to make it easier for academics to share, store, and organize papers they are reading. Besides commercial services (which are usually free to use), there are some open-source social bookmarking programs that can be installed on local Web servers. One of these, Unalog, was created by librarian Daniel Chudnov and is used by some systems librarians and software developers who work in libraries to share bookmarks.

Social bookmarking applications appear in other Web sites as well. *Nature's* Connotea is a free online reference management service available to researchers, scientists, and clinicians that incorporates social bookmarking features. Social bookmarking has also been added to the University of Pennsylvania's library catalog via PennTags. PennTags is a social bookmarking tool developed by librarians at the University of Pennsylvania that can be used to locate, organize, and share online resources. Besides being included in library catalogs, social bookmarking has many other potential applications in libraries. A small college library without an IT staff can use a social bookmarking tool or site to easily create and maintain subject and class guides consisting of Web-based resources. Librarians can also employ social bookmarking to share Web links with colleagues in their library or around the world.

Photo and Video Sharing

Photo sharing Web sites allow people to easily upload photographs to share with others. Like social bookmarking sites, photo sharing sites provide for community tagging of images and image collections. Some photo sharing sites are generic, while others are more focused on the type of photographs they contain. Flickr, for example, has a wide range of images, while a site such as BallofDirt focuses on travel photos.

PictureAustralia is a partnership between the National Archives of Australia, the National Library of Australia, and other culture agencies that contains photographs relating to Australia. The photos included in PictureAustralia have come from organizations throughout Australia and in some cases from other countries that have images they willingly share. Individuals can also contribute to PictureAustralia by posting their photos to Flickr and adding them to an appropriate PictureAustralia group.

Photo sharing can be used by libraries and other community organizations to build digital collections of local history. By allowing community members to upload the photographs they have taken, a digital collection can rapidly be expanded with minimal staff effort. Video sharing is a similar concept to photo sharing; however, video is shared instead. Video sharing offers additional technical challenges since streaming video from a site like YouTube can take up a significant amount of network resources and may require additional software to be installed on public computers in order for patrons to be able to view the videos.

Creative Commons licenses, although not directly linked to photo and video sharing or even social software in general, are often applied to photographs and videos on resource sharing sites. These licenses can also be applied to videos, clip art, blog entries, wiki pages, and other documents as well. While there are varying versions of Creative Common licenses, they typically are used by copyright holders to allow other people to legally reuse works they created under certain circumstances. One popular license is the Attribution-NonCommercial-ShareAlike 2.0 license, which allows anyone to reuse content for noncommercial purposes as long as attribution is made and the resulting work is licensed under the same open terms. Creative Commons–licensed content can typically be used on academic library Web sites, tutorials, handouts, and other documents at no cost.

Many of these images are of high quality and available to small libraries without access to a graphic designer to create professional-looking materials.

Challenges that photo sharing bring to libraries include preservation and collection development issues. Should libraries collect digital materials this way, and if they do, how can they be assured that the photographs are properly licensed? How do libraries make sure that the content is preserved and can still be viewed in the years to come if file formats become out of date?

Podcasting

Podcasting is a method of making audio (and, increasingly, video) content available for downloading to personal audio and video players and computers. Unlike many other forms of social software, podcasting is usually more of a one-to-many communication format instead of being collaborative. In this way it is less social than many of the other forms of social software. Podcasting content can be almost anything from songs by amateur musicians to television shows to the president's weekly radio address. Some colleges and universities, including Stanford University, even offer course lectures through podcasts. People who create podcasts can either distribute them via their Web site or via a service such as Apple's iTunes. Podcasting is different then placing an MP3 or other audio file on a Web because podcasts have metadata and can be syndicated. One way to think of a podcast is as a combination of RSS feeds and audio files.

Libraries can create podcasts for library tours or bibliographic instruction sessions. Some libraries have even made library news available through podcasts. Like video sharing, podcasting offers additional technical challenges to libraries. In order for people to view or listen to a podcast, software may need to be installed on public computers, and headphones may need to be made available. Another issue is what libraries should do to preserve and archive podcasts. If a professor creates a podcast of a lecture for a course, should the library be involved to preserve it and/or provide access to it?

Social Networking Web Sites

There are a growing number of Web sites that are designed for people to connect with each other using various techniques and ideas from social software and Web 2.0 applications. Millennials are typically very comfortable in these online environments and visit them frequently. MySpace, Facebook, and Friendster attract high numbers of users who post photographs and music, write blog posts, and share other information about themselves for their friends and the world to see. These users are mostly young adults and teenagers. While many of these Web sites focus primarily on social relationships, some sites, such as LinkedIn, are more geared toward creating and sharing professional networks. Since our patrons are in these spaces, it begs the question, Should we be in there as well? Some libraries, including the Brooklyn College Library and the Morrisville College Libraries, have created a presence on MySpace in an effort to connect with students by bringing the library to where the students live online. Other libraries have created groups on Facebook. At Elmira College, Elizabeth Wavle (2007) has found that the group she created for the Gannett-Tripp Library "is an excellent way to introduce library staff to the college community" (322).

Mashups

Sometimes there is content from one or more Web 2.0 sites that libraries would like to combine with their own content. Many of the different protocols and standards that Web 2.0 and social software applications are built on are open in the sense that they can be known and used without a fee. This makes it possible for people to integrate content from different software applications together to create new or improved services. When content is combined this way, it is known as a mashup. Duane Merrill (2006) describes mashups as "an exciting genre of interactive Web applications that draw upon content retrieved from external data sources to create entirely new and innovative services" (n.p.). Mashups are not just geared toward social software and networking sites, however. The library at the New Jersey Institute of Technology and other libraries have mashed content such as user ratings and book reviews from Amazon and other Web sites into their library catalogs. Some small academic libraries have taken advantage of Google's spell-check API license that offers 1,000 free hits per day to add a spell-checking feature to their library catalog. Others have used Amazon's API to include book cover images in the library catalog at no cost.

STAYING CURRENT

One of the challenges of librarianship is trying to stay current with all the information that is available. While the Internet has in some ways made keeping current easier, at the same time it has drastically increased the amount of information that librarians need to consume. Steven Cohen (2003), in his book *Keeping Current: Advanced Internet Strategies to Meet Librarian and Patron Needs*, details ways that the Web and social software can help deliver information about librarianship. Many of his methods can be used to stay informed about social software and Web 2.0.

There are places and ways to keep current with social software and Web 2.0 technology. Some of these rely on tried-and-true methods that existed before the Internet, some rely on Web 2.0, and some lie somewhere in between. Two of the methods librarians used before the Web were reading trade journals and attending conferences. These two avenues are still productive tools. Trade publications such as *Computers in Libraries* and *College and Research Library News* often include articles that describe how libraries are using social software and Web 2.0 technologies. *Educause Quarterly* (2005) "is a practitioner's journal about managing and using information resources in higher education" (n.p.). While not focused on libraries, *Educause Quarterly* has many articles of interest to librarians that deal with new technologies, including social software and Web 2.0 applications.

Attending conferences is also a good way to keep current with Web 2.0 and social software and their uses in libraries. Information Today, Inc., the publishers of *Computers in Libraries* magazine, also puts on a series of annual conferences that deal with library technologies. These conferences—Computers in Libraries, Internet Librarian, and Internet Librarian International—have many sessions on Web 2.0 and social software in libraries. Educause also has conferences with sessions dealing with Web 2.0 on college campuses that may be of interest to librarians. National and international library organizations often have conferences that will have sessions on these technologies as well. One obvious choice in the United States is the Library and Information Technology Association (LITA) National Forum, which focuses on new technologies, but local and state conferences shouldn't be overlooked, as they will often have multiple sessions on these topics.

Local and regional library associations often offer quality training, workshops, and symposiums on new technologies at low cost. A good resource for keeping informed on upcoming conferences, workshops, and other professional development opportunities in librarianship is the "Beyond the Job" blog. While "Beyond the Job" is not focused solely on new technologies, it is updated often and has numerous listings of Web 2.0 and social software professional development opportunities.

Using social software to keep track of developments in social software is an obvious way of keeping up with the topic. There are numerous blogs in addition to "Beyond the Job" that discuss Web 2.0 and social software from a library perspective. While it is not possible to list them all, some more popular ones include the "Librarian in Black" maintained by Sarah Houghton, "Library 2.0: An Academic's Perspective" maintained by Laura B. Cohen, and "Panlibus" maintained by the staff of Talis. Another great resource is Planet Code4lib, which aggregates blogs from many different systems librarians and others who write code or implement new technologies in libraries.

There are some wikis that deal with social software, Web 2.0, and libraries as well. The "Ambient Librarian" wiki is designed to help information professionals and students learn more about Web 2.0 technologies for libraries. LITA also has a wiki focused on this topic called "LITA Library 2.0 Wiki." Another good social software resource to use to stay informed about developments in Web 2.0 and social software for libraries is the *Library 2.0 Reading List* created by Jenny Levine and Michael Stephens.

While the previously mentioned journals, conferences, blogs, and wikis are all very useful for keeping up with Web 2.0 and social software technologies for libraries, nothing replaces actually using these applications and services. Librarians should set up a social bookmarking account, use IM, edit a wiki, keep or at least read a blog, or use these other technologies (at least occasionally). By doing, one is learning. All these applications are designed to be easy to use, and one doesn't have to spend much time to learn about them. Experiencing them may be the best way to understand them—especially for hands-on learners.

CONCLUSIONS

Library 2.0 is a term used as a way to apply Web 2.0 principles to libraries—and more specifically to library catalogs and other electronic resources. Miller (2006) believes that Library 2.0 is a concept that has provided stimulus to conversations about "the changing ways that libraries should make themselves and their services visible to end users and to one another" (n.p.). Librarians need to consider the challenges Library 2.0 brings with it. One of the challenges is how (and if) to respond to social software, social networking sites, and Web 2.0. If they don't respond, librarians risk being left behind and not being able to adequately support patrons in online social environments. If the small academic library is unable to support scholars in these online social environments, it risks being overlooked by these scholars who are comfortable in these environments. The loss of mind share may not only be in terms of content based on Web 2.0 and social software. It may also affect the scholar's awareness about more traditional resources and services available through the college library, such as online journal databases and possibly even the library's print collections.

If librarians and libraries are to expand their roles into online social environments using social software and Web 2.0 technologies, they will need support from library and other administrators. This support does not have to come in the form of increased funding, although encouraging librarians and other library staff to attend workshops and conferences that focus on Web 2.0 and social software will make the learning curve easier and faster. One of the most effective means that administrators can employ is to encourage librarians and staff to experiment with and learn about these technologies. In most cases, since social software (or at least limited versions of it) is usually available for free, this involves allowing staff to take time out of their workday to master these technologies. For some projects, however, additional equipment or service contracts may need to be acquired. This is true particularly with more advanced or larger projects and ones where local branding is required or desired.

FINAL THOUGHTS

Social software, by design, is intended to be used for collaboration and sharing. People around the world can easily create, modify, and respond to content created by others. Someone may write an entry on a blog in the United States, and people from France and New Zealand can post comments within minutes. In this respect, one of the strengths of social software is that it is able to leverage the wisdom of the crowds. Whether we like it or not, social software and Web 2.0 are here and are not going to go away. If anything, they will become more prevalent. While looking at new technology with a skeptical eye is not a bad thing, librarians cannot put their heads in the sand hoping they'll wake up and it will all go away. Librarians need to be informed about these technologies in order to make decisions about when, what, if, and how social software should be implemented in the library so that it meets the role of the library as the intellectual hub of the college community.

ACKNOWLEDGMENTS

This chapter is in honor of John Iliff, who originally was going to write it. He unfortunately passed away before the chapter was written. John was always enthusiastic about social software and new technologies for libraries and will surely be missed.

The author gratefully acknowledges James Robertson, with whom he has presented at conferences about social software and libraries in the past.

REFERENCES

Cohen, Steven. 2003. *Keeping Current: Advanced Internet Strategies to Meet Librarian and Patron Needs*. Chicago: American Library Association.

Corrado, Edward M., and Heather L. Moulaison. 2006. "Integrating RSS Feeds of New Books into the Campus Course Management System." *Computers in Libraries* 26 (9): 6–9, 61–64.

Educause Quarterly. 2005. Available at: http://www.educause.edu/apps/eq/about.asp. Accessed April 30, 2007.

Giles, Jim. 2005. "Internet Encyclopedias Go Head to Head." *Nature* 438: 900–901.

Merrill, Duane. 2006. "Mashups: The New Breed of Web App." *IBM developerWorks*. Available at: http://www-128.ibm.com/developerworks/library/x-mashups.html. Accessed September 26, 2006.

Miller, Paul. 2006. "Coming Together around Library 2.0: A Focus for Discussion and a Call to Arms." *D-Lib Magazine* 12 (4). Available at: http://www.dlib.org/dlib/april06/miller/04miller.html. Accessed September 27, 2006.

O'Reilly, Dennis. 2004. "Users Direct the Next Big Thing." *PC World*. Available at: http://www.pcworld.com/article/id,114855-page,1/article.html. Accessed September 22, 2006.

O'Reilly, Tim. 2005. *What Is Web 2.0: Design Patterns and Business Models for the Next Generation of Software*. Available at: http://www.oreillynet.com/pub/a/oreilly/tim/news/2005/09/30/what-is-web-20.html. Accessed September 22, 2006.

Seigenthaler, John. 2005. "A False Wikipedia 'Biography.'" *USA Today* (November 30). Available at: http://www.usatoday.com/news/opinion/editorials/2005–11–29-wikipedia-edit_x.htm. Accessed July 21, 2006.

Shirky, Clay. 2003. "Social Software and the Politics of Groups." *Networks, Economics, and Culture*. Available at: http://www.shirky.com/writings/group_politics.html. Accessed August 7, 2006.

Sweeney, Richard T. 2005. "Reinventing Library Buildings and Services for the Millennial Generation." *Library Administration and Management* 19 (4): 165–75.

Wavle, Elizabeth. 2007. "From Midnight Breakfast to Facebook.com: Social Networking and the Small College Library." In *Sailing into the Future: Charting Our Destiny: Proceedings of the Thirteenth National Conference of the Association of College and Research Libraries*, 317–24. Chicago: Association of College and Research Libraries.

SELECTED WEBLIOGRAPHY

43 Things: http://www.43things.com

Action Potential (*Nature Neuroscience* Blog): http://blogs.nature.com/nn/actionpotential

"Ambient Librarian" wiki: http://www.ambientlibrarian.org

AOL Instant Messenger (AIM): http://www.aim.com

BallofDirt: http://ballofdirt.com

Brooklyn College Library on MySpace: http://www.myspace.com/brooklyncollegelibrary

CiteULike: http://citeulike.com

Connotea (from *Nature*): http://www.connotea.org

Creative Commons: http://creativecommons.org

Del.icio.us: http://del.icio.us

Facebook: http://www.facebook.com

Flickr: http://flickr.com

Friendster: http://www.friendster.com

"Information Wants to be Free" blog by M. Farkas: http://meredith.wolfwater.com/wordpress

iTunes (from Apple): http://www.apple.com/itunes

Jabber (IM): http://www.jabber.org

"Librarian in Black" blog by S. Houghton-Jan: http://librarianinblack.net

"Library 2.0: An Academic's Perspective" blog by L. Cohen: http://liblogs.albany.edu/library20

"Library 2.0 Reading List" by J. Levine and M. Stephens: http://www.squidoo.com/library20

LinkedIn: http://www.linkedin.com

"LITA Library 2.0 Wiki": http://wikis.ala.org/LITALibrary2.0

"Lorcan Dempsey's Weblog": http://orweblog.oclc.org

Morrisville College Libraries on MySpace: http://www.myspace.com/morrisvillecollegelibrary

MySpace: http://www.myspace.com

NJIT Library catalog: http://librarius.njit.edu

"One Big Library" blog by D. Chudnov: http://onebiglibrary.net

"Panlibus" blog maintained by the staff of Talis: http://blogs.talis.com/panlibus

PennTags: http://tags.library.upenn.edu

PictureAustralia: http://www.pictureaustralia.org

Planet Code4lib: http://planet.code4lib.org

Planet Debian: http://planet.debian.org

"The Shifted Librarian" by J. Levine: http://www.theshiftedlibrarian.com

TCNJ Library RSS Feeds: http://www.tcnj.edu/~library/rss

TrackBack Specification: http://www.movabletype.org/docs/mttrackback.html

Unalog: http://unalog.org
Wikipedia: http://wikipedia.org
Yahoo! Messenger: http://messenger.yahoo.com
YouTube: http://www.youtube.com

II

THE INTEGRATION OF FORM AND FUNCTION: BUILDINGS AND SERVICES

3 PLACE PLANNING FOR LIBRARIES: THE SPACE NEAR THE HEART OF THE COLLEGE

Eleanor Mitchell

It is said by college presidents and others, particularly on the occasion of the completion of an expensive building project, that the library is the heart of the college. These and other ribbon-cutting comments validate this use of institutional resources; the very substance of the bricks and mortar (or concrete and glass), in turn, reinforces the solidity and wisdom of the investment. There is, however, a countervailing notion that the library building, rather than residing at the heart, is losing its centrality on the campus and beyond, as digital formats and seemingly ubiquitous access offer virtual alternatives for at least some activities formerly in the province of the physical library. Barbara Doyle-Wilch (2005), dean of the Library at Middlebury College, wrote, "The library is the 'heart of the academic community,' yet we constantly question if there will be libraries in the future" (n.p.). Campbell (2006) noted, "Today, however, the library is relinquishing its place as the top source of inquiry. The reason that the library is losing its supremacy in carrying out this fundamental role is due, of course, to the impact of digital technology" (16). Noting the services that have emerged in academic libraries in the digital age—including "providing quality learning spaces"—Campbell writes, "these services are derivative and diffuse. . . . As a group, they do not constitute a fundamental purpose for the future library, and they lack the ringing clarity of the well-known historic mission in which they are rooted" (20). He suggests, "It may be that as scholarship becomes more interdisciplinary and classrooms become more virtual, colleges and universities will need more high-quality *library-like* space for student interaction, peer learning, collaboration, and similar functions. But it may also be that institutions will need the space for other priorities . . . it will remain unclear what part the physical library space will play in a context where virtual communities and activities are increasingly utilized and prominent" (20, emphasis added).

The role and place of the library in the life of the college have altered dramatically in the past decade in response to technological, informational, economic, and social phenomena. Teaching and learning, core campus missions, continue to be transformed by technology, and so has library space. This is evident in the increase in electronic classrooms within library buildings but also in the rapid development of information commons, wired buildings and now wireless computing, library equipment ranging from loaner laptops to desktop scanners, and a host of library spaces and functions that support and shape collaboration, exploration, discovery, access, synthesis, and creation of information. New information formats require different and additional equipment, furniture, spaces, and support, which must be accommodated and housed alongside and harmoniously with the exponentially increasing printed sources and the technological remnants of past formats. There is a cost beyond the materials themselves; library space must be differentiated for quiet and collaborative uses of resources, for example, or for viewing, listening, digitizing, or production. The onset of the digital has not lightened the load of print: libraries continue to house print collections, though increasingly with some off-site storage or in compact shelving. Accommodating their access and use can be a costly business. The social component has perhaps the most far-reaching impact on planning for college libraries. Library services, resources, and spaces must be informed by what we know about the social framework in which our students operate and the "information-age mindset" (Frand 2000, 14–24) of our Millennial student population. Frand has described some of these qualities: constant connectivity, comfort with "input-output devices," a preference for activity and interactivity (offered by Web-based resources), learning through "Nintendo over logic" trial and error or the discovery method rather than in-depth analysis, and zero tolerance for delays. There has been a bleeding of edges around their academic, social, and personal dimensions. Lippincott (2005) captures it well:

> Walking into a busy information commons on a weekday evening, an observer would likely see groups of students clustered around computers, some chatting, others talking on cell phones, some with headphones listening to audio while they work on computers, and some working on their own, perhaps on a laptop, with coffee and snacks, books and notebooks spread out on a table. It would be difficult to tell, without peering over their shoulders, exactly what types of activities the students were engaged in, particularly whether they're recreational or academic. Today's students mix academic and social activities. Some see their multitasking as a troublesome lack of ability to concentrate, but it is a logical strategy for students who grew up in a world with media in many formats at their fingertips 24 hours a day. Information commons with their large numbers of computers, range of software, and spaces configured for groups, provide an ideal environment for students to collaborate with others and multitask. (7.5)

Library staff might do well to begin a consideration of space with just such observations of students in their natural habitats; if they are not in the library, seek them out in the dorms, in the student centers, or in the coffee shops.

In years past, before the digital age, the notion of the value of the library was inextricably tied to the physical collections and the predominantly solitary scholarly activities that depended on them. Of late, the preeminence of the print collections is challenged by the cost, ubiquity, and flexibility of the digital environment; the lone scholar heading toward the stacks passes fully booked group study rooms on the way, and the silence of the reading room is shattered by the din of the "no shush zone," as Brigham Young University's Harold B. Lee Library labels its reference area. Libraries that sustain their place at the heart of the campus are those that have successfully repurposed themselves to accommodate these dualities.

CHANGING SPACES: IMPETUS AND IMPEDIMENT (OR, THE NEWS OF THE DEATH OF THE LIBRARY HAS BEEN GROSSLY EXAGGERATED)

In his 2001 article "The Deserted Library," Carlson observed, "Gate counts and circulation of traditional materials are falling at many college libraries across the country, as students find new study spaces in dorm rooms or apartments, coffee shops, or nearby bookstores. . . . The shift leaves many librarians and scholars wondering and worrying about the future of what has traditionally been the social and intellectual heart of campus" (A35). If the decreased library usage that Carlson describes (which did not go unchallenged by the library community) was a compelling argument against investment in construction, it did not appear to be reflected in curtailment of library building activity. The period from 1992 to 2001 was marked by continued investment on the part of colleges and universities in library space. "The age-old truth about libraries—that they always grow in size and demand more space—remained fully in force. It is hard to find evidence that breathtaking innovation in information technology and the 'virtual space' it occupies slowed traditional investment in library bricks and mortar" (Bennett 2003, 7). The argument has been made that as libraries assume a more virtual role, electronic resources will obviate the need for investment in library buildings. Yet the availability of library content electronically, anywhere, anytime, has not sounded the death knell for libraries as places (nor has it eliminated most libraries' continued acquisition of printed materials). Investment in library spaces has continued in the face of the electronic revolution and despite rumors of significant changes in use patterns.

There are many compelling drivers for space changes in libraries. More than a decade ago, Fraley and Anderson (1990, 15) identified four situations that prompted library space reorganization: lack of collection growth space, lack of space for people, a change in direction or mission of the organization or community served by the library, or the introduction of new services. Bennett (2003, 7), writing about the library building projects of the previous decade, notes five motivators identified by library directors, several indicative of changing roles for libraries. In addition to growth of collections and changes in public services (other than reference), he adds the changing character of student study space needs, the dysfunctional design of previous space, and changes in or growth of library instruction. Crosbie and Hickey's (2001, 7) analysis of seven academic library building projects provides a more granular list of factors shaping construction decisions, including the growing importance of electronics, the shift to individual and collaborative learning, and uncertainty about the future.

Recent college library construction projects reflect programmatic or organizational changes on campus or in the library, changing user expectations and behaviors, new collaborations and partnerships, technological advancements, and responses to competition for user loyalty. Local campus priorities will inform which of the factors may be most compelling for any given circumstance.

There is now some convincing evidence that investment in space appears to pay off for libraries and their campuses. Beyond the intended benefits (workflow improvements, easing of stack overcrowding, updated systems, and so on), new spaces bring more users into the buildings. A recent query on the American Library Association's College Libraries Section list asked for examples of increases in library traffic following a building project. One library dean noted a 433 percent increase in traffic in the first semester of the new facility; another described doubling gate count in the first six months and a slower but steady increase continuing. Shill and Tonner (2004) confirmed that "the great majority of new and improved libraries have experienced sustained increases in usage of the physical facility following project completion. In addition, some libraries have experienced profound increases in usage, with 25.6 percent of survey participants reporting post project usage gains exceeding 100 percent. In short, a high-quality building does make a difference" (149). Higher gate counts alone, however, may not validate the investment in library space enhancement. Not just greater building usage but also improved educational results may be the more compelling argument for investment in bricks, mortar, cabling, and coffee bars. But the prophecy of the deserted library may be self-fulfilling: if you don't build it, they certainly won't come.

SPACE PLANNING PROCESS: INSTITUTIONAL ALIGNMENT AND USER INVOLVEMENT

It is essential to align the goals and the timing of a library space project with institutional direction. Read the strategic plan; listen to the president's speeches. See where the campus is heading and position the library accordingly. For example, if there is a campus initiative for student–faculty research or a new digital scholarship center, can your library space enhance or support that goal? Making certain that the library and the campus administration share core assumptions is critical in any space project. Think, for example, of the information commons described previously by Lippincott; when your president signed off on a plan with a commons, did he imagine a library full of activity, collaboration, and noise (not to mention food and drink)? Clarifying the vision and the expectations at the outset and continuing to communicate as the project progresses will go a long way toward avoiding surprises at the ribbon-cutting or open-house celebration.

Library space must accommodate both the practical and the symbolic associations with the library on the college campus. A plan to create a commons or incorporate a cafe must tread lightly on those traditional values attached to library space as emblematic of quiet study and serious scholarship. Faculty may be resistant to plans to address stack space constraints with remote storage; gaining public space by relocating staff outside the library building will surely be a sensitive suggestion that needs careful conversation. Most important is to be aware of the library as a "common good": everyone is a stakeholder in its plans. From a global redesign to the repositioning of the reference desk, changes often can elicit unexpectedly vehement and heartfelt responses from faculty and students. Educating the campus community about the roles and purposes of the library in the twenty-first century will help garner support for your plans.

Elements of Space Planning

The team: The planning or coordinating team often includes library staff and administrators, faculty and student representatives, information technologists, and campus facilities personnel. Increasingly, library buildings include other campus functions—student advising, tutoring, and writing centers—and having these partners involved from the beginning is essential to moving from a "landlord–tenant" relationship to a true collaboration and shared sense of building ownership.

Other expertise: Architects, interior designers, space planners, technology experts, engineers, campus budget personnel, and vendors representing everything from compact shelving companies to café seating may be called on as needed, depending on the scope and scale of the project. Some campuses employ a consultant to gather data and produce a background document. Input from other campuses with library space projects can be very helpful. Gather not only the perspective of the directors but also the opinions of library users to find useful reflection on the outcomes of other space projects.

The time line: The time line drives the planning and implementation process for a space change. The plan also needs to predict the time frame or the life expectancy of the new space design: given patterns of acquisitions and funding in the past or allowing for expected enrollment changes in the future, how long will it be before another space project will be necessary? One library director noted, "Looking back, we can now see that the 1963 addition was too small almost from the day it was dedicated" (Michalak 1995, 30). Some space plans include collection growth projections for 5, 10, 15, and 20 years. Robert Kieft, director of college information resources and librarian of the College at Haverford College, noted in an e-mail, "At this point, I am counting on the slowing of growth in the number of printed books we buy in the 5–10 year range, and I am assuming that in the 20 year range we will be seeing for the most part only specialty publishing in print, that is, a very high percentage of our general collections materials will not be published in print anymore. I predicate these numbers on two assumptions (no surprise to anyone), one, that a reading device that most people will accept under most circumstances and for most purposes as being as good as a printed book for academic materials and, two, that the mass of digitized older material will tip most users' reading preferences in the digital direction. Thus, I am counting on partnerships of one sort or another to hold growth to a slow pace, slow enough so that the College does not need to anticipate needing more physical (it may need more electronic) space/architecture for the library."

Assumptions and issues: It is critical to capture the prevailing environmental and institutional circumstances within which the space plan is conceived. This document is a good way to identify places of agreement and to surface misconceptions. For example, Williams College's library space plan, developed by a consultant, incorporated a number of planning assumptions that illuminated factors affecting academic libraries in general (relating to changes in publishing and scholarly communication, for example). One assumption was stated: "there is a continuing and critical role for the library as 'place'" (Lucker 2000, n.p.). The list of such assumptions was summarized as "what the liberal arts college library of the 21st century needs to be and do." This document also included more specific planning issues that related to the local campus community and library.

Goals: What is the impetus for the change, and what are the goals? Stating the goals clearly and referring back to them frequently will keep the process on track throughout myriad decisions and choices that surface. The goal statement will also avoid "mission creep" where a small relocation develops, incrementally, into a budget-breaking large-scale renovation. An example of a goal might be to improve the quality and quantity of study spaces in the library. After gathering data to determine the right mix and attributes for a variety of library study spaces, the goal might be further refined more explicitly: develop a plan for quiet and collaborative study spaces to support the range of student study behaviors.

Data gathering: A space plan should begin with the key documents that describe the library and institutional environment. Fraley and Anderson (1990, 28) suggest gathering information into a space data file, with detailed descriptions of past and present facilities use and data for planning for future use. Among the information to be included (and, as they suggest, dated and labeled) are the following: institutional mission statements and other core planning documents; library core documents, including operational description; budget information, including numbers for proposed and past projects; previous library space studies; current and past photographs, blueprints, and floor plans of the library; collection measures; inventory of equipment and furnishings; and present work flows and service points with statistics.

Gather information to pinpoint where the current space falls short or where opportunities for improvement exist. Probe existing surveys such as *LibQual* or other local questionnaires for relevant items and responses. If you have a feedback or other communication mechanism in the library, such as a suggestion box or a standing advisory group, relevant comments that provide insight into building space gaps and preferences may already exist in library files and minutes. For example, one library suggestion box regularly included student comments about poor lighting, temperature control, and noise in the building. From these informal or qualitative data, one can derive a list of repeated issues that can then be further tested through surveys, observations, and focus groups.

While gate count provides information on library building traffic, it doesn't capture the key issues surrounding building usage. One approach is to survey library users (and nonusers) about their habits. Where do they study? When do they most often use the library? For what activities? Where do they prefer to sit? Why? How would they rate the space in terms of how well it supports a range of activities, from finding resources and services to solitary study to collaborative learning to using technology? What obstacles and frustrations do they encounter? Why do they *not* use the library? Include faculty as well as students; their expectations for student independent research and collaborative work are important data points, and their own use of library space needs to be factored in as well.

Another method used to gather data on building use and needs is observation. Silver (2006, n.p.) described conducting "periodic sweeps" of the collaborative spaces in a recently renovated college library; in his method, the investigator recorded activities and user characteristics on a checklist; brief interviews were also conducted with some users.

Informal observation can also provide useful information. One library director noted that every morning, sofas were found in front of each of the DVD viewing stations in the media room, replacing the chairs intended for that space. Viewing videos, for class work or recreation, was clearly a group activity in that library. While observations will reveal what is taking place, more information may be needed to draw conclusions about reasons and implications for space plans.

Focus groups are also effective ways to identify library space issues and concerns. A student library council at the University of Texas at Austin operates much as a focus group would. Building and space issues mentioned among their minutes include providing side-door access to the library, building hours, safety in the stacks, cleaning of the building, and even a note that the return slot at the interlibrary loan desk was too small for music scores! When the plans to reexamine their undergraduate library were underway, this group provided a sounding board for ideas like the dispersing of the print collections, the location of reserves, and a multifunctional information desk.

Another method for gathering data on your community's use of library space is a usability study. The University of Chicago Library assessed way finding in its multistory, multicollection building by having student subjects "think and act aloud" as they searched for books first in the catalog and then in the stacks. This illuminated many of the already suspected issues: multiple collections with the same call numbers, competing signage, confusing maps, and so on (Kress, Larsen, Olsen, and Tatarka 2006, n.p.). Although it is a time- and labor-intensive approach, this methodology uses a small sample to confirm expected issues and discover unanticipated ones.

No matter which methods are used to gather ideas and data, the library space planning process should seek input from multiple perspectives: experts and generalists, internal and external constituencies, and staff and patrons.

Models and best practices: Reading the professional literature, attending conferences and presentations, and making site visits can help the team develop a portfolio of good ideas and approaches to academic library space. Someone else may have solved a similar problem or devised a creative approach that you might want to adopt. One library has mounted a large, live electronic sign to display the current availability of computers in spaces throughout the library (Brigham Young University); another has a "production and rhetoric" room (Lake Forest College). How about diner-style seating (University of Pennsylvania)? Users tell us (see the *Perceptions of Libraries and Information Resources* report of the Online Computer Library Center [OCLC]) to look to chain coffee shops and superbookstores for well-planned community space, so don't limit your explorations to peer institutions or even libraries.

STUDENT-CENTERED LIBRARY SPACE

"Libraries need to work well. For most students the average academic library is a complex set of systems that does more to confuse than to help the user. A badly designed library increases people's perplexity, wastes their time, and is better avoided" (Edwards 1990, vii).

A poorly designed library space (physical or virtual) frustrates and confuses students. Their first impressions will foretell whether the library experience will be a helpful or a hostile one or will be a struggle or supportive and successful. One historic undergraduate library building on a university campus had a beautiful entrance foyer with no fewer than seven possibilities—doorways or stairways—among which the hapless freshman had to choose; there was not a book in sight, though, to hint at the traditional purpose. Students were awed by the architecture but irked by having to ask in order to find almost anything. Newer library buildings (and Web sites) can have similarly confusing layouts, with neither library service points nor staff visible from the entrance and poorly worded, ill-placed, contradictory, or nonexistent signage to help with way finding.

But beyond the basics of being able to find useful resources, locate appropriate service points and facilities, and enjoy quiet, well-lighted places for study, there are increasingly high expectations from college students for the spaces that they use on campus, including the library. Students at 46 institutions in the United States and Canada participated in the online survey that produced the data for a report, "The Impact of Facilities on Recruitment and Retention of Students." The study, conducted by the Association of Higher Education Facilities Officers, revealed that 56.3 percent of students surveyed felt that the library facility was an extremely or very important criterion when selecting a college. This was second in importance behind facilities for their majors and ahead of classrooms, residence halls, dining facilities, and recreation space (June 2006, A27). What we don't know from this report is what students regard as desirable or essential in a college library space.

Lomas and Oblinger (2006, 5.2) identified five attributes of students that have implications for the design of learning spaces; they are described as being digital, mobile, independent, social, and participatory. Our libraries, then, must be wired and wireless, offering an array of online resources and network access from many vantage points. No more do students want to be tethered to plug-in ports with hard-backed chairs that dictate where and how one must sit. With wireless and laptops, students can lounge on the sofas, group around a study table, or move outside under an umbrella on the patio. But despite the increasing number of wireless libraries—a recent survey reported that 35.9 percent of academic campuses are now entirely wireless—it has been reported by some librarians that students still vie for the wired spaces in their libraries, both for the electricity and for real or perceived robustness of the ports over the wireless connections.

Lomas and Oblinger's independent studiers might seek out the more traditional carrel-type seating and may find the diner-style and other collaboration-inspired seating off-putting. Or such students may want nontraditional spaces—one library has beanbag chairs tucked under a lower-level stairwell, while another has low coffee tables for laptops with cushions on the floor as seats. One librarian noted that rather than occupy a vacant space intended for small groups, some students will run long extension cords to reach individual seats. Other students, although wanting to study alone, settle in the middle of the most trafficked areas; solitary study doesn't necessarily mean isolated. To accommodate all these habits, college libraries offer a range of seating possibilities in both remote and central spaces.

Much has been made of the social nature of today's college students. They are constantly connected; they have embraced social networking and raised it to the level of a phenomenon. Sweeney's (2005) experiences with focus groups of college students found the following: "Millennials stay in constant contact with their friends via e-mail, cell phones, text messaging, or instant messaging (IM) but also meet up frequently with friends to go have fun or work together. Millennials depend upon their friends to help learn new skills, particularly in the information, technology, or gaming arenas. In short, the byproduct of the many Millennial friendships is collaboration that improves their learning" (171). He notes that these students frequent superbookstores, using them much as they might a library, to read magazines and study their own textbooks: "The days and hours of service, location, décor, food and drink, and other amenities all appeal to and are much more convenient to Millennials. In addition to the super bookstores, Millennials can be found in many Starbucks or other coffee houses reading or studying. . . . Will the proliferation of remote information technologies and resources eliminate the need for physical library buildings? The answer is counter-intuitive, just as the growth of television did not eliminate people attending movie theaters. Millennials, like all the generations before them, need and still demand social and public spaces. Everybody has to be somewhere" (174).

The OCLC (2006) document *College Students' Perceptions of Libraries and Information Resources: A Report to the OCLC Membership* provides a wealth of information about student opinion and behaviors that can be incorporated into library space planning. Some of the findings were the following:

- The most frequent use of the library reported by college students was as a place to do homework and to study.
- Only 13 percent of college students had positive associations with their library as a quiet environment, a work environment, and friendly and comfortable surroundings.
- Twelve percent offered negative comments about the library, noting confusing layouts and its being too quiet, too noisy, dirty, and outdated.
- When asked what they thought of when they heard the word "library," 70 percent of college students said "books." Yet when asked what they use the library for in a month, fewer than 40 percent mentioned borrowing books.
- Students' advice to libraries included, among other things, improving lighting and furniture, increasing hours, and allowing food and drink.

Interestingly, the age-group just a step behind this college cohort, the 14- to 17-year-olds, had other requirements, perhaps basing their expectations on the public library environment with which they are more familiar. They ask for more computers, displays of books and encouragement of reading for fun, snacks and drinks, special events to bring people into the library, nice seating, comfortable furniture, and a quiet room.

College librarians can extract much meaning from these and other studies of student needs, habits, and desires. Garten and Williams (2006) noted, "If libraries want to maintain their role as the intellectual center of the campus and as an attractive place where serious students and faculty gather, and interact, they must compete based on their desire to meet the needs of users as the users define them. That may mean developing cafes in the library, varying work spaces to fit the desires of students, identifying places where people can work together without disruption and quiet places that meet the needs of students who work best in that environment" (4). The authors remind us, "Colleges and universities need to put much thought into redesigning their libraries because students have choices" (3).

Carlson (2001) attributes many features of the new library to "librarians . . . fighting back." Nice furniture, cafés, activities, music, and the like, he suggests, are efforts to "attract students back to the physical structures, because the new electronic offerings are here to stay" (A35–38). It may be argued, though, that these elements now increasingly common to the college library are not just stylistic concessions, attempts to lure students and win our market share back from the superbookstores, with lattes and soft seating, but rather are acknowledgments of the ways in which students prefer to learn: collaboratively, electronically, actively, perhaps noisily, late at night, and in comfort.

ELEMENTS OF THE TWENTY-FIRST-CENTURY COLLEGE LIBRARY

Flexibility: The one consistent characteristic noted in the professional literature and dialogue about the college library of today and tomorrow is flexibility. Flexibility in space planning seems more about what to avoid than what to embrace: fixed and permanent walls, single-purpose rooms, static design, immovable furniture, and expensive and concretized commitment to formats, media, wiring, and layouts that may argue against change. Library architects and planners Shepley Bulfinch Richardson & Abbott (n.d.) note in their brochure on library design that "despite careful planning, rapidly changing technology can render leading-edge spaces obsolete within a year. Planning for flexibility and adaptability is no longer the exception: it's the rule."

Collaborations and partnerships: Joint tenancy is not new to college libraries. For reasons of space more than compatibility of mission or method, offices and personnel from a variety of campus departments have been housed within library buildings. In the worst of circumstances, these relationships can be marked by tension and turf wars as nonlibrary personnel flout rules and make demands. From security to signage to service, culture wars between library staff and other campus building mates can erupt around issues large and small. More often, a gentle truce enables neighborly cohabitation if not collaboration. In the best of situations, the partnership is intentional, providing an environment in which different campus entities housed within the library space join forces to provide a seamless and supportive panoply of services for students. Writing centers, tutoring services, services for students with disabilities, and student advising have shared library spaces for years, building a strong local network of referral and support for students. More recently, technology services—centers for teaching and learning, multimedia spaces, digitization spaces, and production facilities—join with library services to provide a range of resources and expertise to enhance and facilitate the teaching and learning process from research through creation and presentation. Campus cultural and social entities such as art galleries and theaters are also increasingly sharing spaces with libraries. Inclusion of all parties in developing goals and sharing decisions—about furniture, arrangement, access, signage, and so on—will do much to move from coexistence to collaboration.

Commons: The commons has been described as "an aggregation of services intended to encourage engagement with information in its various forms, reinforce the value of collaborative inquiry, and create new opportunities for community interactions" (Garten and Williams 2006, 2). There is a great deal of professional dialogue about what an information commons is. How does it differ from a computer lab, a computing commons, a learning commons, or a knowledge commons? Are these just different names for the same spaces? It seems clear that a critical mass of computers does not alone create a commons. The commons generally integrates technology, information, expertise, and other tools and resources to accommodate and encourage a range of computer-enhanced academic activities from solitary study to collaborative creation. In planning a commons, elements to consider include the physical and the virtual: space, service model, technology, arrangement or layout, and the furniture and equipment.

In the early manifestations of these spaces, computers were installed in space-saving rows, in areas away from the other business of the library, where the special needs of equipment and users could be addressed conveniently and efficiently without impinging on the traditional library activities. Over time, additional hardware and software were provided, forming scholars' workstations where research, writing, multimedia production, and presentation activities were supported. Single-person workstations have now morphed into desktops that accommodate several students clustered around monitors and reconfigurable tables that users arrange to fit their current needs.

Should the commons facilities be centralized or dispersed and integrated into other library spheres? Some libraries identify their entire building as "learning commons," with workstations and other technology distributed throughout and research and technical expertise available on demand, by appointment, or virtually. In addition to undifferentiated computing space, commons may incorporate other areas, such as soundproof rooms, presentation practice rooms, group study rooms, and training spaces and classrooms. Stanford University's Meyer Library offers the Meyer TeamSpace, a 24-hour, six-person space that supports networking of laptops for document and information sharing and collective document editing, with the ability to view documents on a 40-inch LCD screen. As Stanford's Web site describes the space, it is not just the technology that matters: "Having a big table with comfortable, flexible chairs in a space dedicated to collaborative work means that it's okay to talk, be loud, and debate things. There has to be a place where a team can do that." Whether your commons is centralized or disbursed, plan for flexibility in furnishings and arrangement so as to meet current needs and adapt as they change. Movable walls, chairs on wheels, whiteboards, large-screen monitors, laptop-lending desks, vending machines for diskettes and CD-ROMs, and other technological and physical appointments provide flexibility and anticipate and support a variety of uses.

Collections: The cost and growth of printed collections has led to creative solutions that impact space planning. On-site collections have been housed in subbasements excavated beneath library buildings and in floors added above; they have been compacted in both public and backroom storage areas. In some libraries, robotic storage and retrieval systems pluck and deliver shelved volumes from storage to requesters mechanically, like dry cleaning. Off-site storage, either dedicated or shared, is another option for managing collection growth without crowding user space. In some libraries with readily accessible off-site storage, newly arrived monographs are automatically routed to storage, and the decision to house them on-site is made on first request for circulation.

Classroom spaces: Library classrooms may be dedicated to information literacy instruction or may be scheduled by the campus for other classes. While instruction librarians strive to have a classroom under their own scheduling control, it is also advantageous for faculty to hold classes on library turf, underscoring the connection of library to curriculum. If the classroom is to be used by instructors other than library staff, it is recommended that the instructor's workstation follow the standard campus classroom setup so as to minimize technical difficulties. Classrooms within libraries may be traditional lecture-style auditoriums, seminar rooms, or, increasingly, spaces that support demonstration, active learning, and collaboration. Tables or "pods" encourage group work, while large monitors and either projection or broadcast capabilities allow the instructor to present or demonstrate. Classrooms offer a range of technology, hardware, and software, from those on the standard library workstation, including Internet, audio, and video, to specialized resources, such as GIS, language-learning programs, and collaboration software. Teleconferencing and videoconferencing capabilities may also be incorporated. Flexibility is again the key, with seating, technology, and arrangement that may be reconfigured to accommodate different teaching methods and learning styles. Unlike other teaching spaces on campus, the library classroom may not be the regular meeting space for a course; it should be located where students unfamiliar with the library spaces can easily find it.

Individual and group study spaces: A variety of seating and study spaces will provide alternatives for library users. Soft seating is increasingly common, from armchairs with ottomans to loveseats and couches (which are often seen, even in busy libraries, occupied by only one user). Some students still prefer hard-backed chairs at study carrels and will seek areas away from the din. Furniture that is portable and reconfigurable into different combinations will enable students to build their own arrangements where they prefer to be.

Students increasingly seek places for collaborative work and study. Within open spaces, tables for four, six, or more will attract group studiers; even those libraries that have added enclosed group study rooms find that the demand exceeds the supply, and students will create their own group study space anywhere if need be. By designating floors or wings of the building as quiet or collaborative, through signage, color, lighting, or seating arrangement, one can minimize the disturbance of those seeking silence. Some libraries are making movable partitions available to encourage students to build their own spaces close to the relevant resources and technology. One librarian noted that her group study rooms have turned into the quiet spaces in her library, while the open areas are increasingly used for collaboration. Group study rooms, when large enough for 6 to 10 users, provide flexibility: they may be used for small-group instruction and reference consultation when not in use for studying. While group study rooms should be soundproof, these spaces often are glass fronted, both for security reasons and to decrease a sense of isolation. They have network connections and may come equipped with computers and large monitors or screens for viewing, or students may bring their own or library-loaned laptops; DVD and VCR players may also be useful.

Even with most user seats wired or the entire building wireless, students will still need electric outlets to power their laptops. In newer space, the wiring is often beneath the floor, enabling greater flexibility in arrangement. Lighting is often mentioned as inadequate in libraries; observing the space use at night reveals which areas are lacking. Natural and artificial light—ambient, overhead, and task—is essential. While considering light, also consider glare and its effect on screen visibility. Even on those happily and completely wired campuses, it is hard to take advantage of outdoor spaces for study unless umbrellas, overhanging roofs, or other structures are available.

Work surfaces—desks, tables, and chair arms—must accommodate an ever-increasing array of student necessities. A typical student may arrive to study with a backpack, books and notebooks, laptop, iPod, cell phone, and perhaps a latte or water bottle. Multiply this by a small group working together, and the tables around which they gather must be large or, preferably, able to be moved together. Students are vocal about uncomfortable seating; there are many manufacturers today producing ergonomic workstation seating that is comfortable, attractive, and mobile.

Social, cultural, and informal learning spaces: Libraries are more intentionally planning for what has long been an informal function of the library space: social connection and informal learning. While students have traditionally found their own spaces for these purposes—the undifferentiated spaces of the library, such as the entrance, the area in front of the circulation desk, and the stairwells—increasingly libraries are embracing this as a central role the library can play on campus. Existing underutilized spaces—those near the noisy entrances, perhaps—may be repurposed for informal uses simply by the placement of small sofas and armchairs clustered around low coffee tables with reading lamps.

A library space may signal a social or cultural purpose by the collections it displays. Dickinson College Library (where this author is director) introduced a "reading beyond the curriculum" section called "Dickinson Reads," where new fiction, graphic novels, and other books of current interest are shelved. Soft seating and a location close to the entrance make this a very popular area (and the circulation of the books has skyrocketed). Other nearby collections—newspapers, news magazines, and DVDs—take their inspiration from the superbookstores and are placed (in good marketing style) to catch the eye of the passerby and result in an impulse "purchase."

College libraries are incorporating spaces for cultural events and activities both by expanding exhibit areas and by defining rooms where presentations, panel discussions, and performances can take place without interrupting the primary library functions. Beyond the exhibit cases located in special collections, libraries showcase their own treasures as well as student and other campus creative works with displays on the main floors and in other library areas. Student art has become permanent in some libraries and rotates through in others. One library has become the gallery for the student photography club; an opening reception is held, photographs are displayed, and a competition determines which will be enlarged for permanent installation on the library's walls. Virtual exhibits parallel those in the physical space.

Academic libraries with appropriate spaces find themselves hosting visiting scholars' presentations, panel discussions, student poetry readings, and other scholarly and cultural events; if a library public event space is available and attractive, opportunities for cosponsorship with other campus offices will abound.

Space for seating, a podium, a sound system, and projection capability are essential; good acoustics and heating and cooling are also critical. Other libraries schedule concerts, performances, and even ballroom dances in their spaces. If the space is open to other areas of the library, guidelines for use—relating to type of event, audience size, and time of the semester and day—are strongly advised. It is worth noting that not every library user embraces this new role for library space; some find it unexpected and disruptive.

Café society: A recent exchange on a college library directors' list began with a query about food and drink policies. Responses flew back within minutes, one after another director indicating that he or she no longer chose to fight this battle with students. Food and drink were permitted in all areas of their libraries, save the special collections, and damage and vermin were not a significant problem. Some college libraries have embraced the notion of refreshments: events and exhibition openings include catered receptions, holidays and significant dates are marked by celebratory cakes, and library-sponsored study breaks—one offering peanut butter and jelly sandwiches—are common.

Having moved beyond forbidding and policing patrons' eating and drinking habits, increasingly academic libraries are incorporating a "food presence" within their spaces. In some instances, it is no more than a bank of vending machines. In others, full-scale operations with baristas and toasted bakery items have found their way inside the doors.

Cafés within libraries are often located on the main level, near the entrance. This limits the disruption of hissing steam and clattering plates to studying students and also attracts business beyond the library users. Those with enough space for tables and chairs report not only that business is booming but also that the café spaces are used for much more than eating and drinking. Faculty hold office hours; students study together and alone; computers provide access and diversion; and chess, checkers, and other game boards offer study break activities. Some libraries schedule events in their cafés, such as poetry readings; others use the walls to showcase student art. Over and again, the directors of these libraries note that their cafés are financially successful and, as one said, "proof positive of the importance of place."

Zoning: The concept of zoning in library space planning provides for differentiated areas in a natural progression moving from entrances and service areas where activity and noise are high, through collaborative study areas where conversation is encouraged, and finally into quiet spaces for individual study where group activities are behind doors. One can signal through lighting, color, furniture, and signage the intent of the individual spaces and also the transitional areas between them. Lisa Kemp Jones, manager of the College Library Instructional Computing Commons at the undergraduate library at UCLA, developed a four-zone concept for the main floor of that historic and complex library building. The first zone, near the entrance, was the active zone where students have first contact with service desks and high-density, stand-up, quick-check computer stations were located. The second zone, adjacent, was a collaborative space where modular group work spaces, with and without computers, and movable walls were provided. This area was a pass through to other library spaces and so was designed for disruption. The third zone, deeper within the building, was labeled "independent" and supported quiet study, with desks, chairs, and soft seating. An enclosed area was created beyond this zone, "collaborative/computing," where students could work together with technology and away from the disruption of traffic.

CONCLUSION

The tension between sustaining the physical and building the virtual library will only increase as technology advances and user expectations heighten; both the bricks and the clicks are essential and not mutually exclusive. Library architects at Shepley Bulfinch speak of three needs for libraries: space for information, space for contemplation, and space for community. We must also continue to plan for space for overflowing book drops, parking for herds of book carts, and the ongoing library processes and activities that will not disappear anytime soon. It is clear that the college library building will continue to serve traditional uses and host unanticipated ones.

In an article titled "Redefining Library Space: Managing the Coexistence of Books, Computers, and Readers," Thomas (2000) wrote, "Perhaps the best way to plan library space at the beginning of the 21st century is to think about the virtual library when planning the renovation of its reality counterpart. What can take place as effectively in the online environment? What services are less effective? What may be presented even more effectively on line? Library managers must gaze into a cloudy crystal ball for the most transient glimpse of the possibilities. By designing for maximum flexibility in any space, perhaps the wise librarian may shape the co-existence of the virtual and the traditional in the future" (415). The "cloudy crystal ball" will, for the foreseeable future, continue to picture the college library as a vibrant, busy, comfortable, and richly resourced place where the coffee flows and the disciplines converge.

REFERENCES

Bennett, Scott. 2003. *Libraries Designed for Learning.* Washington, D.C.: Council on Library and Information Resources. Available at: http://www.clir.org/pubs/reports/pub122/pub122web.pdf. Accessed January 26, 2007.

Campbell, Jerry. 2006. "Changing a Cultural Icon: The Academic Library as a Virtual Destination." *Educause Review* 41 (1): 16–30.

Carlson, Scott. 2001. "The Deserted Library." *Chronicle of Higher Education* 48 (12): A35. Available at: http://chronicle.com/free/v48/i12/12a03501.htm. Accessed January 26, 2007.

Crosbie, Michael J., and Damon D. Hickey. 2001. *When Change Is Set in Stone: An Analysis of Seven Academic Libraries Designed by Perry Dean Rogers and Partners: Architects.* Chicago: Association of College and Research Libraries.

Doyle-Wilch, Barbara. 2005. "What Is a Library?" *Transformations: Liberal Arts in the Digital Age* 2 (2). Available at: http://apps.nitle.org/transformations/?q=node/95. Accessed January 27, 2007.

Edwards, Heather M. 1990. *University Library Building Planning.* Metuchen, N.J.: Scarecrow Press.

Fraley, Ruth A., and Carol Lee Anderson. 1990. *Library Space Planning.* New York: Neal Schuman Publishers.

Frand, Jason L. 2000. "The Information-Age Mindset: Changes in Students and Implications for Higher Education." *Educause Review* 35 (5): 15–19, 22, 24.

Garten, Edward D., and Delmus E. Williams. 2006. "Repurposing Older Libraries for New Times: Creating New Learning Space." *Library Issues: Briefings for Faculty and Administrators* 26 (4): 1–6.

June, Audrey Williams. 2006. "Facilities Play a Key Role in Students' Enrollment Decisions, Study Finds." *Chronicle of Higher Education* 52 (40): A27.

Kress, Nancy J., David K. Larsen, Tod A. Olsen, and Agnes M. Tatarka. 2006. "Wayfinding in the Library: Usability Testing of Physical Spaces." Paper presented at the ARL Library Assessment Conference: Building Effective, Sustainable, Practical Assessment. Charlottesville, Virginia, September 25–27, 2006.

Lippincott, Joan. 2005. "Linking the Information Commons to Learning." In *Learning Spaces*, ed. Diane G. Oblinger. Boulder, Colo.: Educause. Available at: http://www.educause.edu/learningspaces. Accessed January 27, 2007.

Lomas, Cyprien, and Diana G. Oblinger. 2006. "Student Practices and Their Impact on Learning Spaces." In *Learning Spaces*, ed. Diane G. Oblinger. Boulder, Colo.: Educause. Available at: http://www.educause.edu/learningspaces. Accessed January 27, 2007.

Lucker, Jay K. 2000. *Williams College: Library Space Planning for the 21st Century.* Available at: http://www.williams.edu/go/stetsonsawyer/consultantrpt.pdf. Accessed December 10, 2006.

Michalak, Sarah C. 1995. "Planning a Main Library Addition for an Academic Research Library." In *Planning Additions to Academic Library Buildings: A Seamless Approach*, ed. Pat Hawthorne and Ron G. Martin, 28–45. Chicago: American Library Association.

OCLC Online Computer Library Center, Inc. 2006. *College Students' Perceptions of Libraries and Information Resources: A Report to the OCLC Membership.* Dublin, Ohio: OCLC Online Computer Library Center, Inc. Available at: http://www.oclc.org/reports/pdfs/studentperceptions.pdf. Accessed January 30, 2007.

Shepley Bulfinch Richardson & Abbott. n.d. *Library Design at Shepley Bulfinch.* Boston: Shepley Bulfinch Richardson & Abbott.

Shill, Harold B., and Shawn Tonner. 2004. "Does the Building Still Matter? Usage Patterns in New, Expanded and Renovated Libraries, 1995–2002." *College and Research Libraries* 65 (2): 123–50.

Silver, Howard. 2006. *Use of Collaborative Spaces in a College Library.* Available at: http://web.mit.edu/~hsilver/www/simmonsproject/Collaborative%20Spaces.htm. Accessed January 27, 2007.

Sweeney, Richard T. 2005. "Reinventing Library Buildings and Services for the Millennial Generation." *Library Administration and Management* 19 (4): 165–75.

Thomas, Mary August. 2000. "Redefining Library Space: Managing the Coexistence of Books, Computers, and Readers." *Journal of Academic Librarianship* 26 (6): 408–15.

4 THE NEW 3R'S: REVOLUTION, REORGANIZATION, AND RENOVATION

Susan M. Campbell

THE STRATEGIC PLAN SETS THE STAGE

Schmidt Library at York College of Pennsylvania (YCP) is a dynamic, vibrant space where staff members provide a multitude of services from a highly visible central desk in the main lobby. The new services, staffing model, and space are the products of effective, deliberate, and careful long-range strategic planning and assessment employed by YCP for more than a decade. York College is a small, private, liberal arts college with a number of professional majors. During the 10 years and two planning cycles discussed, the college grew from 4,082 full-time-equivalent (FTE) students and 215 FTE faculty members to 5,023 students and 260 FTE faculty members.

In 1996, when the college's Academic Senate Long Range Planning Committee, whose members included faculty, students, administrators, and the president, initiated the five-year planning process for 1997 to 2002, library faculty and staff convened that summer to create vision and mission statements, consistent with the YCP mission. Using the Schmidt Library's assessment plan, the York College mission statement, the Schmidt Library's 1994 mission statement (Appendix A), and the 1996 Middle States Association evaluation report section on the Schmidt Library, five groups of three to four staff and faculty met to complete these exercises:

Examine the York College mission statement—How do our current assessment criteria fit?

Examine the Schmidt Library mission statement—Does it fit the York College mission statement? Does it need revisions, especially with respect to our criteria? Look at the assessment document for each criterion and determine how it relates to the college's mission statement. Talk about where we should be in the next one to five years—again, with respect to these criteria. In early fall of 1996, the same groups met to do the following:

- Write a final draft of a vision statement for their assigned assessment area
- Determine strategic objectives for each criterion for further study that year
- Determine objectives we might want to highlight in a presentation to the Long Range Planning Committee (e.g., need for new building)

The director compiled these statements into the 1996 revised mission statement. "The faculty and staff of Schmidt Library are committed to providing high quality classroom and individual instruction in research skills, state-of-the-art technology for information retrieval, balanced collections in support of the curriculum, and excellent physical space for research and study." This statement and the following objectives were presented to the Long Range Planning Committee on October 14, 1996.

Research Skills

- Insure that students meet goals of information literacy core course
- Provide excellent faculty and staff, well-designed classrooms, and state-of-the-art technology
- Continue providing exceptional one-on-one instruction in reference services
- Offer advanced instruction as necessary

Technological Skills

- Insure students' ability to use information technology in support of learning
- Maintain state-of-the-art workstations
- Provide state-of-the-art classroom for information literacy core courses
- Increase number of public terminals

Balanced Collections

- Acquire, maintain, and provide access to balanced collections in support of the curriculum
- Monitor changes in curriculum
- Systematically analyze collection
- Acquire materials to correct imbalances

Physical Facilities

- Provide atmosphere conducive to active learning through well-designed user, staff, and collection spaces
- Plan a new library building or an expansion/renovation project

- Insure Americans with Disabilities Act (ADA) accessibility
- Supply electronic resources at reasonable pricing and licensing to be available to YCP users anywhere on campus or off campus whenever possible

The committee overwhelmingly approved the plan and the library filed an addendum in January 1997 that contained supplemental data to support the strategic needs. The Long Range Planning Committee's 1997–2002 Strategic Plan for the college targeted the library for a capital building project.

REVOLUTION

Before discussion of the plan's tenets and their execution, it is critical to note two things. First, while developing this plan, the Schmidt Library faculty was simultaneously designing a new two-credit core curriculum course in information literacy (IFL 101) mandated by the General Education Task Force and approved by the Academic Senate as part of a new core to be offered for the first time in the fall 1997 semester. The seven full-time librarians and 4 to 11 adjunct faculty members teach from 27 to 37 sections of 24 students each both fall and spring semesters, plus additional smaller sections in each of YCP's three summer terms every year. In order to provide time for class preparation, teaching, office hours, and grading, all librarian and staff duties were realigned in 1995–1996, with many clerical staff members getting not only revised position descriptions but also changes in job classifications. The Schmidt Library faculty and staff, in addition to dealing with the tremendous changes wrought by the burgeoning World Wide Web, were offering a credit course and planning for total revolution of services, staff, and building.

Second, while the plan was developed in 1996 and approved in 1997, constraints of YCP's largest-ever capital campaign delayed implementation of some major components of the plan until the 2002–2007 planning cycle. Thus, the 1996 plan withstood two complete YCP five-year planning cycles. Each year from 1998 to 2004, the library staff and faculty continued to revisit the plan, reviewing and revising it as necessary, based on ongoing assessment and review by the Academic Senate Library Committee.

The director of physical plant and personnel retained the college's architects, Reese, Lower, Patrick and Scott, to begin design plans for the totally renovated library. As that work began, the ongoing project of ensuring research skills through instruction in IFL 101 and through one-on-one reference interaction continued. Several IFL faculty members created the online eText, which is still in use today. The library faculty met regularly with composition faculty to explore ways to strengthen the core curriculum through collaboration. Both the Writing Program (WRT) and IFL began offering joint sessions for honors students. Collaboration has now expanded to all core coordinators to address issues raised in the 2002 core curriculum review.

The faculty and staff also undertook a number of important projects to balance and improve the collections. The first collection analysis provided collection statistics for each discipline, including numbers of books and periodicals, average price of each, and numbers of items circulated, including periodicals from closed periodical stacks. The annual periodicals project, which had added 25 to 50 new periodicals annually since 1986, was revamped for the aggregated database age, and an ongoing "Wish List" was created by the library faculty and Academic Senate Library Committee. A massive weeding initiative identified more than 40,000 titles that had not circulated since 1991, and a cooperative venture was launched where faculty could visit weeding Web sites or physical shelves to ascertain whether books should be retained. All paper journals over five years old were moved to storage on the new part of campus. Many print and microform journal subscriptions were canceled in favor of online access. A library faculty member chaired the Academic Senate Curriculum Committee through most of this time, so curriculum changes and collection needs were carefully monitored. In 2004, the library used the collection analysis tools of the Online Computer Library Center for a more systematic overview of the collections.

In the technology arena, there were many changes as well, with two massive Web redesigns, migration from DRA to SIRSI, and installation of a proxy server. An e-journal management system, link resolver, and two federated search platforms were launched. In what was then audiovisual (AV) delivery, many classrooms were outfitted with permanent installation of television monitors and video and DVD players. The AV staff took on responsibility as well for delivery of PC carts with portable digital projectors to classrooms. Approximately 14,000 electronic journals and 5,000 e-books were added to the collection, requiring a dizzying array of management protocols for library systems staff.

REORGANIZATION

Staff

As all these initiatives took place and the architects' work on the building renovation proceeded, the dean of academic affairs charged the librarians to examine our written plan and our current organizational chart to create a strategy model that better matched our new mission. The old structure reflected many changes and additions in staffing, made more for expediency than organizational sense, and further did not really reflect either the work we were doing, the work we said we were going to do, and, perhaps most important, the level of work we were expecting from everyone when we envisioned combining all services in a central location.

After months of exploration and difficult deliberations with a new academic dean and the director of physical plant and personnel, this structure was approved. (See old and new organization charts in Appendix C.) The dean recognized new titles and responsibilities for the librarians in their contracts, and the personnel director effectively eliminated all 13 clerical staff positions, creating 11 new full-time positions and two new part-time positions. All full-time positions were created at the administrator level, requiring a bachelor's degree, and were assigned to a specific unit to be managed by a librarian. Those employees without the degree were moved to the top of the job classification scale and received raises akin to those in the new administrative positions. All employees interviewed for the new slots. Many took similar positions in the new organization, but all had many new responsibilities working at the new central service desk, Information Services. There were hurdles in the transition, at first because not everyone got administrative status, because clerical staff had managed departments in the previous organization, and finally because the new jobs were exceptionally complex, requiring every staff member to learn a broad range of new skills to provide the new centralized service. It was also challenging for the librarians to manage a much different kind of organization with higher expectations for both them and their staffs.

Services

It was easy to see that offering services at five different areas on two different floors—circulation and reference in different places on the main level and AV, closed stack periodicals, and interlibrary loan in three different places on the lower level—was very confusing. There was 100 percent agreement on moving to a single service point. If reimagining staffing was a challenge, so also was planning the integration of services. Long-standing autonomy was difficult to abandon, but both assessment data and anecdotal evidence bear strong testimony to the ease of use for students and faculty alike. To their great credit, in spite of growing pains, staff readily acknowledge that they are working together to provide better service to our community. Most relish the administrative-level responsibilities of their new positions and play a vital role in planning and budgeting for new services, both for their particular areas of expertise and for Information Services.

RENOVATION

No one can believe that Schmidt Library was totally renovated in three and a half months for $3.5 million. Construction began in the middle of the spring 2004 semester. Contractors eventually removed all walls; wiring; plumbing; lighting; heating, ventilating, and air-conditioning (HVAC); ceilings; and most flooring. All furniture was given away. All collections and computers were stored. The staff moved into classrooms after commencement, operating a minilibrary with limited services for the summer terms. The Schmidt Library welcomed students and faculty back in late August for the fall semester to a totally new facility. The transformation provided everything that required staff assistance on the main level in Information Services—our version of a learning or information commons—circulation, reserves (print and electronic), periodicals, media, microforms, media production, document delivery, workstations and wireless laptops, black-and-white and color copiers, scanners, and poster printers.

What about reference? Although we spent months designing the physical space and service, the physical space was never occupied. The library decided to offer research services on call, responding to requests on an IP wireless telephone.

THE PRESENT AND FUTURE

There is no way to do justice in one chapter to the magnitude of the implementation of the plan born of the enormous vision of the Schmidt Library faculty and staff. I have been overwhelmed and indeed astounded by their foresight from 1996 forward, how their thoughtful approach not only has withstood the test of time through Generations X and Y and the Millennials but also has been flexible enough to be adaptable as we enter the 2007–2012 planning cycle.

Interviews with more than 700 students in 35 classes in all departments, meetings with all senior administrators, and working and consulting with the Instructional Resources Committee to solicit broad faculty input and with our information technology colleagues have served as a valuable environmental scan, confirming yet again what our astoundingly consistent 10 years of assessment data told us and what the library faculty and staff did early in this planning process, namely, reaffirm the major tenets of our now long-standing long-range plan. Through the long-range planning process, including assessment, we have forged a document that has enabled us to embrace change and use it effectively to better serve the YCP community.

APPENDIX A

Schmidt Library
York College of Pennsylvania
Susan M. Campbell
Library Director

MISSION AND GOALS

It is the mission of Schmidt Library to provide access to recorded knowledge through materials, services, and equipment that support the career-oriented liberal arts curriculum of York College of Pennsylvania. To that end, the library faculty and staff will:

Work with other faculty members to develop well-rounded collections of print and nonprint materials to support all facets of the curriculum.

Acquire, process, and organize all materials for efficient user access; provide means of access to these materials as well as to those not owned by Schmidt Library; and maintain all collections and equipment in good condition.

Teach students to become knowledgeable, confident, self-sufficient library users through desk assistance, orientation, and classroom library instruction.

Provide online searching to support faculty teaching and research and develop and promote programs to introduce online searching to students.

Recruit and train personnel whose knowledge and skills facilitate the library's mission, encourage staff development at all levels, and systematically evaluate the performance of all individuals.

Develop budget requests to support the continuing growth of all collections, provide all necessary equipment, and maintain all services.

Maintain open forums of communication within the library; use a library newsletter, the library handbooks for faculty and students, discussions with the Faculty Senate Library Committee, and other means to keep users informed and to gather information; and maintain an awareness of college developments that might have an impact on the library.

Provide adequate facilities and an appropriate environment for users, staff, collections, and equipment.

Continue to foster interlibrary cooperation and resource sharing to provide users with materials not available in Schmidt Library.

Support an integrated, automated library system and promote knowledge of current developments in information technology.

Ensure availability of equipment that is easy to use and that is standardized when possible within format to facilitate user recognition.

Maintain AV production facilities and provide production materials at minimum or no cost to users.

Maintain the archival documents and historical records of York County Academy, York Collegiate Institute, York Junior College, and York College of Pennsylvania.

Preserve collections to insure that important resources are available to future users.

Promote knowledge and information and take an active role in the intellectual life of the college through sponsorship of exhibits, lectures, and other programs.

Examine and revise policies and procedures to provide accurate, prompt, and friendly service.

Examine these goals regularly and revise them as necessary.
September 1994

APPENDIX B

Schmidt Library
York College of Pennsylvania

Long-Range Plan

Schmidt Library Faculty and Staff
Academic Senate Library Committee

May 2000
Schmidt Library

Long-Range Plan

May 2000

Table of Contents

INTRODUCTION

The 1997–2002 Long-Range Strategic Plan mandates that the library director, the dean of academic affairs, and the Library Committee of the Academic Senate will coordinate a study and review process of academic libraries to produce a vision plan for a remodeled library facility by the end of the 1999–2000 academic year. Working from a revised vision plan created during the 1996–1997 academic year, the library faculty and staff and the Library Committee conducted a thorough review of Schmidt Library's facilities and services. We brainstormed with the faculty from other departments on campus, solicited suggestions from students, and visited other academic libraries to create a vision plan for Schmidt Library. The following report highlights the results of this investigation. The library faculty and staff and the Library Committee agree that Schmidt Library must become a dynamic facility, providing different kinds of study spaces to meet the variety of users' needs. We must maintain traditional collections and manage new electronic resources. We must take advantage of current technology by consistently updating network connectivity and AV production facilities yet also prepare to accommodate future technologies. In addition, to meet the ongoing research needs of the York College of Pennsylvania community, Schmidt Library must provide an inviting yet intellectually stimulating environment that is user-friendly and has a comfortable ambience. Schmidt Library must also offer excellent core services that the entire college community can access from any geographical location, on campus, at home, or around the world.

ORGANIZATIONAL OVERVIEW

The Schmidt Library Vision Statement asserts:

The faculty and staff of Schmidt Library are committed to providing high-quality classroom and individual instruction in research skills, state-of-the-art technology for information retrieval, balanced collections in support of the curriculum, and excellent physical space for research and study. This document is organized by the four categories in the Schmidt Library Vision Statement:

Research Skills
Technological Skills
Balanced Collections
Physical Facilities

The vision statements appear in bold, highlighted text, followed by the projects necessary for each category. Supporting data and documents are available in the library director's office.

RESEARCH SKILLS

Vision

- Insure that students meet goals of Information Literacy core course
- Provide excellent faculty and staff, well-designed classrooms, and state-of-the-art technology
- Continue providing exceptional one-on-one instruction in Reference Services
- Offer advanced instruction as necessary

Projects

- Provide print and online materials equitably across disciplines in and out of the library, on and off campus
- Improve the Schmidt Library Web
- Customize searching by discipline
- Customize searching profile for individual users
- Provide single search interface for all databases

- Continue development of IFL 101 for students
- Provide students with all current research skills and integrated presentation techniques
- Provide state-of-the-art electronic classrooms (see also Physical Facilities)
- Provide online and hands-on training for all faculty in new Schmidt Library Web tools, including licensed and locally created databases
- Increase involvement of library faculty liaisons with faculty across all disciplines

TECHNOLOGICAL SKILLS

Vision

- Insure students' ability to use information technology in support of learning
- Maintain state-of-the-art workstations
- Provide state-of-the-art classroom for Information Literacy core courses
- Increase number of public terminals

Projects

- Expand network access with more network connectivity throughout the library, including individual carrels (see also Physical Facilities)
- Continue to build online services such as reference, reserves, interlibrary loan, AV delivery, and acquisitions as well as self-checkout
- Provide technology-enhanced group study rooms for students to prepare multimedia presentations (see also Physical Facilities)
- Provide state-of-the-art AV production facilities and equipment

BALANCED COLLECTIONS

Vision

- Acquire, maintain, and provide access to balanced collections in support of the curriculum
- Monitor changes in curriculum
- Systematically analyze collection
- Acquire materials to correct imbalances

Projects

- Encourage strong faculty involvement in building all collections
- Expand book collections, particularly where demonstrably weak in 1997 benchmark collection study
- Continue development of periodicals collection by judicious addition of print and online subscriptions, document delivery, and licensing of full text index databases

- Add CD, video, DVD, and other emerging formats in support of the curriculum
- Address YCP archives in an ongoing, systematic way, providing Schmidt Library Web access to digitized documents
- Build the fast-tracks feature of the Schmidt Library Web to further support faculty and student research across disciplines
- Provide recreational and self-help collections in all formats

PHYSICAL FACILITIES

Vision

- Provide atmosphere conducive to active learning through well-designed user, staff, and collection spaces
- Plan a new library building or an expansion/renovation project
- Insure ADA accessibility
- Supply electronic resources at reasonable pricing and licensing to be available to YCP users anywhere on campus or off campus whenever possible

Function and Atmosphere

- Create inviting and dynamic environment
- Create one central service desk (eliminating four existing desks)
- Provide space and open stacks for all collections (including books, periodicals, all existing and new AV formats, education materials, and juvenile collection) and providing off-site storage as necessary for older materials
- Create facilities for student use
- 24-hour study room
- Cybercafe
- 24-hour PC lab
- Technology-enhanced group study rooms
- Provide two state-of-the-art IFL classrooms
- Provide better patron space with mix of types of seating and network-connected carrels
- Provide staff work space
- Redesign all building security, installing new gate/detection system
- Combine Lincoln Room, Archives, and Special Collections and provide improved exhibit, display, and student art gallery space
- Provide adequate storage in all necessary campus buildings for AV equipment infrastructure
- Remove all existing interior walls and redesign all space
- Replace roof
- Improve physical access to front of building, entering on lower level
- Add windows to all sides of buildings on levels 2 and 3

- Add network connectivity as noted previously and as necessary for current and future upgrades
- Replace HVAC with attention to humidity and temperature control
- Replace lighting
- Replace flooring
- Improve soundproofing

APPENDIX C

Figure 4.1
Schmidt Library

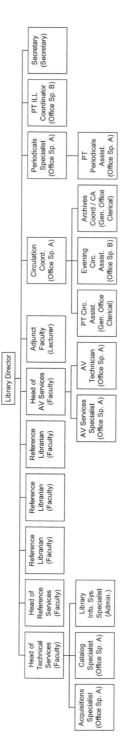

Figure 4.2
Proposed Organization

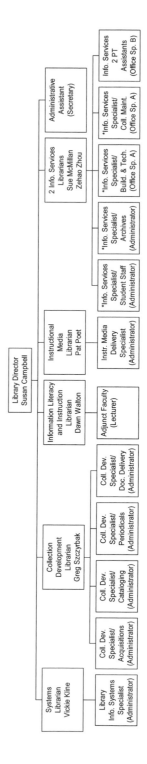

5 A FUTURE PLACE FOR US: RESULTS OF A SURVEY ON THE ACADEMIC LIBRARY "AS A PLACE"

Jason Martin

Academic libraries have faced a plethora of changes over the past 15 years, not the least of which is the ongoing shift to online research resources. Online information today is more readily available, reliable, and sophisticated than in the past. Today's library users, especially current college students, are much more adept at online searching, and the databases that they are searching, for the most part, have been designed with the end user in mind. Book-reliant subject areas such as the humanities and social sciences are seeing their numbers of student majors steadily decline, while majors in the science and business fields, which are more dependent on journal and online resources, explode. Because of these changes, fewer students and faculty actually need to enter the physical space of the library to find information and perform research. In fact, print materials, which were once the heart and soul of the library's research collection, are now seen as secondary and complimentary by today's academic library users (Anderson 2003, n.p.).

It is not just the academic library that is feeling the winds of change. Today's college students, known as "Millennials," are changing the nature of higher education altogether. These students prefer "blended learning" to traditional face-to-face classroom settings and expect frequent use of technology in their classes to keep them engaged. In many cases, it is not practical for students to purchase this technology, so they need a place on campus where they can use the latest computers and software. Not all of their computer use is for class projects, however. Instant messaging programs, Web sites like Facebook and MySpace, and software applications like Limewire and iTunes are just a few of the nonacademic reasons college students have for using high-speed Internet connection. Students also want a place where they can study in groups, snack, and be comfortable. Ideally, this place would be the library, but many libraries place bans on food and drink, forbid lounging on the furniture (assuming the furniture is even comfortable and inviting), provide much more quiet space than group study areas, and for security purposes lock down the computers. The Millennial college student, however, does not settle for what services he or she can get but rather will search for the place that offers all the services he or she wants or needs. If the library will not allow students to drink an espresso while studying in a group, they will simply go where they are allowed to engage in such behavior.

Added together, these factors have created a first for libraries across college campuses: they are seriously facing the threat of becoming irrelevant "as a place" in the world of academia. All hope is not lost, of course. Lynch and colleagues (2000) remarked that libraries must be "creatively led and strategically targeted at the interests and preferences of differentiated audiences" (69). They suggest that libraries need to establish the "right vision" and implement it (70). This means that library directors must step up and become leaders who not only re-define the role of the library "as a place" but work to secure its future as well. Thus, in order to gauge the severity of the threat that academic libraries "as a place" are becoming irrelevant and to gain an understanding of what academic library leaders are doing to combat it, I surveyed library directors from small and medium-sized academic institutions to gather their opinions on the current and future state of the academic library "as a place."

THE SURVEY

After completing the final draft of the survey, I submitted it, along with all the necessary paperwork, to the University of Central Florida's Institutional Review Board (IRB) for approval to use on human subjects. Once permission from the IRB was granted, I set about defining the limitations of those schools I wished to include in the survey. It was decided that all schools with a student enrollment of no less than 1,200 and no more than 10,000 would be eligible. A list of these eligible schools was downloaded from http://www.petersons.com, and the list was edited to include only American, four-year, place-specific (no "virtual" schools) colleges and universities. Once this list was complete, it was divided into separate lists by size to ensure equal representation. A random generator was applied to each list, and a total of 200 schools were selected for participation. The library director for each selected institution was sent one initial e-mail and one follow-up e-mail containing information about the survey with a link to it. The number of usable responses I received was 49 for a return rate of 24.5 percent.

The survey itself consisted of 45 questions. The first nine were demographic questions pertaining to the size of the institution, the number of librarians em-ployed, and the total library budget. The remaining 36 questions featured 27 Likert-scale questions on various aspects of the academic library "as a place." It also featured five qualitative or short-answer questions, three "yes or no" ques-tions, and one multiple-choice question. Of the 49 usable completed surveys re-ceived, all were of a very honest and extremely helpful nature. Library directors at 23 public and 26 private institutions responded. On average, these institutions carried a student enrollment of 5,122, employed nine librarians, housed 331,156 volumes in their libraries, and spent an annual total library budget of $2,103,550. (See Appendix A for the complete survey results.)

QUANTITATIVE RESPONSES

Library as a Place

When asked if they thought the importance of the academic library "as a place" had changed over the past 15 years, 68 percent of respondents thought the library "as a place" was much or somewhat more important, 20 percent felt that the importance of the physical library was somewhat less important, and 12 percent believed no change had occurred at all. Asked to describe the current relevancy of the library, 62 percent of directors responded by proclaiming that the library was very or somewhat relevant, while 29 percent felt that it was somewhat or very irrelevant. Ten percent believed that currently the physical library is neither relevant nor irrelevant. (Since percentages are rounded, not all totals will equal 100%.)

In response to the statement "My library has a physical inviting space," 67 percent strongly or somewhat agreed, 16 percent somewhat or strongly disagreed, and 16 percent neither agreed nor disagreed. When asked whether their library actively promoted the library "as a place," 78 percent strongly or somewhat agreed, 6 percent somewhat or strongly disagreed, and 16 percent neither agreed nor disagreed. Participants were also asked if their library actively promoted its online resources. An overwhelming 90 percent strongly or somewhat agreed with the statement, 6 percent were undecided, and only 4 percent somewhat disagreed with the statement. No one strongly disagreed that their library actively promotes its online resources. From these results, it seems clear that while today's academic library places more emphasis on promoting the "virtual" aspect of their library, the library "as a place" is readily included in marketing materials.

Virtual Library

When asked if their library had a strong online presence, 94 percent of respondents either strongly or somewhat agreed. Only 4 percent were undecided, and a paltry 2 percent strongly disagreed. Eighty-two percent of survey participants either strongly or somewhat agreed that their library's resources were easy to use. Six percent somewhat or strongly disagreed with the above statement, while 12 percent were undecided. Regarding the "Googlization" of academic research, 80 percent of library directors surveyed responded that they strongly or somewhat agreed that students relied too much on Google or other nonlibrary Internet sources. 12% neither agreed nor disagreed, while 8% of the respondents somewhat or strongly disagreed. When asked to rate the statement "A virtual library provides the same level of research support as a physical library," 28 percent strongly or somewhat agreed, 58 percent somewhat or strongly disagreed, and

14 percent neither agreed nor disagreed. In response to the statement "Twenty years from now enough information will be online to render physical libraries obsolete," only 16 percent strongly or somewhat agreed compared with 76 percent who somewhat or strongly disagreed. Ten percent of respondents neither agreed nor disagreed with the above statement.

Patron Wants

One of the big advantages to working at a small or medium-sized academic institution is the intimate setting and direct contact it affords with so many of the campus community. One great way to make contact with the students and faculty is to poll them as to their library wants and needs. It appears that many libraries have been doing just that. In response to the statement "My library has conducted studies of our patrons' needs and wants," 90 percent replied they had, with 10 percent saying they had not. The statement "My library meets the wants and needs of my patrons" generated 86 percent agreement (either strongly or somewhat) among library directors responding, while only 8 percent somewhat or strongly disagreed. Six percent neither agreed nor disagreed with the statement. Yet when asked if their library had a strong grasp of the wants and needs of its patrons, 78 percent of respondents strongly or somewhat agreed that they did, and 8 percent somewhat or strongly disagreed. Fourteen percent neither agreed nor disagreed that their library had a firm grasp of its patrons' wants and needs. It is unclear how more librarians can claim to meet patron wants and needs than have a firm grasp on exactly what those wants and needs are.

Library Usage

Eighty-two percent of those surveyed said they keep statistics of the number of questions asked at the reference desk, while 18 percent did not. Of those libraries that keep statistics, only 30 percent reported a great or somewhat increase in usage over the past five years, while 47 percent said their reference desk statistics have decreased somewhat or greatly. Six percent of respondents reported no change over that same time period. The same percentage of respondents also reported keeping library gate counts. But while the reference desk statistics were on the decline, gate counts were on the upswing. Sixty-four percent of those libraries that keep gate counts reported a great or somewhat increase over the past five years. Only 12 percent reported a somewhat or great decrease with 10 percent of respondents reporting no change at all.

Library Function

What function does the academic library play in a world of digitization and remote servers? Is its mission still the same, or do all librarians need to rethink their purpose and place? The answers provided by the responding library directors help shed some light on the issue. Ninety-four percent of those surveyed believe their library plays an important role in the education of the college or university's students, while only 6 percent disagreed in some fashion. A whopping 96 percent of respondents think that their library provides a service on campus that no other department does compared with a paltry 4 percent who disagree with this statement. Question 29—"At university X a large building exists on campus where undergraduate admissions is located on the first floor, financial aid is on the second floor, and the third floor consists of books for free check-out. University X declares the third floor to be a library. Do you agree with University X?"—provided some interesting answers. Seventy-four percent of library directors either somewhat or strongly disagreed with this statement. Ten percent disagreed to some degree, and 16 percent neither agreed nor disagreed. Almost three-quarters of the respondents believe that a library is much more than a warehouse for books. So then what is the function of the library?

When given the statement "An important function of an academic library is to provide access to information," an overwhelming 98 percent agreed either strongly or somewhat agreed with the statement. This is far and away the most consensus on one question in the entire survey. Eighty-seven percent of library directors think that an important function of the library is to select and preserve knowledge, with 10 percent neither agreeing nor disagreeing with this statement. When asked if an important function of an academic library is to provide reading materials, 89 percent believed it was, with 10 percent unsure. And an outstanding 96 percent of library directors surveyed think that an important function of the library is to provide research materials. When these four functions of a library (provide access to information, select and preserve knowledge, provide reading materials, and provide research materials) were combined with the ubiquitous "Other" in a list and library directors were asked to choose the most important function of the academic library, 71 percent chose "Provide Access to Information," 6 percent chose "Provide Research Materials," while 22 percent selected "Other." Of those answers given for "Other," almost half were "Information Literacy," with one person responding that the most important function of an academic library was all four of those functions. These answers fall in step with what Anderson (2003, n.p.) posits as the purpose of a library today. He states that the library is a portal for access to information. If this is the case, do libraries run the risk of being replaced by a server maintained somewhere in Missoula, Montana, or New Delhi, India? Not according to the library director's surveyed here. Seventy-four percent of them somewhat or greatly disagreed with the statement that libraries would become irrelevant in the future. Fourteen percent neither agreed nor disagreed with the statement, while 12 percent, to some degree, feared for the demise of the academic library. This might seem very well, indeed, to those who are in the profession and passionate about libraries. But how will this be put into practical use? How will librarians and library directors ensure that academic libraries will still be standing 20 or 100 years from now? The answers to those questions were broached in the qualitative, or short-answer, questions in the survey. Those responses are summarized below and help shed light on the thinking of academic library directors as they guide the library profession to its future horizon.

QUALITATIVE RESPONSES

Extras

The online revolution was victorious, but librarianship was designed for a print world. In order to accommodate this shift, libraries need to fundamentally alter their service (Anderson 2003, n.p.) This sentiment is echoed by Deiss (2004, 17) when she asserts that libraries that can anticipate and meet the needs of their patrons and the changing world are the ones that will meet with success and thereby attract more resources and talent. So what will these changes look like? Well, if it is fair to say that a revolution in library services is afoot, then it is clear that the revolution will be well caffeinated. When asked if they have implemented or were considering implementing any "extras" to attract patrons to the library, almost every respondent remarked they had either installed a coffee shop, were in the midst of installing a coffee shop, or would like to install one but cannot because of limitations in space and/or budget. Although one director expressed concerns over whether the acidic aroma from the coffee would damage the collections as well as the effect of spillage and insect infestation, it seems most librarians see the library coffee shop as a blessing, especially those librarians needing regular java fixes.

Piggybacking on the coffee shop is the allowance of food and drink in the library. It seems like such a simple idea, especially when considering how many libraries now house coffee shops, would be one that should have been welcomed at the same time the image of the hair-bunned spinster as librarian was ushered out the door. But this policy still has its ardent defenders and can cause even the most rational of librarians to lose their proverbial cool. That being said, more and more libraries are allowing outside food and drink as a way to make the library more welcoming. In this vein, many libraries are also adding plush chairs and couches where students can sit or lie and study comfortably.

Another popular answer—and to some degree dovetailing on the coffee shop idea as well—is art exhibit space in the library. Many directors commented that they have created spaces in their libraries where students, faculty, or members of the outside community may display artwork. These displays are rotated on a regular basis and in some cases consist of a variety of media. This simple idea has many positive benefits. First, it creates foot traffic in the library. Many students will go to see their friend's artwork or to support their fellow students or simply because they love art. Second, it allows the artist the all-important chance to display his or her art, a chance for which the artist will always be grateful. Third, it is another way for the library to become a vital part of the larger campus community and life.

Some other "extras" have come by the way of collaboration that are vital to the survival of libraries in this day and age of limited funds and resources. Many libraries are collaborating with their college's writing centers, giving the writing centers space in their libraries to conduct consultations and workshops. Some libraries also allowed peer tutoring, and many are working with computer services, most notably in the form of learning commons. This answer was not as popular as one would suspect. Of course, it could be because learning commons are now so commonplace in academic libraries that it seems anathema at this point to not have one. Libraries were also collaborating with or, maybe more appropriately, embedding themselves in campus culture by hosting various campus events and receptions.

A few small academic libraries also took a bold step and started to act more like a public library. And if truth be told, to many students who may be out of state or out of the area, the academic library is their public library. These libraries were offering "popular" materials, either noneducational videos and/or best-selling books. Some libraries paid for these items through book sales and overdue fines, while others worked in conjunction with their local public libraries. Some libraries were also offering more traditional public library programming, such as book talks, author readings, and adult literacy programs. Many of these programs bring together disparate parts of the campus and outside community and are great ways for the library to create a sense of community.

Some of the more progressive responses from library directors included having televisions, hosting concerts in the library, and having a student liaison who would communicate student concerns, wants, and needs to library administration. One library even went so far as to hold a seminar on campus made up of librarians, library administration, college faculty, and administration to discuss the role of the library on campus. Part of this seminar would include a discussion on library "as a place." Critics have argued that while comfortable chairs, music, and hot espresso might attract patrons to the library, it does little to enhance their learning (Carlson 2001, A35). This misses the point. The first objective of librarians should be to get the patrons in the door. Once they are there, the librarians and library staff can set about educating them on the vast resources and uses of the academic library so that one day when the student does need to learn, he or she will know where to go and what to use to do it.

Reference Desk Usage

As was stated earlier, 30 percent of survey respondents declared that their reference desk usage had greatly or somewhat increased over the past five years, while 47 percent said their numbers had somewhat or greatly decreased. When asked what factors they think contributed most to these changes, the answers were enlightening.

For those libraries that saw an increase in reference desk usage, all showed a great deal of agency in the matter. Each library believed they could control this matter and implemented "library-centered" methods to improve these numbers. When the students would not come to the library, the library simply went to them in the form of either increased marketing of the library's resources, especially reference, or by teaching more library instruction classes. These same libraries also reported embracing the Web and its technology (read Google) instead of banishing it to the hinterlands of serious academic research. Some libraries reported that they started library instruction classes with a brief overview of Google and how great it is for certain information needs and then steadily worked their way toward the library's subscription resources.

Information literacy, however, was probably the most popular and important answer given by respondents as to the reason for their resurgence in use. Information literacy is in many ways the most vital service a library can offer on today's college campuses. With the wealth of information now at our fingertips, information seekers need to know how to navigate this sea of information and find a harbor of proper and useful information. This goes beyond the one-shot library classes into a campuswide information literacy initiative. Information literacy is in the librarian's domain and should be spearheaded by librarians. This is a way for libraries to do more than collaborate; it is a way for libraries to embed themselves in the campus curriculum.

The libraries that reported decreases in reference desk usage seemed to be evenly split between those libraries that reported that the number of questions has gone down and the questions that were being asked were much simpler and those that reported that the remaining questions were now much more sophisticated. Clearly this is a matter of perspective and varies depending on the programs offered and students enrolled in each school, but it is clear that almost all the libraries that experienced a decline in their reference desk usage took a "student-centered" approach to the phenomenon. These libraries reported either that the students were more technologically savvy and therefore did not need a librarian's help to perform searches, that the students were not prepared for serious academic research and therefore had no idea that "Googling" all their resources for a paper was not adequate, or that college students today were simply lazy, impatient, and intellectually uncurious.

A few who reported declines, however, seemed on the cusp of a breakthrough, namely, that traditional library service is proving inadequate for the Millennial generation that makes up the vast bulk of today's college students. One director wrote, "The rewired brains of our students seek information and learn differently today," while another responded, "The traditional model used to connect with Millennial students is outdated and outmoded; we need to develop intervention tools, online tutorials, and broadcast news lists." These answers show a shift toward the library-centered approach that emphasizes the power libraries have to correct declining usage.

General Library Usage

It was previously recorded that in contrast to the reference desk usage, library gate counts of those libraries surveyed actually increased. Sixty-four percent of respondents reported their gate counts had increased greatly or somewhat, while only 12 percent reported a decrease of any kind. When asked to give reasons for the change in gate counts, some answers were as simple as increased enrollment. Here again libraries at small and medium-sized academic institutions have an advantage over libraries at larger institutions. If the current enrollment at an institution is 1,500 students and enrollment jumps by 250 students, that is an impact that can be felt all over campus. But an increase of 2,000 students at a large university with 30,000 to 40,000 students will not make a dent on campuswide service.

Information literacy also emerged as a large contributing factor to increased library usage. In a campuswide information literacy initiative, many of the faculty will integrate at least one library component in their classes. As the students matriculate through school and start taking more advanced classes, these library assignments become more specialized and sophisticated, often taking the student to the library to use the resources there.

The main reason for increased gate counts included in these responses, however, seems to be that the library is a meeting place for students. At the library they can interact, study, and research together. This is due to the fact that these library directors and their staff have worked hard to make the library more inviting and comfortable. In some cases, it was a matter of building a new library or, at the very least, remodeling or renovating the existing structure. Those libraries that could not afford this route chose to make the environment welcoming through greater customer service. Librarians and staff no longer acted as the food police or shooshed all those about them. Instead, the library staff became the helpers of the patrons.

Some other libraries attributed their increase to more classes, both library and academic, being taught in the library. This allowed students to feel comfortable in the library environs, and it brought them to the library, where they could take the chance to use the library's resources and learn what the library has to offer. Another important factor in these increases has been the amount and level of technology offered in the library. Those libraries that housed computer labs or offered a great number of computers and computer services saw large numbers of students flock to the library to write papers, prepare presentations, or simply e-mail friends and family back home.

The libraries that reported a decrease in gate counts over the past five years almost unanimously attributed this decline to both free and fee-based online sources. The only other reason given was the poor condition of the library building itself. Some libraries that reported a constant drop since the late 1990s saw a marked increase in gate counts when they remodeled their existing library or opened a new one altogether.

When asked how they planned to combat these lowered usage numbers, most libraries responded with similar ideas as those that have seen their gate numbers escalate: increased service, added technology, and allowing outside food and drink into the library. Many libraries also reported they are planning on increasing their marketing and outreach and plan to push information literacy—or at least basic library instruction—across the campus curriculum. Almost all respondents to this question, though, remarked that they must first improve the condition of the building. And this means not renovating the library or adding comfortable chairs or a coffee bar but simple things, like vacuuming, dusting, and cleaning spots on the existing furniture. This leads one to wonder how the academic libraries of our nation became so dirty and dingy in the first place. If librarians are as passionate about libraries as they so loudly proclaim, then they must be proactive in making sure the basic day-to-day cleaning needs of the library are met.

THE FUTURE

The purpose of libraries is not changing; rather, the "relative importance of different aspects, given a different context, are shifting" (Akeroyd 2001, 80). More and more library directors are starting to see the importance of the library as a social setting (Carlson 2001, A36). These quotes are quite apropos of the responses received to the final survey question, which simply read, "What does the future hold for academic libraries 'as a place'?" Some directors suggested that academic libraries "as a place" would survive as repositories of archival material and special collections. Quite a few more suggested the often-cited information literacy as holding the key to the future of academic libraries. But almost every single answer from the surveyed library directors mentioned in someway that libraries will survive as a social gathering place. Humans are by nature social animals and have a desire to be around other humans engaged in similar activities and interests as ourselves. When we engage in research, eventually we will want to surround ourselves with other researchers. Added to this is the growing number of group and team projects prevalent across college campuses today. These groups need a place to meet where they can work and collaborate. Students without access to a reliable computer, new software, or a high-speed Internet connection also need a place where they can type papers, create presentations, e-mail, and access online courseware. But the question still remains as to why a student would choose the physical library over other buildings on or off campus. This question is further complicated by the response of one library director who said that other buildings on campus are now offering "library-like spaces." The answer is, as another library director wrote, "not rocket science."

In order for students to come to the library, librarians need to give them what they want and need. Simply holding on to the belief that students will come to the library because it is there not only is unhelpful but also can present a danger to the future and vitality of the profession. And remember that this does not mean that librarians give the students what we think they want and need. Librarians need to first listen to students and faculty. Hold surveys, focus groups, and open houses to find out the needs and wants of your patrons. Or simply make a note of their questions, complaints, and concerns that are overheard or brought directly to a librarian. Librarians need to constantly assess programs and library functions. The days of a "one-size-fits-all" approach to library service are over. Libraries no longer exist in a vacuum. Research alternatives to libraries are now prevalent, and just because they do not have all the rich resources that a library does is beside the point. What matters is that many library patrons consider them, if not as equal to libraries, at least as viable alternatives. And if today's students are not having their needs met, they will go elsewhere. But above all, libraries need to be responsive to change. Some endeavors will fail, but others—many others—will soar and succeed. Libraries can be whatever we want them to be, and they can be as different from one another as day and night. Let's throw out all the old rules and ideas and make new ones. But if librarians can listen, assess, and respond, then the library "as a place" will always be an important part of college campuses. Granted, students might not be doing what was once considered "traditional library work," and in all likelihood the generations that follow them will find new and varied uses for the library as well. But what is important is that the students make use of the library and that we, as librarians, find new ways to reach out to them, teach them, and help them learn.

REFERENCES

Akeroyd, John. 2001. "The Future of Academic Libraries." *Aslib Proceedings* 53 (4):79–84.

Anderson, Rick. 2003. "The Library Is Dead, Long Live the Library: Why Everything Is Different Now and What We Can Do about It." Available at: http://www2.library.unr.edu/Anderson/molospeech.htm. Accessed June 16, 2006.

Carlson, Scott. 2001. "The Deserted Library." *Chronicle of Higher Education* 48 (12): A35–A38.

Deiss, Kathryn J. 2004. "Innovation and Strategy: Risk and Choice in Shaping User-Centered Libraries." *Library Trends* 53 (1): 17–32.

Lynch, Clifford, Patricia Batin, Richard Lucier, Carol Mandel, Deanna Marcum, and Duane Webster. 2000. "Panel on the Future of Libraries." *Educause Review* 35 (1): 69–71.

APPENDIX A

LIBRARY AS A PLACE SURVEY

1. What is the current enrollment at your institution?   **Avg 5,122**
2. What is the total number of faculty employed at your university?   **Avg 207**
3. How many librarians does your library employ?   **Avg 9**
4. How many library staff does you library employ?   **Avg 16**
5. What is the size of your acquisitions budget?   **Avg 694,112**
   Your total library budget?   **Avg 2,103,550**
6. How many volumes are in your library?   **Avg 331,156**
7. To how many electronic databases do you subscribe? (Include both institutional and consortial subscriptions.)   **Avg 95**
8. To how many electronic journals does your library subscribe? (Include both institutional and consortial subscriptions.)   **Avg 11,662**
9. Are you a public or private institution?   **22 Public 26 Private**
10. Has the importance of the academic library "as a place" changed over the past 15 years?

33%	35%	12%	20%	0%
5	4	3	2	1
Much More Important	Somewhat More Important	Neither More Important nor Less Important	Somewhat Less Important	Much Less Important
16	17	6	10	0

11. How relevant is the academic library as a place today?

31%	31%	10%	27%	2%
5	4	3	2	1
Very Relevant	Somewhat Relevant	Neither Relevant nor Irrelevant	Somewhat Irrelevant	Very Irrelevant
15	15	5	13	1

12. My academic library provides a sense of community on the campus.

47%	41%	4%	6%	2%
5	4	3	2	1
Very Much Agree	Somewhat Agree	Neither Agree nor Disagree	Somewhat Disagree	Very Much Disagree
23	20	2	3	1

13. My library meets the wants and needs of its patrons.

27%	59%	6%	6%	2%
5	4	3	2	1
Strongly Agree	Somewhat Agree	Neither Agree nor Disagree	Somewhat Disagree	Strongly Disagree
13	29	3	3	1

14. My library plays an important part in the education of the university's students.

61%	33%	0%	4%	2%
5	4	3	2	1
Strongly Agree	Somewhat Agree	Neither Agree nor Disagree	Somewhat Disagree	Strongly Disagree
30	16	0	2	1

15. My library is located in a central place on campus.

67%	14%	4%	10%	4%
5	4	3	2	1
Strongly Agree	Somewhat Agree	Neither Agree nor Disagree	Somewhat Disagree	Strongly Disagree
33	7	2	5	2

16. My library figures prominently in the future plans of the campus.

39%	37%	4%	4%	2%
5	4	3	2	1
Strongly Agree	Somewhat Agree	Neither Agree nor Disagree	Somewhat Disagree	Strongly Disagree
19	18	2	2	1

17. My library is the most technologically advanced department on campus.

14%	49%	20%	12%	4%
5	4	3	2	1
Strongly Agree	Somewhat Agree	Neither Agree nor Disagree	Somewhat Disagree	Strongly Disagree
7	24	10	6	2

18. My library has a strong online presence.

55%	39%	4%	0%	2%
5	4	3	2	1
Strongly Agree	Somewhat Agree	Neither Agree nor Disagree	Somewhat Disagree	Strongly Disagree
27	19	2	0	1

19. My library's online resources are easy to use.

33%	49%	12%	4%	2%
5	4	3	2	1
Strongly Agree	Somewhat Agree	Neither Agree nor Disagree	Somewhat Disagree	Strongly Disagree
16	24	6	2	1

20. I fear students rely too much on Google and other nonlibrary Internet resources.

41%	39%	12%	6%	2%
5	4	3	2	1
Strongly Agree	Somewhat Agree	Neither Agree nor Disagree	Somewhat Disagree	Strongly Disagree
20	19	6	3	1

21. A virtual library provides the same level of research support as a physical library.

6%	22%	14%	31%	27%
5	4	3	2	1
Strongly Agree	Somewhat Agree	Neither Agree nor Disagree	Somewhat Disagree	Strongly Disagree
3	11	7	15	13

22. My library actively promotes the library's online resources.

53%	37%	6%	4%	0%
5	4	3	2	1
Strongly Agree	Somewhat Agree	Neither Agree nor Disagree	Somewhat Disagree	Strongly Disagree
26	18	3	2	0

23. My library has a physically inviting space.

43%	24%	16%	12%	4%
5	4	3	2	1
Strongly Agree	Somewhat Agree	Neither Agree nor Disagree	Somewhat Disagree	Strongly Disagree
21	12	8	5	2

24. My library actively promotes the library as a physical place.

39%	39%	16%	4%	2%
5	4	3	2	1
Strongly Agree	Somewhat Agree	Neither Agree nor Disagree	Somewhat Disagree	Strongly Disagree
19	19	8	2	1

25. Have you implemented, or are considering implementing, any "extras" (i.e., a coffee shop) to attract more patrons to the library? If so, please briefly explain.

26. Academic libraries lead the way in making use of technological advancements.

31%	55%	10%	0%	4%
5	4	3	2	1
Strongly Agree	Somewhat Agree	Neither Agree nor Disagree	Somewhat Disagree	Strongly Disagree
15	27	5	0	2

27. My library has a firm grasp of the wants and needs of its patrons.

29%	49%	14%	6%	2%
5	4	3	2	1
Strongly Agree	Somewhat Agree	Neither Agree nor Disagree	Somewhat Disagree	Strongly Disagree
14	24	7	3	1

28. My library provides a function on campus no other department does.

86%	10%	0%	2%	2%
5	4	3	2	1
Strongly Agree	Somewhat Agree	Neither Agree nor Disagree	Somewhat Disagree	Strongly Disagree
42	5	0	1	1

29. At University X a large building exists on campus where undergraduate admissions is located on the first floor, financial aid is on the second floor, and the third floor consists of books for free checkout. University X declares the third floor to be a library. Do you agree with University X?

4%	6%	16%	31%	43%
5	4	3	2	1
Strongly Agree	Somewhat Agree	Neither Agree nor Disagree	Somewhat Disagree	Strongly Disagree
2	3	8	15	21

30. Twenty years from now enough information will be online to render physical libraries obsolete.

6%	10%	10%	31%	45%
5	4	3	2	1
Strongly Agree	Somewhat Agree	Neither Agree nor Disagree	Somewhat Disagree	Strongly Disagree
3	5	5	15	22

31. Does your library keep reference desk statistics?

82%	18%
Yes	No
40	9

32. If so, how have those statistics changed over the past five years?

14%	16%	6%	33%	14%	16%
5	4	3	2	1	0
Greatly Increased	Somewhat Increased	Neither Increased nor Decreased	Somewhat Decreased	Greatly Decreased	Nonapplicable
7	8	3	16	7	8

33. What factors do you think have contributed to these changes?

34. Does your library keep gate counts?

82%	18%
Yes	No
40	9

35. If so, how have those statistics changed over the past five years?

33%	31%	10%	10%	2%	14%
5	4	3	2	1	0
Greatly Increased	Somewhat Increased	Neither Increased nor Decreased	Somewhat Decreased	Greatly Decreased	Nonapplicable
16	15	5	5	1	7

36. What factors do you think have contributed to these changes?

37. If your overall library usage (gate counts + reference desk statistics) is in decline, what strategies are using to combat this?

38. My library has conducted studies of our patrons' needs and wants.

90%	10%
Yes	No
44	5

39. An important function of an academic library is to provide access to information.

90%	8%	0%	2%	0%
5	4	3	2	1
Strongly Agree	Somewhat Agree	Neither Agree nor Disagree	Somewhat Disagree	Strongly Disagree
44	4	0	1	0

40. An important function of an academic library is to select and preserve knowledge.

65%	22%	10%	0%	2%
5	4	3	2	1
Strongly Agree	Somewhat Agree	Neither Agree nor Disagree	Somewhat Disagree	Strongly Disagree
32	11	5	0	1

41. An important function of an academic library is to provide reading materials.

67%	22%	8%	0%	2%
5	4	3	2	1
Strongly Agree	Somewhat Agree	Neither Agree nor Disagree	Somewhat Disagree	Strongly Disagree
33	11	4	0	1

42. An important function of an academic library is to provide research materials.

88%	8%	2%	0%	2%
5	4	3	2	1
Strongly Agree	Somewhat Agree	Neither Agree nor Disagree	Somewhat Disagree	Strongly Disagree
43	4	1	0	1

43. The most important function of an academic library is:

    Provide Access to Information   35–71%
    Select and Preserve Knowledge   0–0%
    Provide Reading Materials   0–0%
    Provide Research Materials   3–6%
    Other:_____   11–22% (5 IF) (1 Educate) (1 Support the Mission of the University) (2 Research Assistance) (1 ALL) (1 A Learning Environment for Students)

44. I fear academic libraries as a place may become irrelevant in the future.

4%	8%	14%	41%	33%
5	4	3	2	1
Strongly Agree	Somewhat Agree	Neither Agree nor Disagree	Somewhat Disagree	Strongly Disagree
2	4	7	20	16

45. What does the future hold for academic libraries "as a place"?

III

COLLABORATION FOR LEARNING: MANAGING INFORMATION LITERACY

6 RHETORIC VERSUS REALITY: A FACULTY PERSPECTIVE ON INFORMATION LITERACY INSTRUCTION

Arthur H. Sterngold

Most readers will agree that library instructional programs should do more than develop students' bibliographic skills and awareness of library resources. These services should help students master the information resources and technologies that drive our knowledge-based society and are important to the students' life-long learning and professional development. Library instruction should enhance the students' information literacy (IL), including the ability to employ a variety of strategies and tools to acquire, evaluate, and use information to solve problems and gain knowledge as well as an understanding of the role of information technologies and resources in modern society.

Developing students' IL is as important to their future effectiveness as is increasing the students' subject-matter knowledge, much of which may become outdated soon after the students graduate from college or be irrelevant when students switch jobs and careers. As explained by Larry Spence (2001), the founder of the Schreyer Institute for Innovation in Learning at Pennsylvania State University, to succeed in today's information-rich society, a college student "does not need to learn more facts but how to think, decide, judge, create, and learn" (12). Developing students' IL contributes to these higher-order abilities.

For IL instruction to be effective, I believe that it must be firmly embedded in an institution's academic curriculum and that the faculty should assume the lead responsibility for developing and delivering IL instruction. I propose that librarians' roles and rhetoric reflect this emphasis and that librarians serve more as consultants to the faculty than as direct providers of IL instruction.

OVERVIEW

Led by librarians, many colleges and universities have adopted campuswide IL programs, and more are doing so now that regional accrediting bodies include IL standards in their evaluative criteria. Despite its importance, however, many faculty members remain uninformed and apathetic about IL and do not appreciate the value of library-provided instruction. As Badke (2005) says, "The accrediting bodies may be rumbling in the distance about the need for information literacy in the curriculum, but the continuing experience of most academic librarians is that information literacy is only a small blip on the radar of most professors and their academic administrators. Faculty culture remains a tough nut to crack" (70).

Given this situation, it is understandable that some librarians favor using accreditation standards to try to compel faculty to cooperate and to more fully recognize the status and influence of librarians. This position is forcefully expressed by Kempcke (2002), who states, "No longer are we in business just to support teaching. In a sense, the tables have been turned. Undergraduate teaching needs to support the library and its instructional mission of IL" (Badke 2005, 66).

As one way to meet IL accreditation requirements, Badke suggests embedding credit-bearing IL instruction in academic departments, even if the courses must be supported by college libraries as elective courses at first. Badke (2005) insists that these IL courses be taught by librarians because only they have the specialized knowledge and training required to view information as its own discipline and to create a broadly based IL curriculum.

I fear that providing stand-alone library-based IL instruction, even if individualized, may not be as effective in developing students' IL as some anticipate. Even if faculty do support this approach, students and faculty may not take the instruction seriously if it is not integrated into regular academic courses and grading. Perhaps more important, library-controlled programs may not be able to adequately develop the students' appreciation for the inherently context-specific aspects of IL, just as English composition courses sometimes fail to fully develop students' ability to write in their disciplines.

For IL instruction to be effective, faculty must believe that developing students' IL is an important aspect of their school's academic mission and programs, and the faculty also needs to assume the primary responsibility for incorporating IL instruction in their teaching and curricula. As Miller and Bell (2005) argue, IL instruction should be "woven into the fabric of courses, rather than added on somewhat awkwardly after the fact" (n.p.) To gain this faculty cooperation and support, librarians should soften their rhetoric about IL, and they should concentrate more on serving as consultants to the faculty than as providers of IL instruction. Rather than viewing IL accreditation requirements as a tool to pressure the faculty to cooperate, librarians should use the accreditation process as an opportunity to enhance faculty understanding and support and to improve their own insights into how they can help faculty members more effectively incorporate IL instruction into their teaching and courses.

WHY IL MUST BE EMBEDDED IN REGULAR ACADEMIC CLASSES

Students Must Believe IL Instruction Counts

Librarians are painfully aware of the problems that occur when faculty members, who may know little about library resources and services, request library instructional services. Despite a genuine desire to cooperate with the program, faculty may not realize how to incorporate the training into their courses and teaching. Understandably, many students do not take such instruction seriously because they do not see how it is relevant to their course work and grades, or they cannot understand the connections between general IL instruction and their specific assignments. Such "one-shot" instruction is made even more ineffective if the classroom faculty do not follow up on the IL training throughout the rest of the semester.

A further hindrance to the students' perception of value is that the librarians who teach the programs may have little in-depth knowledge about the specific courses and assignments for which they are providing the instructional services. Librarians, especially at small colleges, must cover many disciplines and follow a rigorous instruction schedule through much of the semester. Miller and Bell (2005) conclude, "There is every indication that information literacy instruction for students, as a one-size-fits-all, exclusive domain of librarians, is at best a hit-or-miss, haphazard proposition which is valued by few, still leaves many underserved, is far too labor-intensive, and overall is a paradigm of how to work dumber instead of smarter" (n.p.).

Faculty Must Believe That IL Counts

Last year, I interviewed several faculty members at my institution to find out what they think about IL and how they incorporate IL instruction into their courses. These interviews confirmed the common assumption that most faculty members are preoccupied with covering as much subject matter as possible in their courses, and they are not interested in devoting any more time to developing students' information competencies. (This is similar to the problem that plagues writing-across-the-curriculum programs in many schools.) Several faculty members told me that there is hardly enough time during the semester to cover all the course topics and textbook chapters listed in their syllabi. Some instructors told me that they simply do not have the interest or temperament to employ the kinds of process-oriented or student-centered teaching that may be required to develop their students' IL. Some of these faculty members explained that they were hired for their subject-matter expertise and that their job is to convey this knowledge rather than develop skills. In the absence of strong institutional incentives to change their pedagogical styles, many faculty members will continue using lecture-based teaching methods that are easier, safer, and less time consuming to practice.

As part of the outcomes assessment system that the accounting and business departments at my college developed to satisfy our accreditation requirements, we adopted a set of learning objectives a few years ago that included developing students' abilities to use business-oriented software programs, such as Microsoft Excel, PowerPoint, and Access. During our initial discussions and on subsequent occasions, I proposed that we include the goal of developing our students' research and information skills, using the more modest definition of IL described later in this chapter. I argued that this goal could be rather easily integrated into our academic programs, and I cited statements by the American Institute of Certified Public Accountants and other business groups indicating the importance of developing students' information competencies. Despite my efforts, the accounting and business faculties decided against adding IL as a learning objective, partly because they were not convinced that developing students' IL was important and partly because they were not interested in making the necessary changes to their teaching and curricula.

As Spence (2001, 12) explains, most faculty members learn to teach through a process of trial and error ("sink or swim" may be more fitting), employing the same lecture-based methods of teaching their professors used, who employed the instructional techniques which their professors used, and so on. Based on interviews with doctoral students working as teaching assistants, Austin (2002, 102) found that only rarely did the students' faculty advisers discuss instructional issues or practices with them and that the discussions usually focused on preparing lectures, writing exams, and other fairly mechanical issues. While many other professions have changed considerably over time, Spence (2001) suggests that a fifteenth-century teacher from the University of Paris would feel right at home in a Berkeley classroom because most professors continue to believe that "teaching is telling, learning is absorbing, and knowledge is subject matter content" (12).

True IL Is Inherently Context Specific

Information literacy is inherently context specific—that is, determining what information strategies and tools should be employed depends on the specific research situations in which the strategies and tools will be applied. To a considerable degree, each discipline has its own ideas about how research should be conducted and what information sources and methods are appropriate. In undergraduate education, these contextual elements are defined by the academic faculty members who teach the students' courses and by the academic disciplines and fields in which the courses are embedded.

Just as effective writing requires authors to assess their audiences and their writing situations early in the composition process, so true IL requires an ability to assess different research situations and then to adapt one's information strategies and tools accordingly.

This is similar to the rationale for the writing-in-discipline (WID) movement, which argues that writing instruction and practice should be embedded in disciplinary communities so that the students learn each community's preferred discourse, such as its vocabulary, argumentative styles, uses of evidence, and other rhetorical methods (McEwen 2003, 7; Miller, Myers, and Olson 2001, ix). Early proponents of WID believed that general composition courses, typically taught in English departments, were too context free and did little to improve students' writing in other disciplines.

For example, to produce a research-based article for publication in a scholarly journal, a historian may use somewhat different methods of finding, evaluating, and citing data sources than does a business analyst who must quickly brief managers on how her company should respond to a competitor's new product. While the historian must thoroughly assess well-defined bodies of knowledge to write a credible literature review, the marketing analyst may have to search for relevant data about the competitor's new product in popular and commercial sources that many scholars would reject out of hand because they are biased or unreliable, such as company Web sites and sales materials, articles in popular magazines, or even personal blogs and comments posted in online discussion forums. Furthermore, while the historian must fully identify his sources and follow strict guidelines for formatting references, the marketing analyst knows that her readers may not care how she identifies her sources or even whether she cites them at all.

As this suggests, history students must learn how to conduct research and use information resources like historians, while marketing students must learn how to conduct investigations and use information resources like marketing researchers and managers.

From the student's perspective, the most important contextual elements are defined by the research assignments for which the student must gather and use information, the course in which the assignments are used, and the pedagogical style and grading criteria of the faculty member who teaches the course. These include the specific topics, goals, and requirements of the assignments, the actual or implied audiences to which the students will report their research findings, the instructors' criteria for grading the assignments, and the contents and requirements of the academic courses in which the assignments are given.

Beyond these, the information context is also shaped by the academic discipline in which the course is embedded. This is because every academic discipline and profession comprises a unique community of practice that has its own specialized language, practices, and norms that determine what kinds of research questions are important, what research methods and tools are suitable for addressing the questions, what criteria should be used to evaluate information sources, and how those sources should be used and acknowledged when presenting research results to other practitioners.

In my introductory marketing course, the students are required to investigate the marketing strategies of well-known U.S. companies as well as the competitive circumstances in which the firms operate and then to present recommendations for improving the companies' marketing performance to hypothetical groups of managers. For this assignment, students mostly use information sources written for business managers and professionals, such as articles in trade publications, business databases, and policy-oriented journals. To evaluate these sources and the information they contain, the students must properly distinguish between information that is operational or tactical and information that is truly strategic (e.g., seasonal variations in a company's advertising and pricing versus long-term changes in the firm's product offerings and market segments). Most scholarly books and articles are not very useful for this assignment because they tend to be overly general, theoretical, or untimely. For their papers, I encourage the students to explicitly acknowledge their sources in the bodies of their reports rather than using formal citation formatting styles and to do so in a manner that suggests potential biases or inaccuracies in the source materials (e.g., "According to the company's Web site . . . ," "An informal survey of local shoppers suggests . . .").

These aspects of the assignment reflect my personal (and perhaps idiosyncratic) preferences, and they differ greatly from what many librarians would stress in library instructional sessions they designed on their own. Yet these content-specific elements are ones I believe are important based on my experiences from working in business, marketing, and advertising.

LONG-TERM SOLUTIONS

Soften the Rhetoric of IL

While IL is a popular concept and catchphrase among librarians, current definitions may unnecessarily confuse or even alienate some faculty because the definitions are too complex or contain too much jargon. At present, it seems that most of the academic research and discourse about IL occur among librarians with little participation of faculty members in other disciplines. To elicit greater faculty understanding and support, more members of the academic community must participate in the dialogue.

This may require defining IL in ways that are easier for faculty to understand and that make sense in specific academic situations. In *Characteristics of Excellence in Higher Education*, the Middle States Commission on Higher Education (2002) uses the definition of IL developed by Association of College and Research Libraries (ACRL):

> Information literacy is an intellectual framework for identifying, finding, understanding, evaluating and using information. It includes determining the nature and extent of needed information; accessing information effectively and efficiently; evaluating critically information and its sources; incorporating selected information into the learner's knowledge base and value system; using information effectively to accomplish a specific purpose; understanding the economic, legal and social issues surrounding the use of information and information technology; observing laws, regulations and institutional policies related to the access and use of information. (32)

This definition is overly complex and encompassing, and it is couched in language that may confuse many faculty members or reinforce suspicions that the IL movement is a ploy to expand the library's influence and role. How many faculty members understand "the economic, legal and social issues surrounding the use of information and information technology" and how important is this to developing the IL of undergraduate students? Is "incorporating selected information into the learner's knowledge base and value system," which may involve students' cognitive, moral, and emotional development, truly an aspect of IL itself?

I believe that librarians should adopt a more modest definition of IL that is easier for faculty to understand, that can provide a practical basis for integrating library instruction into academic courses, and that faculty are less likely to view as self-serving and encroaching on their domains. In particular, I suggest that we define IL as the ability to use a variety of research methods and tools to acquire, evaluate, identify, and apply information to help solve problems, answer questions, and gain new knowledge. Compared to the ACRL definition, this construct is more modest in scope, and it is similar to one proposed by Sterngold and Hurlbert (1998, 244).

Information Literacy and the Oberlin Education (1996, n.p.), a report by a library committee at Oberlin College, is a highly readable explanation of IL that is similar in scope and includes these elements: (1) understand how information is produced, disseminated, and organized; (2) know how to formulate questions; (3) know how to access information; (4) know how to evaluate information; and (5) understand how to make use of information.

Of course, each school should define IL in the manner that best fits its own situation and academic culture. Last year, my college's Information Literacy Sub-Committee decided to use the term "research and information literacy," or RIC, instead of IL. We did this because "research" is a familiar and valued concept in academe, connoting a systematic process of inquiry to discover new facts, to interpret existing knowledge and thinking, or to evaluate evidence and arguments. Most academic departments offer research methods courses, and many courses about discipline-specific topics include research projects and exposure to research studies.

Librarians as Consultants to Faculty

My faculty interviews confirmed what librarians already know—at most institutions, faculty members depend on librarians to plan and teach IL instructional sessions, limiting faculty involvement to describing the research assignment for which the sessions are held. This approach too easily lets faculty become disengaged, resulting in library sessions that may focus too narrowly on the technical or mechanical aspects of IL. As discussed earlier, faculty often do not integrate these library-controlled programs into their teaching and courses, and students do not take them seriously. As Miller and Bell (2005) argue, this approach is "far too labor-intensive and overall is a paradigm of how to work dumber instead of smarter" (n.p.). They assert further that to solve this problem, librarians should "concentrate less on teaching students directly, and more on helping primary instructors to do so, and developing tools and resources that faculty would use to integrate information literacy skill building into their courses" (n.p.).

Although this change will require librarians to relinquish some of their control over IL instructional programs, it does not imply that librarians will lose influence and status. In the business world, management consultants often enjoy greater professional status (and earn more money) than do their business clients, even though the consultants' roles are to serve and advise those clients. Furthermore, serving more as consultants is consistent with the managerial culture of academic librarians (Badke 2005, 65).

Professional consulting does require different skills and behaviors than does teaching. To be an effective consultant requires strong interviewing, listening and collaboration skills, and a sincere willingness to understand each faculty member's unique problems, goals, and circumstances and then to develop solutions that fit those situations. This requires that librarians view IL and IL instruction through the eyes of the academic faculty rather than just from the perspective of information professionals. This may also require librarians to spend more planning time with faculty members to elicit answers to the following kinds of questions:

1. Exactly what is the purpose of your research assignment, and what do you want students to learn from it?
2. How does this assignment relate to your overall course objectives and contents? How important is the assignment to the course?
3. What must the students do for this assignment, and how will their work be evaluated?
4. What are the products or outcomes which the students must produce for this assignment, and when are they due (e.g., theses statements, paper drafts, annotated bibliographies, oral presentations)?
5. What research and IL tasks must students perform to successfully complete the assignment, and for which of these do you think the students will benefit from library instruction and assistance?
6. How many sources must the students use, and what kinds of sources are permissible and preferred (e.g., scholarly books and articles, writings in popular magazines and newspapers, information from nonacademic Web sites)?

By asking these types of questions early in the consultation process and by continuously probing for specific explanations and examples, librarians can become sufficiently knowledgeable about the contents and contexts of the faculty's research assignments to help develop IL instruction tailored to fit instructors' specific assignments, courses, and teaching styles. In turn, faculty are more likely to integrate such instruction into their curricula, and students are more likely to take the instruction seriously.

For several years, the current director of Lycoming College's library and I worked collaboratively to plan and deliver library instructional sessions for research assignments in my marketing classes, as we described elsewhere (Sterngold and Hurlbert 1998, 246). Having worked in business before pursuing an academic career, I am skeptical about the validity and usefulness of some of the academic theories described in the marketing literature, so I require students to use information sources written for business practitioners. The librarian understood my views, and she was extremely helpful in providing instructional workshops that chiefly used practitioner-oriented source materials, even if she may have personally felt I was overly dismissive of academic sources. Furthermore, the librarian conveyed a sincere interest in my research assignments and in the outcomes of the students' research efforts, and this steadily enhanced my appreciation for her expertise and services, eventually leading to our coauthoring an article (Sterngold and Hurlbert 1998).

Of course, there is no guarantee that serving more as consultants than instructors will greatly increase faculty cooperation, but I believe it is a better strategy than providing library-based instruction in the absence of adequate faculty involvement and support.

Use Accreditation Process to Build Faculty Rapport

Now that regional accreditation bodies are emphasizing IL in their outcomes assessment criteria, colleges and universities are likely to increase their use of surveys, audits, and other assessment instruments to measure the scope and nature of IL instruction on their campuses. Although these methods don't always generate accurate results (Sterngold 2005), they can be invaluable tools for building librarian–faculty partnerships and for eliciting greater faculty support. Regardless of what assessment tools are used, librarians should use them as opportunities to talk to faculty members about the importance and meaning of IL and to explore ways to incorporate IL instruction into the faculty's teaching and curricula.

Understandably, some librarians may feel hesitant to use assessment tools for these purposes because they fear many faculty members may refuse to share information or discuss their teaching and assignments with librarians. It may comfort readers to know that even within academic departments, faculty members often avoid discussing their courses, assignments, and teaching with each other! To a large extent, this reflects the faculty's preoccupation with academic freedom and autonomy.

Information Literacy across the Curriculum

The next step is to systematically incorporate IL instruction into the school's academic programs on a department-by-department basis and in a manner that progressively improves the students' IL. To accomplish this, Miller and Bell (2005) suggest using a matrix approach in which librarians, faculty, and administrators decide together what aspects of IL should be included in which courses and programs. Miller and Bell argue that using this approach can encourage faculty to assume greater responsibility for IL and that it can "set the stage for taking course-integrated, faculty-taught information literacy to the next level" (n.p.). One solution is to build an IL-across-the-curriculum program that is similar in purpose and form to the institution's writing-across-the-curriculum program, or WAC, if it has one (Badke 2005, 74). (As suggested earlier, it may make sense to call this a RIC program that emphasizes both research and information competencies.)

If the faculty will not support this approach, then they might support formally incorporating IL objectives and instruction into the school's existing WAC program. During my interviews with faculty and students, I discovered that writing-intensive courses at my school tend to include more research assignments and IL focus than do most other courses, so formally incorporating IL into WAC programs may be a natural fit. If many of a school's academic majors and departments require students to take research methods courses, then these are also good vehicles for formally incorporating IL instruction.

Just as most WAC programs require or encourage faculty to include a variety of informal and formal writing assignments in their courses, so IL instruction should require "time-on-task" assignments that are integrated into individual courses and coordinated across the discipline.

At our institution, we found that classroom management software (CMS), such as Blackboard or Moodle, is a useful tool for helping faculty to design and embed IL instruction into their courses. While many people may view CMS chiefly as an online or distance learning resource, it can also be used to enhance courses and teaching in residential learning environments.

Classroom management software can be used to customize IL instruction for individual courses and to make IL instruction more appealing to students. For example, the students can be required to write short information essays using links to resources that are preselected by instructors and to engage in informal online discussions about their information-seeking experiences and problems. Using CMS, specific course content can be incorporated into these IL activities using the knowledge and skills of both reference librarians and teaching faculty. The faculty members remain in charge of their courses, but the librarians are involved in designing information activities and providing advice. This further educates faculty members about the range of informational technologies that can be used in their courses and how they can be adapted to fit their teaching and curricula.

At Lycoming College, a reference librarian creates modules in Moodle on such topics as plagiarism, the research process, and searching techniques. These modules can be placed within the classroom management system as an introduction to a more discipline-specific activity that will follow. A faculty member chooses which modules are appropriate for a particular course and then works with the librarian to design assignments that the students complete after reviewing the IL module.

CONCLUSION

Developing effective IL programs may require serious changes in how faculty members view and practice their teaching and in the academic goals and culture that underlie these pedagogies. By toning down the rhetoric about IL, by serving more as IL consultants than as direct providers of IL instruction, and by using

IL accreditation requirements to reach out to faculty, librarians can contribute to these more fundamental changes.

REFERENCES

Austin, Ann E. 2002. "Preparing the Next Generation of Faculty: Graduate School as Socialization to the Academic Career." *Journal of Higher Education* 73 (1): 94–122.

Badke, William B. 2005. "Can't Get No Respect: Helping Faculty to Understand the Educational Power of Information Literacy." *Reference Librarian* 89/90: 63–80.

Information Literacy and the Oberlin Education. 1996. A Report by the GF Library Committee. Available at: http://www.oberlin.edu/ library/reference/infolit/report.html. Accessed June 10, 2006.

Kempcke, Ken. 2002. "The Art of War for Librarians: Academic Culture, Curriculum Reform and Wisdom from Sun Tzu." *portal: Libraries and the Academy* 2 (4): 529–55.

McEwen, Beryl C. 2003. "Improving the Writing Skills of Business Majors: The Collective Responsibility of All Courses and Professors." Proceedings of the 2003 Association for Business Communication Annual Convention. Available at: http://www.businesscommunication.org/conventions/Proceedings/2003/PDF/13ABC03.pdf. Accessed September 5, 2007.

Middle States Commission on Higher Education. 2002. *Characteristics of Excellence in Higher Education: Eligibility Requirements and Standards for Accreditation*. Philadelphia: Middle States Commission on Higher Education.

Miller, William, and Steven Bell. 2005. "A New Strategy for Enhancing Library Use: Faculty-Led Information Literacy Instruction." *Library Issues* 25 (5).

Spence, Larry D. 2001. "The Case against Teaching." *Change* 33 (6): 11–19.

Sterngold, Arthur H. 2005. "Battling Bias: Beware of Surveys That Overstate People's Attitudes, Activities, and Future Behavior." *Planning* 71 (7): 42–46.

Sterngold, Arthur H., and Janet M. Hurlbert. 1998. "Information Literacy and the Marketing Curriculum: A Multi-Dimensional Definition and Practical Application." *Journal of Marketing Education* 20 (3): 244–49.

7 FACULTY AND INFORMATION LITERACY CASE STUDY

Emmett Lombard and Sally LeVan

Library information literacy often focuses on students—after all, they account for the majority of overall library usage. As important as it is to understand students and their learning styles, though, it is at least as important to understand faculty and their expectations—they account for the actual student need for the types of resources and services associated with information literacy via assignments. Students might come to the library for refreshments and study rooms; however, without faculty assigned research, it is doubtful that they will fully use their academic library for its intended purposes (Baker 1997, 177).

In medium-sized colleges and universities, there seem to be two tiers within which faculty require information literacy support from the library: scholarship and teaching.

Tier 1: Scholarship

Expectations based on the Boyer model require information literacy for peer-reviewed, communicated, and professional scholarship (Boyer 1990). Faculty conduct research within their disciplines but are also encouraged to conduct collaborative, cross-disciplinary research. In order to accomplish these scholarship expectations, faculty must orient themselves to the print and technological library sources available. Often such faculty orientation must be pursued through individual effort and time, as there is not an institutional mechanism, or when the library offers something, it is sometimes dismissed.

Faculty research is usually in the library or online and is much like the loneliness of the long-distance runner. Faculty rarely consider librarians as "colleagues" in the research process, coaches to a degree. Instead, they see librarians as the water boys, offering help and support as requested by the "runner/scholar."

Contrarily, as in the example of this chapter, the authors have become partners in research and teaching and have demonstrated that for this to occur faculty must first trust librarians' expertise in matters of information literacy. Additionally, academic librarians should celebrate their expertise, especially in the area of technological literacy and the library, but must also understand that the mission they follow hinges on faculty validation. This can best be accomplished through continuous orientation and collaboration with and for the faculty in both research and teaching.

For example, in collaborating with Lombard on this chapter, LeVan must be literate regarding information sources and processes for accessing scholarship in librarianship, whereas Lombard must be aware of her needs and expectations, which, as an English professor, differ from the typical freshman doing term paper research on affirmative action or abortion.

Tier 2: Teaching

An excellent example for this tier is the traditional freshman composition course where students write a term paper (i.e., affirmative action or abortion). In this course, faculty are expected to orient students to the types of scholarly sources (and the processes for accessing and using them) and primary research (e.g., interviews, observation, focus groups, and surveys) in order to complete a professional research project. This course is also designed to familiarize students with the information literacy process and tools to complete projects throughout their undergraduate course work. A problem is that faculty themselves sometimes do not grasp the necessary process or skills because of the same disconnect in tier 1.

This chapter demonstrates how much information literacy perception conflicts with information literacy reality in a college setting. One assumption is that faculty, students, administrators, and librarians agree and have articulated the definitions and expectations for information literacy process and product. However, in the authors' experiences, individual definitions of such terms as "information literacy," "primary sources," "secondary sources," and "technological sources" differ. As a result, inconsistent understandings can be perpetuated at all levels since it is often assumed that (1) all agree on the terms and outcomes and that (2) all faculty gear their research presentations to accomplish the same outcomes with the same definitions.

LITERATURE REVIEW

Combinations of *library*, *faculty*, and *information literacy* retrieved unique articles that dealt with faculty/library collaboration. Most included aspects of at least one of the following: teaching, technology, critical thinking, and assessment. In addition, most were case studies in which information literacy practices of specific colleges and universities were discussed.

Ruess's (1994) article described an undergraduate core course developed to emphasize library/information skills. It also considered ways to assess its effectiveness.

Cox and Vanderpol (2004) described librarian marketing initiatives at the University of Nevada—Las Vegas that catered to faculty interests. Their article was extremely relevant to this study because the academic library focus was on faculty. They recognized that without faculty buy-in, information literacy initiatives lack potency.

Exceptionally insightful to this study was Mackey and Jacobson's (2005) acknowledgment of the importance of faculty to library information literacy initiatives. They reminded readers that accrediting agencies are increasing their interest in information literacy. In order for schools to effectively meet the standards, collaboration between faculty and librarians is essential. They presented two processes for such collaboration at work at the University at Albany.

An interesting note: many of the case studies were community colleges. For example, Bower (2000, 15) described how librarians at Pellissippi State Technical Community College used technology to familiarize faculty with library resources and services. Zeszotarski (2000) distinguished computer literacy from information literacy and suggested combining the two in library instruction. She cited many different community college examples, including Florence-Darlington Technical College and Miami-Dade Community College, where administrators, librarians, and faculty worked together to incorporate technology into various learning processes, including the classroom and library. Such articles provide excellent examples of how to encourage faculty involvement in traditional library matters. However, they do not deeply delve into faculty understandings or assumptions concerning the library and/or information literacy. In order to truly collaborate, it is important for librarians to first understand what faculty perceives and where their struggles lie. To help in this effort, we conducted a perceptional study of faculty at a private Carnegie Classified Master's I University in northwestern Pennsylvania regarding library and information literacy concepts and connections.

METHODOLOGY/RATIONALE

Overall faculty perceptions were gauged using an electronic survey via e-mail. The survey posed eight questions/statements with Likert ratings or multiple choices for response (see Appendix A). A focus group succeeded the survey to acquire more qualitative data (Appendix B). In addition to information literacy, survey respondents were asked to provide the following demographic data:

1. Department. The university is composed of two colleges: the College of Humanities, Business, and Education (CHBE) and the College of Sciences, Engineering, and Health Sciences (CSEHS). Faculty in science-oriented fields rely differently on information (and different types) than colleagues in humanities. Therefore, perception comparisons among departmental faculty within the two colleges regarding information literacy and its relationship to the library could be useful.
2. Gender. Numerous studies document differences in thought patterns between the two genders that warrant survey distinction.

3. Rank. Faculty with different ranks or status (e.g., full professors, associate professors; tenured, nontenured) could have different research requirements and/or expectations. How the library accommodates those expectations might affect perceptions among the ranks.

RESEARCH RESULTS—SURVEY DATA

Overall

Sixty faculty responded to the survey. Table 7.1 offers response averages to the survey's first question and three succeeding statements. The numbers reflect agreement or disagreement with the question/statements. For example, if a person responded "strongly disagree," then a value of 1 was assigned; "disagree"=2, "agree"=3, "strongly agree"=4. Note that two of the 60 did not respond to statement 4.

Table 7.1

Survey Question 1 and Statements 2–4	Average response
1. ALA information literacy definition agreement	3.23
2. Library crucial to information literacy	3.4
3. Faculty input is crucial to library information literacy initiatives	3.33
4. Library effectively supports faculty information literacy	3.15

Questions 5 through 8 were not assigned Likert-scale ratings. Instead, faculty were provided multiple choices. As Table 7.2 shows, seven faculty responded that information literacy impacts them most as "scholar" and 13 as "teacher," and 40 stated that information literacy "equally" impacts them as teachers and scholars; none stated that information literacy has "no impact."

Table 7.2

5. How does information literacy most impact you?	Scholar	Teacher	Equally	No impact
Number of responses	7	13	40	0

None of the respondents identified "recognizing information need" as the information literacy component with which they most struggle; 33 identified "locating information," four "evaluating information," and six "incorporating information"; five identified "all" these components as a struggle, and 11 identified "no struggles" (see Table 7.3). Note that one did not respond to question 6.

Table 7.3

6. With which information literacy component do you most struggle as a scholar?	Recognizing information need	Locating information	Evaluating information	Incorporating information	All	No struggles
Number of responses	0	33	4	6	5	11

For most information literacy struggle as a teacher, 18 faculty identified "creating assignments," 12 "grading assignments," and 14 "explaining assignments"; 15 responded that information literacy has "no impact" in terms of struggle as a teacher (see Table 7.4).

Table 7.4

7. With which information literacy component do you most struggle as a teacher?	Creating assignments	Grading assignments	Explaining assignments	No impact
Number of responses	18	12	14	15

The last question was "Who do you perceive as the information literacy experts?" Twenty-seven faculty identified "Librarians," 26 "subject scholars," four "tech experts," one "other," and zero "students" or "administration" (see Table 7.5). Note that two did not respond to question 8.

Table 7.5

8. Who do you perceive as the information literacy experts?	Librarians	Subject scholars	Tech experts	Administration	Students	Other
Number of responses	27	26	4	0	0	1

College

Thirty-four faculty from CHBE responded. Identified departments included English (five respondents), History/Political Science (two respondents), Foreign Languages (one respondent), Business (one respondent), Education (one respondent), Criminal Justice (one respondent), Social Work (three respondents), Theology (one respondent), Psychology (four respondents), Legal Studies (one respondent), and Theatre/Communication Arts (one respondent).

Twenty-six faculty from CSEHS responded. Identified departments included Nursing (four respondents), Biology (four respondents), Physical Therapy (two respondents), Environmental Science Engineering (one respondent), Mathematics (three respondents), Occupational Therapy (two respondents), and Computer and Information Science (one respondent). Many departments in both colleges have no response identification.

Table 7.6 compares the response averages to the survey's first question and three succeeding statements between the two colleges. Note that two of the 26 CSEHS faculty did not respond to statement 4.

Table 7.6

Survey Question 1 and Statements 2–4	CHBE	CSEHS
1. ALA information literacy definition agreement	3.24	3.23
2. Library crucial to information literacy	3.5	3.27
3. Faculty input is crucial to library information literacy initiatives	3.35	3.31
4. Library effectively supports faculty information literacy	3.29	2.96

Table 7.7 shows that three CHBE faculty responded that information literacy impacts them most as "scholar" and eight as "teacher"; 23 responded that information literacy "equally" impacts them as teachers and scholars, and none stated that information literacy has "no impact." For CSEHS, four identified "scholar," five "teacher," 17 "equally," and zero "no impact."

Table 7.7

5. How does information literacy most impact you?	Scholar	Teacher	Equally	No impact
CHBE	3	8	23	0
CSEHS	4	5	17	0

None of the CHBE faculty identified "recognizing information need" as the information literacy component with which they most struggle; 20 identified "locating information," one "evaluating information," and four "incorporating information"; four identified "all" these components as a struggle, and four identified "no struggles." Zero from CSEHS identified "recognizing," 13 "locating," three "evaluating;" two "incorporating," and one "all"; seven identified "no struggles" (see Table 7.8). Note that one of the CHBE faculty respondents did not answer question 6.

Table 7.8

6. With which information literacy component do you most struggle as a scholar?	Recognizing information need	Locating information	Evaluating information	Incorporating information	All	No struggles
CHBE	0	20	1	4	4	4
CSEHS	0	13	3	2	1	7

For most information literacy struggle as a teacher, 13 CHBE faculty identified "creating assignments," seven "grading assignments," and eight "explaining assignments"; six responded that information literacy has "no impact" in terms of struggle as a teacher. Five CSEHS identified "creating assignments," five "grading assignments," six "explaining assignments," and nine "no impact" (see Table 7.9). Note that one of the CSEHS faculty respondents did not answer question 7.

Table 7.9

7. With which information literacy component do you most struggle as a teacher?	Creating assignments	Grading assignments	Explaining assignments	No impact
CHBE	13	7	8	6
CSEHS	5	5	6	9

The last question was "Who do you perceive as the information literacy experts?" Eighteen CHBE faculty identified "librarians," eleven "subject scholars" or faculty, three "tech experts," and one "other"; no faculty identified "students" or "administration." For CSEHS, nine identified "Librarians," 15 "subject scholars," and one "tech experts"; none identified "administration," "students," or "other" (see Table 7.10). Note that two faculty members (one from CHBE; one from CSEHS) did not respond to question 8.

Table 7.10

8. Who do you perceive as the information literacy experts?	Librarians	Subject scholars	Tech experts	Administration	Students	Other
CHBE	18	11	3	0	0	1
CSEHS	9	15	1	0	0	0

Gender

Table 7.11 represents the response averages to the survey's first question and three succeeding statements according to gender. Thirty faculty identified

Table 7.11

Survey Question 1 and Statements 2–4	Female	Male
1. ALA information literacy definition agreement	3.3	3.08
2. Library crucial to information literacy	3.4	3.3
3. Faculty input is crucial to library information literacy initiatives	3.26	3.35
4. Library effectively supports faculty information literacy	3.24	3.13

themselves as "female" and 23 as "male." Note that two faculty (one female and one male) did not respond to statement 4.

Table 7.12 shows that information literacy impacted two female faculty most as "scholar" and eight as "teacher," 20 stated that information literacy "equally" impacted them as teachers and scholars, and no one stated that information literacy has "no impact." Four males identified "scholar," four "teacher," 15 "equally," and none "no impact."

Table 7.12

5. How does information literacy most impact you?	Scholar	Teacher	Equally	No impact
Female	2	8	20	0
Male	4	4	15	0

No female faculty identified "recognizing information need" as the information literacy component with which they most struggle; 14 identified "locating information," four "evaluating information," and three "incorporating information"; three identified "all" these components as a struggle, and five identified "no struggles." No males identified "recognizing," 13 "locating," none "evaluating," three "incorporation," and two "all"; five identified "no struggles" (see Table 7.13). Note that one of the female respondents did not answer question 6.

Table 7.13

6. With which information literacy component do you most struggle as a scholar?	Recognizing information need	Locating information	Evaluating information	Incorporating information	All	No struggles
Female	0	14	4	3	3	5
Male	0	13	0	3	2	5

Nine female faculty identified "creating assignments" as their major information literacy struggle as a teacher, seven "grading assignments," and five "explaining assignments"; nine responded that information literacy has "no impact" in terms of struggle as a teacher. For males, six identified "creating assignments," five "grading assignments," seven "explaining assignments," and four "no impact" (see Table 7.14). Note that one of the male respondents did not answer question 7.

Table 7.14

7. With which information literacy component do you most struggle as a teacher?	Creating assignments	Grading assignments	Explaining assignments	No impact
Female	9	7	5	9
Male	6	5	7	4

For "Who do you perceive as the information literacy experts?" 19 female faculty identified "librarians," nine "subject scholars," and one "tech experts"; none identified "administration," "students," or "other." Six males identified "Librarians," 14 "subject scholars," two "tech experts," and one "other"; none identified "administration" or "students" (see Table 7.15). Note that one female did not respond to question 8.

Table 7.15

8. Who do you perceive as the information literacy experts?	Librarians	Subject scholars	Tech experts	Administration	Students	Other
Female	19	9	1	0	0	0
Male	6	14	2	0	0	1

Rank

Table 7.16 represents response averages to the survey's first question and three succeeding statements based on academic rank. Ten faculty identified themselves as "instructor," 14 as "assistant professor," eight as "associate professor," and three as "professor."

Table 7.16

Survey Question 1 and Statements 2–4	Instructor	Assistant	Associate	Professor
1. ALA information literacy definition agreement	3.2	3.29	2.75	3.67
2. Library crucial to information literacy	3.3	3.43	3.75	3.67
3. Faculty input is crucial to library information literacy initiatives	3.1	3.36	3.5	3.33
4. Library effectively supports faculty information literacy	3.1	3.14	3.75	3.33

Table 7.17 illustrates that one instructor believed information literacy impacts him or her most as "scholar" and four as "teacher," five stated that information literacy "equally" impacts them as teachers and scholars, and no one stated that information literacy has "no impact." Of the 14 assistant professors, two identified "scholar," three "teacher;" nine "equally," and none "no impact." One associate professor identified "scholar," one "teacher," six "equally," and none "no impact." Finally, no professors identified "scholar," one "teacher," two "equally," and none "no impact."

Table 7.17

5. How does information literacy most impact you?	Scholar	Teacher	Equally	No impact
Instructor	1	4	5	0
Assistant	2	3	9	0
Associate	1	1	6	0
Professor	0	1	2	0

No instructors identified "recognizing information need" as the information literacy component with which they most struggle, six "locating information," none "evaluating information," one "incorporating information"; one identified "all" of these components as a struggle, and one identified "no struggles" (note that one instructor did not respond). No assistant professors identified "recognizing," nine "locating," none "evaluating," one "incorporating," two "all," and two "no struggles." No associate professors identified "recognizing," three "locating," one "evaluating," two "incorporating," one "all," and one "no struggles." Finally, no professors identified "recognizing," two "locating," none "evaluating," none "incorporating," none "all," and one "no struggles" (see Table 7.18).

Table 7.18

6. With which information literacy component do you most struggle as a scholar?	Recognizing information need	Locating information	Evaluating information	Incorporating information	All	No struggles
Instructor	0	6	0	1	1	1
Assistant	0	9	0	1	2	2
Associate	0	3	1	2	1	1
Professor	0	2	0	0	0	1

For the most information literacy struggle as teacher, four instructors identified "creating assignments," two "grading assignments," and one "explaining assignments"; two responded that information literacy has "no impact" in terms of struggle as a teacher. Six assistant professors identified "creating assignments," two "grading assignments," four "explaining assignments, and" two "no impact." One associate professor identified "creating assignments," two "grading assignments," two "explaining assignments," and three "no impact." One professor identified "creating assignments," none "grading assignments," two "explaining assignments," and none "no impact" (see Table 7.19).

Table 7.19

7. With which information literacy component do you most struggle as a teacher?	Creating assignments	Grading assignments	Explaining assignments	No impact
Instructor	4	2	1	2
Assistant	6	2	4	2
Associate	1	2	2	3
Professor	1	0	2	0

The last question was "Who do you perceive as the information literacy experts?" Six Instructors identified "librarians," two "subject scholars," and two "tech experts"; none identified "administration," "students," or "other." For assistant professors, nine identified "librarians," four "subject scholars," and one "other"; none identified "tech experts," "administration," or "students." One associate professor identified "librarians," six "subject scholars," and one "tech experts"; none identified "administration," "students," or "other." Finally, two professors identified "librarians" and one "subject scholars"; none identified "tech experts," "administration," "students," or "other" (see Table 7.20).

Table 7.20

8. Who do you perceive as the information literacy experts?	Librarians	Subject scholars	Tech experts	Administration	Students	Other
Instructor	6	2	2	0	0	0
Assistant	9	4	0	0	0	1
Associate	1	6	1	0	0	0
Professor	2	1	0	0	0	0

Survey Comments

CHBE

Female assistant professor (English): "I want to comment on question number 8, which I found difficult to answer as stated. I believe that, in terms of sub-specialty areas, faculty probably are the experts about finding material in that limited area of information, but overall, the librarians are more informed and have the broader big-picture perspective."

Male assistant professor (English): "One of the points of confusion for some faculty who teach LENG112 Critical Analysis & Composition is the classification of information. For example, what constitutes and differentiates an online source from a library source that is accessed online? Are our notions about primary and secondary sources the same as they were 20 years ago? Are these distinctions even necessary anymore? Perhaps there is no agreed-upon answer to these sorts of questions. However, I do think that many faculty would benefit from more instruction in information literacy before they try to help students become more literate, whether those faculty teach freshmen or graduate students."

Male (Psychology): "I answered these questions regarding what I think the notion of literacy meant . . . but I think I might not have a solid definition. . . . also, I teach mainly grad students, so my experiences may be a bit different."

Female assistant professor (Social Work): "I think the **** library is a spectacular support but requires more resources. I'd like to see more on-line journal subscriptions & expanded book holdings. However, I do think our library staff does a wonderful job with their current limited resources."

Unknown (Foreign Languages): "I hope that somehow this survey brings more books, videos, DVDs, CDs, journals, etc., on my field to our library."

Unknown: "Couldn't answer question #8; information literacy is too broad to be the designated, closed territory of only librarians, only subject scholars, or only IT folks. It takes all three."

CSEHS

Female (Nursing): "I did have a problem with question # 8. I believe that all of us contribute to information literacy. With so much information on the Web and electronically, it is increasingly difficult to be an expert."

Female (Physical Therapy): "Question 8 was left blank because all are (or should be) information literacy experts to function successfully in the world today. Question 4 was answered specific to the library services available at ******. There are adequate resources with regard to textbook accessibility in the stacks or via interlibrary loan, however access to on-line journals is lacking. As I am enrolled in an advanced degree program at another university I have access to thousands of on-line journal from home or work. This is a valuable resource which should be available to ****** faculty and students as they pursue scholarly activity."

Female (Computer and Information Science): "While librarians are the custodians and experts in collections of information, the awareness about and retrieval of specialized information is also a responsibility of domain experts—like faculty. HOW to actually obtain and interact with some of the specialized information often requires technology-savvy. This need for a blend of capabilities tempered with information validity-critiquing makes information literacy more challenging in 2006 than in 1906."

Focus Group

All faculty who included their names on the survey were invited to participate in a follow-up focus group. One male assistant professor and two female instructors, all CHBE faculty, participated. Before actual discussion commenced, the faculty responded in writing to the following eight italicized questions drawn from the original survey:

1. *Do you agree with the American Library Association definition that an information literate person is one who can ". . . recognize when information is needed and have the ability to locate, evaluate, and use effectively the needed information" (1989)?*

Two of the faculty wrote "yes," and another underlined the word "evaluate" and commented "italicize?"
Do you have a better definition?
None provided an alternative.

2. *How crucial is the library to information literacy?*

One wrote "vital," another "very critical because the written sources are accurate," and the third "very crucial."

3. *How crucial is faculty input to library information literacy initiatives?*

One wrote "very crucial," another "critical to advise what sources should be available," and the third "very crucial."

4. *Does the library effectively support your information literacy needs?*

Two wrote "yes" and the third "yes, resources are excellent."

5. *How does information literacy most impact you?*

One wrote "necessity to constantly update my own knowledge—a *good* thing," another "students entering the field must have accurate sources to cite . . . need help recognizing what is accurate info; and the third "searching for information for courses & helping students to locate & evaluate information."

6. With which information literacy component do you most struggle as a scholar?

One wrote "efficiency in saving information, manipulating data in personal files," another "n/a," and the third "locating material."

7. With which information literacy component do you most struggle as a teacher?

One wrote "guiding students with no visual knowledge of what makes up databases," another "students don't like to read books, but will spend time watching videos, power-points & listening to CD's etc.," and the third "locating material."

8. Who do you perceive as the information literacy experts?

One wrote "librarians who can help students find accurate sources of info. & classroom direction (examples of sites)," another "librarians," and the third "professional librarians & teachers."

Despite there being only three, the group discussion provided insights that the survey numbers could not illuminate. After writing their responses to the questionnaire, the three discussed aspects of information literacy the survey did not anticipate. Categorical headings used to best describe the essence of this discussion are Resources, Administration, Pedagogy, Terminology, and Citation.

Resources

The consensus was that the "library does well with what it has (resources and service)." One problem a faculty member identified was "source visibility: due to electronic 'resources' 'sources' are not as evident. This impacts evaluation of type and quality." Another noted that "students need help—better coordina-tion between Writing Center and Library." Finally, it was stated that the "library as institution has changed (no more physical boundaries—online information); librarians should also change (no longer confined to library; work out of different departments, become more involved in curriculum development)."

Administration

One faculty member who is also a department chair shared how upper administration wanted him to investigate "trends" related to his field. For ex-ample, if he were in nursing, administration wanted him to identify concepts and statistics indicative to nursing as a profession. All chairs were given this charge, and this particular faculty member observed that certain fields were better rep-resented in terms of information quantity than others. For example, professional disciplines, such as nursing, engineering, and accounting, were easier to measure and find than liberal arts disciplines, such as history and philosophy.

The type of information administrators sought might not directly affect teaching or scholarship, but it does affect advising and other service-related duties for which faculty are also responsible. Depending on the discipline, locating useful information for administrative demands can be daunting and requires different search techniques and resources than those typically employed for scholarly or pedagogical pursuits.

Another issue was certification and/or accreditation. External agencies evaluate schools or individual programs for library resource capability; thus, it is outside requirements that sometimes determine budgetary allotment. A concern was the composition of such certification teams. The belief within the focus group was that it is mostly professional administrators and not faculty.

The last item had to do with overall Internet regulation. It was noted that while the accessibility of information on the Internet makes it easier to locate, the ways in which it is regulated and monitored could compromise academic freedom and privacy. Such problems could develop at the institutional and/or global levels.

Pedagogy

A major pedagogical issue was accommodating both undergraduate and graduate students. Undergraduates, especially in liberal studies core courses, offer demographic diversity (e.g., different majors) and topical diversity (e.g., 25 students, of differing majors, in a freshman composition class writing about 25 different topics for their research papers). Whereas undergraduates challenge faculty knowledge breadth, graduates require more depth. It is difficult to juggle the literacy needs and expectations when teaching two undergraduate and graduate courses each in a semester, which is not atypical for many faculty in Master's I Carnegie class schools.

Terminology

The idea that there is a lot of research jargon and that it is inconsistently applied creates problems. An instructional example is "you are not allowed to use the Web for this research assignment." Technically, that statement includes articles retrieved from EbscoHost. Some faculty and students cannot overcome the semantics that confuse research processes. What most professors might mean by such an instruction is that students are not allowed to cite *Web sites* found using a search engine like Google rather than articles found using indices that are *Web-based* like EbscoHost.

It was agreed that resources and sources need to be better categorized and defined in terms of both quality and hierarchy (i.e., primary, secondary, and tertiary). The question then became "who should define": librarians, faculty, or administration? Should it be campus to campus, or should associations decide at a national level? Additionally, with more consistently and tightly defined terminology, a procedural understanding for the roles of the different players involved in the information literacy process needs to exist. If a college develops an information literacy definition and a policy with procedures to implement it, then all involved in its implementation need to understand their roles and their relationships to other colleagues. For example, if it were decided that every freshman composition course was to have a three-class research orientation in the library, then faculty must accommodate the needed time in their syllabi/schedules, and the administration must provide the library with the necessary resources (e.g., personnel, space, and technology) to support it. Policies and procedures are more the realm of the administration category, but they can grow and work only from consistently determined terminology. Without effective communication, effective implementation is unrealistic.

Citation

There was disagreement as to whether citation should be explicitly stated in an information literacy definition. However, all agreed that it is implicitly a part of the process.

Citation within information literacy included two aspects: style documentation and ownership acknowledgment. That there exist hundreds of citation styles is confusing enough, but compounding the problem are multiple interpretations of the more popular styles (e.g., the style of the Modern Language Association and that of the American Psychological Association). This becomes particularly problematic in a classroom situation. Students are often unfamiliar or uncomfortable with citation as a process and struggle with the detail-oriented aspects of it. However, some professors are uncomfortable with it, too, leading to communication problems. Most of the time, faculty know what they do not want to find on works-cited pages but sometimes cannot definitively express what they do expect. Students pay with lowered grades.

The confusion over documentation often leads to acknowledgment dilemmas. However, one faculty member went philosophically further. She suggested that some faculty do not even understand what constitutes intellectual ownership. In fact, there was disagreement over specific examples of ownership within the group. One professor believed that anything borrowed by one faculty member from another needs to be cited (e.g., class notes and committee work). Another faculty member dismissed this notion. His argument was that citation is unnecessary in instances that do not involve scholarship (i.e., publication) and that it can actually be a distraction in terms of presenting the material within the campus community.

It was agreed by all present that librarians should take the lead in any discussions or policies regarding intellectual property, including citation, but with significant faculty input.

DISCUSSION

Survey Results

Between the two colleges, three response rates noticeably differed. For statement 2, "library crucial to information literacy," CHBE rated 3.5 compared to 3.27 for CSEHS. Both similarly rated agreement with the American Library Association's information literacy definition (CHBE: 3.24; CSEHS: 3.23), but the CHBE respondents placed a higher premium on the library within the information literacy framework. Indicative of this perception is the fact that 85 percent of library instruction provided in 2006 at this school was requested by CHBE faculty.

Another noticeable difference occurred with statement 4's "library effectively supports faculty information literacy" (CHBE: 3.29; CSEHS: 2.96). This could be in response to resources rather than services. All respondents, regardless of discipline, were not overly impressed with what their library has in terms of books and periodicals, as evidenced by some of the commentary (e.g., female assistant professor [Social Work]: "I think the **** library is a spectacular support but requires more resources"). However, science-related resources are much more expensive than humanities and thus more difficult to subscribe or attain—CSEHS library perception could be compromised.

Finally, college response to question 8's "who do you perceive as the information literacy experts" differed. Eighteen CHBE respondents identified "librarians" compared to nine CSEHS. Granted, more CHBE faculty responded to the question than CSEHS (33 to 26), but 15 CSEHS faculty identified "subject scholars" compared to only 11 CHBE. This indicates a much different perception of librarians in relation to information literacy. It could again be attributed to the library's ability or inability to meet resource needs or also to disciplinary differences within collegiate departments concerning information.

For example, CHBE faculty in disciplines such as history and literature rely heavily on books and articles (i.e., secondary sources) for their information, whereas CSEHS faculty in disciplines such as biology and engineering rely heavily on experiments and laboratory tests (i.e., primary sources). The library is better suited to secondary research and is traditionally the main information repository for humanities faculty. Many CSEHS faculty, though, have their own laboratories (complete with laboratory technicians) that are better suited to their primary research needs. Therefore, perceptions concerning research, information literacy, and the library's role would differ.

Female respondents rated higher the first four question/statements than males with the exception of statement 3. They agreed more strongly than their male counterparts with the American Library Association's information literacy definition, the notion that the library is crucial to information literacy and that the library effectively supports faculty information literacy needs. However, males agreed more strongly that faculty input is crucial to library information literacy. This suggests that the female respondents had more confidence in librarians when it comes to information literacy. Again, library instruction numbers can validate this suggestion perception: 74 percent of faculty who scheduled library classes at this university in 2006 were female.

Statement 8 again provided sharp response contrast: 19 females identified "librarians" as the information literacy experts compared to six males, and 14 males identified "subject scholars" compared to nine females. These responses do not contradict responses to the first four survey items.

Although there are interesting responses among the ranks, because of the small identification, it is not feasible to draw any insights.

Overall, no one identified administration or students as information literacy experts. This is important to recognize when developing information literacy policy and assessment. Information literacy is mostly pedagogical and scholarly; thus, faculty and librarians deal with it more than others on campus. Therefore, it is imperative that faculty have confidence in the policy rationale and assessment relevance, or it could compromise teaching and scholarship morale.

Technically, two people identified "technology experts" as information literacy experts (one selected them as their question 8 choice; another commented that "information literacy is too broad to be the designated, closed territory of only librarians, only subject scholars, or only IT folks. It takes all three."). This demonstrates the need for Zeszotarksi's (2000) distinction between information and computer literacy. Many people, including librarians, associate information literacy with computers; however, computer technology is only one possible variable in the information literacy equation. As already noted, the components of information literacy that the American Library Association identifies have been in use for a long time. Perhaps it is the heightened awareness of information literacy parallel to the rise of the Internet that prompts thinking of them in combined terms by default. Regardless, it is important to remember that an information-literate individual must be able to do more than "Google" key words.

Four of the nine survey comments explicitly addressed question 8: information literacy experts. In fact, two respondents did not select a choice on the survey yet commented on the question at the end. The consensus was that no one group is the information literacy expert—it takes combined efforts of faculty, who, as one wrote, are the "domain experts," and librarians.

This might sound like common sense, but it is not often applied in the teaching tier. Many times, faculty cultivate knowledge in their classrooms and leave information retrieval to one or two library sessions, if any. The two should not be mutually exclusive. First, faculty who assign research should involve librarians in the curriculum if they do not already; if they do, it should be for more than one or two classes. Second, librarians should adjust instruction to the particular class (not only discipline but class). For example, if the class is working on the proposal stage of their assignments, emphasis might be on key word and controlled vocabulary search strings and the hierarchy of information concepts and sources. Once the students start writing, the focus can switch to resources (e.g., catalog or indices).

Frequently, faculty rush to schedule library orientations in the beginning of the semester. This is ineffective because the librarian, knowing that she will not again see the students in class, tries to jam as much information (mostly on locating sources) into that session. By the time the students understand exactly what they are going to write about and begin to think about the types of sources they will need (usually not until a few weeks into the semester), they will have forgotten a lot of what they learned during the orientation. Librarians should be a part of the research pedagogy from beginning to end, and faculty should not be idle observers while the librarian is at work: subject expertise dialect during source retrieval lecture reinforces both sides of the process.

Focus Group

Citation was a surprising topic to arise within the discussion because, though justified within the American Library Association's definition ("use effectively the needed information"), it is not explicitly stated and often gets lost in the shuffle of accommodating recognizing, locating, evaluating, and other use aspects. Faculty discussed it in terms of their own scholarship needs; however, it was observed that some faculty could benefit from a better pedagogical citation approach in the classroom. "It's all in the style manual" is not an uncommon answer to a student's citation question, nor is it adequate. Style manuals do not account for every citation possibility that exists. More dialogue about the "whys" behind citation will make the "hows" easier for students to fathom.

The discussion concerning plagiarism included not only student problems but also colleague problems. Citation is a detail-oriented chore, and with the advent of electronic resources and sources, new, complicated, and sometimes multiple interpretations of citation guidelines have evolved. An example is the Modern Language Association: depending on where one looks on the Web or in various composition handbooks, different examples exist on how to cite items. This does not serve anyone well, especially research and citation novices. Some faculty could struggle with it in their own scholarship, and mechanical failings could be misinterpreted as ethical failings.

CONCLUSION

These numbers cannot be used for anything other than simple indication of how some faculty perceive the information literacy process at a particular school. However, the indication is probably not surprising to most, and this study itself could be easily replicated in any school for insights about its own faculty.

Concepts composing information literacy have been a part of academics since the beginning, and information literacy will never disappear. Of late, it has experienced a vigorous scrutiny, and there appear to be perceptional inconsistencies about what it is, how to integrate and support it, and how to assess it. If more consistency is not established, then positive outcomes will be difficult to achieve. We suggest three ways to achieve consistency and effective implementation of information literacy.

1. *Faculty and librarians should play the lead roles in information literacy policy development at both internal and external levels.* It seems that most college and university policy decisions come from administration or faculty who are heavily associated

with administration. If many faculty are to take information literacy initiatives seriously, they should feel that "their own kind" laid the foundation. This might require administrative adjustment. Regardless of who sets policy, it will be faculty and librarians who implement the resulting initiatives, and if they were the ones who established the rationale, then they will more effectively achieve the desired results.

One procedure that should follow is library orientations for all faculty—not the "dog and pony show" where the catalog and citation indices are displayed and explained but rather a pedagogical forum on how to implement library resources (including librarians) into curricula. Instead of spectators, faculty with strong research skills and proven teaching success should be copresenters in this forum with librarians. Sally LeVan anticipates that the results of such an initiative would be "teachnological": an effective combination of library technology and faculty subject expertise.

External implies outside accreditation teams, and the same thinking applies to their personnel composition: more faculty and librarians. If this is already the case, then it should be emphasized to faculty for morale purposes.

II. *The comment that the "library does well with what it has" is an insufficient faculty perception for establishing information literacy confidence; it needs to read "library meets all my research and literacy expectations."* There are four reasons why the former perception exists: (1) faculty ignorance of actual library information literacy resources and policies, (2) library ignorance of faculty information literacy needs, (3) insufficient fiscal support, and (4) combinations of the first three.

Faculty ignorance is remedied through continued library orientations and faculty outreach; however, the faculty must take advantage. If they cannot determine the importance of the library's role in scholarship and pedagogy, then administrative "incentive" should be applied.

Library ignorance is remedied by going beyond traditional departmental liaison procedures: perhaps librarians should take classes within their disciplinary assignments or maybe even teach some classes. This has worked extremely well for Lombard: he completed the Master of Arts degree in English at the school where he works as a librarian and teaches as an adjunct in the English department's freshman writing program. As a result, he knows better how to do the following: orient composition students to the library, pedagogically prepare composition faculty for creating research opportunities for students, and work with students at reference on specific assignments. Earning a subject master's degree is often a promotion requirement for academic librarians; we find it is more relevant that they earn the degree in the actual university in which they work to build better departmental relationships and understandings if at all possible.

Finally, the easiest way to remedy insufficient college or university support is with increased funding. This is not a surprise but often is unrealistic. A more practical alternative would be for the college to truly acknowledge its library's strengths and weaknesses and assess faculty scholarship in lieu of the library. It is unlikely that a faculty member teaching 12 credit hours per semester, served by a library of fewer than 1,000 periodicals, is going to be a publication giant. Therefore, the college should appreciate this when evaluating scholarship quantity.

This in turn might prevent resentment on the parts of faculty with publishing quotas who are not getting their scholarship needs met by the library.

Strides toward this have already begun with the adoption of Boyer's scholarship model by some schools. It stresses quality and relevance over quantity; however, implementation must become a part of campus culture and permeate into all aspects of scholarship, including information literacy, because Boyer's principles are not exclusively absolute—all of them connect to form a scholarship mosaic.

III. The topic of citation arose during the focus group discussions, and it was agreed by faculty present that librarians should take charge. The idea has merit and is not without precedent: some libraries currently offer citation services where librarians will check bibliographies. Sinclair Community College, at one time, offered citation workshops.

The question centers on what citation responsibilities libraries should adopt and to what extent. For example, should libraries focus exclusively on bibliography formats and offer workshops on creating them, or should they also be involved in in-text citation and composition? Either possibility would rely on faculty approval; the second, though, would also require much closer in-class collaboration.

REFERENCES

Baker, Robert K. 1997. "Faculty Perceptions towards Student Library Use in a Large Urban Community College." *Journal of Academic Librarianship* 23 (3): 177–82.

Bower, Rick J. 2000. "The Development of an Online Instruction Tutorial at Pellissippi State Technical College." *Community and Junior College Libraries* 9 (2): 15–24.

Boyer, Ernest. 1990. *Scholarship Reconsidered: Priorities of the Professoriate.* Princeton, N.J.: Carnegie Foundation for the Advancement of Teaching.

Cox, Jennifer L., and Diane Vanderpol. 2004. "Promoting Information Literacy: A Strategic Approach." *Research Strategies* 20 (1/2): 69–76.

Mackey, Thomas P., and Trudi E. Jacobson. 2005. "Information Literacy: A Collaborative Endeavor." *College Teaching* 53 (4): 140–45.

Ruess, Diane E. 1994. "Library and Information Literacy: A Core Curriculum Component." *Research Strategies* 12 (1): 18–23.

Zeszotarski, Paula. 2000. *Computer Literacy for Community College Students.* Los Angeles: ERIC Clearinghouse for Community Colleges. ED438010.

APPENDIX A

1. How strongly do you agree with the American Library Association definition that an information literate person is one who can ". . . recognize when information is needed and have the ability to locate, evaluate, and use effectively the needed information" (1989)?

   a) strongly disagree
   b) disagree
   c) agree
   d) strongly agree

2. The library is crucial to information literacy.

   a) strongly disagree
   b) disagree
   c) agree
   d) strongly agree

3. Faculty input is crucial to library information literacy initiatives.

   a) strongly disagree
   b) disagree
   c) agree
   d) strongly agree

4. The library effectively supports faculty information literacy needs.

   a) strongly disagree
   b) disagree
   c) agree
   d) strongly agree

5. How does information literacy most impact you?

   a) as a scholar
   b) as a teacher
   c) both equally
   d) no impact

6. With which information literacy component do you most struggle as a scholar?

   a) recognizing information need
   b) locating information
   c) evaluating information
   d) incorporating information
   e) all above
   f) no struggles

7. With which information literacy component do you most struggle as a teacher?

   a) creating assignments
   b) grading assignments
   c) explaining assignments
   d) no impact

8. Who do you perceive as the information literacy experts?

   a) librarians
   b) subject scholars (i.e., faculty)
   c) technology experts (e.g., ITS personnel)
   d) administration
   e) students
   f) other

9. Name (not required):

10. Rank:

    a) instructor
    b) assistant professor
    c) associate professor
    d) professor

11. Gender:
12. Department:

Comments regarding this survey or research initiative:

APPENDIX B

1. Do you agree with the American Library Association definition that an information literate person is one who can ". . . recognize when information is needed and
   have the ability to locate, evaluate, and use effectively the needed information"
   (1989)?
   Do you have a better definition?
2. How crucial is the library to information literacy?
3. How crucial is faculty input to library information literacy initiatives?
4. Does the library effectively support your information literacy needs?
5. How does information literacy most impact you?
6. With which information literacy component do you most struggle as a scholar?
7. With which information literacy component do you most struggle as a teacher?
8. Who do you perceive as the information literacy experts?

8 THROUGH THE INFORMATION LITERACY LENS: MANAGING THE COLLEGE LIBRARY IN THE TWENTY-FIRST CENTURY

Susan Swords Steffen

Directing a college library at the beginning of the twenty-first century is an exhilarating undertaking. The dramatic growth of the World Wide Web and the vast array of resources that can be accessed via the Internet have rapidly transformed college libraries into information- and technology-rich environments. Students and faculty can access an extraordinary array of information resources and learn and practice critical and information literacy skills. At the same time, college libraries must continue to meet the more traditional responsibilities of developing resources and services that support and achieve the educational mission of the institution. College libraries still have to collect, organize, and provide access to the resources needed by students and faculty to directly engage in an intellectually broad undergraduate curriculum.

Managing that same library is also a daunting undertaking. In many ways, the brave new world of the college library feels a very unsafe place. The increased technological sophistication of the college library's constituencies has given rise to a general skepticism across the academy about the continued importance of or even need for the library's services and resources. Increased pressure on tuition-dependent colleges to control costs has restricted the funds available and forced the library into active competition with other parts of the institution for limited funding. Regional accrediting agencies that used to be content evaluating college libraries on their commitment of resources now measure a college library's success on the achievement of student learning outcomes, which are no easier to discern in the library world than they are in the classroom. In the face of these challenges, the managers of college libraries must continually strive to position the library, its resources, and its staff at the center of the college's mission.

Information literacy programs have become both core initiatives that academic libraries are expected to provide and one of the primary methods of enhancing the library's role within undergraduate colleges. Information literacy goals to teach students to identify and articulate a need for information, to locate and access information, to critically evaluate sources, and to effectively use, analyze, and present information advance the educational mission of undergraduate institutions. At the Association of College and Research Libraries (ACRL) President's Program, Gary Radford (2006, n.p.), professor of communication studies at Fairleigh Dickinson University, asserted that, through learning to be information literate, his undergraduate students learn a way of being in the world of information that prompts them not only to think about, evaluate, and use information but also to get excited about and become engaged in learning and ideas. The ACRL (2000) has adopted a comprehensive set of information literacy competency standards for higher education and best practice guidelines for instruction programs that describe standards of quality to which libraries can aspire. All the recent recipients of the Excellence in Academic Libraries awards have had significant information literacy programs. Regional accrediting bodies look for the existence of a successful information literacy program as one of the key indicators of an effective college. The Council of Independent Colleges, the major national service organization for small and midsized, independent liberal arts colleges and universities in the United States, is so committed to information literacy as a powerful instrument in effecting institutional change in small colleges that it has provided more than half a million dollars to almost 200 colleges to assist teams of librarians, faculty, and academic administrators in developing information literacy programs through its Transforming the Library and Learning Spaces and Technology workshops.

However, in an era of significant challenges to the college library, some library leaders still argue that information literacy instruction is an unnecessary extra that competes with other library programs and services for limited resources. And they make a persuasive case that balancing the requirements of technological developments with more traditional library goals while at the same time spending large amounts of financial and staff resources teaching students what may be redundant skills may be subvending an unaffordable luxury (Bell 2006, n.p.). College libraries, they argue, can make better use of their limited resources by creating, managing, and interpreting the resources of the library and leaving the students and faculty to develop their own expertise in searching and finding information without direct instruction from librarians (Wilder 2005, n.p.).

So how can college library leaders who believe in the benefits of information literacy learning incorporate information literacy goals into the management of the college library and still have adequate resources to meet the demands of the twenty-first-century library? Perhaps the answer to this dilemma can be found in the best practices of information literacy instruction as outlined by the ACRL (2003). The methodology of information literacy instruction advocates that faculty integrate information literacy goals into their course learning objectives. In a similar way, college library managers should integrate information literacy learning into the management of the college library and use it as an organizing philosophy to refocus library programs and services. As Bennett (2005, n.p.)

advocates, the twenty-first-century library must make a paradigm shift from an institution that exists to deliver services to an institution that produces learning. Weaving information literacy goals into the management of the college library creates an information environment where students can learn and practice such skills through their interactions with the library as well as through direct instructional experiences. A college library focused through the lens of information literacy will result in a library that produces better student learning outcomes and contributes more effectively to the achievement of the educational mission of its institution.

Refocusing the management of the college library through the lens of information literacy has important implications for many areas of library practice. To better understand the consequences of this reorientation of the work of the college library, it is useful to examine the areas of user services, space planning, library technology, and the organizational culture of the library.

USER SERVICES

In a traditional model of college library organization, user services commonly include reference, instruction, and access services. Each of these areas facilitates users' access to information resources by giving research assistance, teaching research skills, or providing access to library materials through circulation of the library's own materials or interlibrary loan. In most cases, each of these functions operates relatively independently, even in libraries where a small staff dictates that the same individuals may perform more than one function. Using information literacy learning as a focus for user services draws these functional areas closer together and makes them more interdependent and complementary.

In this model, facilitating information literacy learning becomes the central theme of all user services and the library's highest priority. The 2005 strategic plan for the ACRL states that "ACRL and its members are recognized as collaborative leaders in teaching lifelong learning skills, improving techniques for assessing learning outcomes, and in creating environments for discovery." To accomplish this goal, college librarians need to be teachers of information literacy skills, both formally and informally. They will need to work hard to become effective teachers who create learning experiences that will compel students to become active learners who make information literacy skills their own. They will partner with classroom faculty to coordinate student learning outcomes with appropriate information literacy skills and experiences.

Accordingly, I would argue that formal information literacy instruction must become the first priority of all user services staff and will take precedence over more traditional reference service. Whether this instruction is integrated into the regular curriculum or delivered as separate credit courses, the shift in focus will have a major impact on the scheduling and deployment of staff resources throughout user services. Traditionally, in most libraries, the reference desk schedule structures and organizes the work of the library, and all other services are scheduled around the desk schedule, but in an information literacy–focused library, instructional activities have priority. Because assisting users is still very important, it will be critical to develop innovative means of providing reference assistance that accommodate the demands of a teaching library. For instance, this may mean a more flexible reference desk schedule or greater use of paraprofessional and student staff to provide backup assistance. When the library makes the learning and teaching of information literacy skills its highest priority, students and faculty will recognize the importance of these skills to their success as learners and teachers and be more likely to take them seriously.

Second, the nature of reference service in a library employing information literacy as an organizing principle will be different. Interactions with users will evolve from simple question answering to inquiry and discovery. Reference librarians will become information collaborators with students. Rather than merely providing answers to questions, librarians will help users shape their research questions, talk with them about their ideas and information needs, and have ongoing, in-depth conversations with users (Steffen and Bell 2005, n.p.). They will not only focus on manipulating print and electronic resources to retrieve information but also help users evaluate the sources they are finding and guide them in choosing among available options. Reference service will not stop with locating and evaluating information but will also include assistance with the analysis, synthesis of information, and presentation of information. Reference librarians will also provide instruction in the use of and assistance with the productivity software that is so essential to educated people today and will not think about this type of assistance as extra or "someone else's job." In this model of reference service, librarians are not tied to the reference desk but may even choose to "rove" on occasion and take reference to the residence halls and the cafeteria, meeting students on their home ground in order to reinforce what we know so well—as good as students think they are, they are not as good as when we are there to assist.

Third, an information literacy–focused library will make use of liaison librarians to deliver library services to students and faculty. In this method of service delivery, librarians assume responsibility for providing instruction, reference consulting, collection development, and information technology support to a particular academic department or discipline. Students are introduced to the liaison librarian for their discipline through formal information literacy instruction and then can continue to develop formal and informal relationships through interaction in the library, one-on-one meetings, and in-depth research consultations. By focusing their work in specific disciplines, librarians become experts in the ways of knowing a subject area, shape the library's resources to meet the needs of the discipline, and guide students in their learning and inquiry. Through this personalized contact with a librarian, students gain important experience in when and how to use expert information support as part of the research process.

Fourth, to fulfill all these expectations, reference librarians will need new knowledge and skills. They will continue to be experts in navigating information resources, understanding the structure of disciplines, evaluating the worth and usability of materials, and interpreting content and quality. They will need to be excellent and accomplished teachers. But in order to help students and faculty become truly information literate, they will also need to teach and provide assistance with an array of software that enables users to synthesize, manipulate, and present information in a variety of formats, such as Web authoring, publishing, digital image and audio editing, and social networking software. They must also become experts in the areas of ethical information use, particularly plagiarism, copyright, and documentation of sources. Anyone who talks to faculty members has heard their frustration when they speak of the rise in student plagiarism. Instead of imagining that the morals of the country are sinking, college librarians are in a unique position to show faculty the perils of the new information-loaded environment and are in the exact position to teach students how to plot a course through the new knowledge world without consciously or unconsciously borrowing the work of others.

Finally, a library organized around an information literacy philosophy will have a user-oriented customer service philosophy focused more on assisting users with meeting their information literacy goals than on optimizing the operation of the library. It will have transparent policies and procedures that help users understand how and why service is provided in a particular way. Service should be delivered in a way that helps students learn how to negotiate library systems in order to get the information they need and to teach students how to work with library and information systems to achieve the results they are seeking.

LIBRARY SPACE

Rethinking a college library through an information literacy lens requires reexamining and, in most cases, reorganizing library space to facilitate information literacy learning. First, a well-designed, well-equipped, and highly visible instructional space is essential because it communicates the centrality of information literacy learning to the operation of the library. By highlighting formal instructional space, users of the library can observe both librarians in their teaching role and students actively engaged in learning information literacy skills. Second, space for reference assistance should be redesigned to be open and barrier free so that students and librarians may work collaboratively on research projects. Although librarians will likely need some type of work space and students should know where they can find a librarian, serious consideration should be given to eliminating or at least redesigning the reference desk to make it a more open and less authoritative place where librarians and students can share the research process. To facilitate collaboration between and among students and librarians, the reference area should also include display equipment, including large-screen monitors, projection equipment, or whiteboards where students and librarians can work together to explore and interact with information as well as furniture that can be easily moved and rearranged to accommodate different-sized groups. Third, library spaces should be designed to support a variety of approaches to learning, including working in groups, multitasking, and quietly studying and reading. Electronic and traditional library resources should be juxtaposed so that students are encouraged to choose between and among a wide variety of resources. Spreading information technology throughout the building encourages students to integrate technology and print materials. Finally, an information literacy–focused library should have an inviting and comfortable atmosphere that encourages engagement, creativity, and productivity, all qualities that foster active student learning. As Bennett (2005, n.p.) argues in his CLIR report, library space that allows students to collaborate, continue conversations beyond the classroom, and celebrate the communal character of inquiry and knowledge promote effective learning.

LIBRARY TECHNOLOGY

Library technology is an area of library management that absorbs a great deal of time, money, and energy and has an impact on every area of library operations. Library technology includes the technology resources that the library acquires, electronic resources, Web tools and other software that the library provides, and the technology expertise of librarians and other library staff. An information literacy management philosophy has implications for planning and decision making in all these areas.

A library with an information literacy focus will provide computer access that is efficient, easy to use, and up to date so that inadequate technology does not become a barrier that detracts from the user's ability to identify, access, evaluate, and use information. Ideally, there should be state-of-the-art computer resources with current versions of software as well as easily usable wireless access, and these resources should be well maintained and in good repair. Because information literacy is also about analyzing, synthesizing, and presenting information, there should be access to an integrated suite of productivity software consistent with a campuswide standard and other hardware and software that facilitates the synthesis and presentation of information, including the ability to access and edit music, video, and still images; to do color printing; and to analyze and visualize data.

The library's own Web site should also be reexamined through an information literacy learning lens. Because many of the college library's users will access the library virtually as well as physically, it is important that the Web site reflect and facilitate the library information literacy learning goals. In addition to providing efficient and effective access to the library's electronic resources, the library's Web site should be designed to encourage users to make choices between and among different types of information resources. It should provide users with tools that help them critically evaluate the information they identify and to make choices between the library's electronic resources and other information accessible via the World Wide Web. The Web site should also provide virtual assistance with the analysis, synthesis, and presentation of information by including links to documentation and tutorials about these software tools. Finally, in order to encourage the ethical use of information, the library's Web site should include information about copyright and plagiarism as well as links to assistance with writing and citing.

The role of technology leadership is a natural one for the information literacy–centered college library. Whether an institution has administratively combined information technology and the library or has decided to keep these functions structurally separate, librarians bring critical expertise in the academic use of information technology and in the management of information to the larger campus. Through their experiences integrating information literacy learning goals into the management of the library, librarians comprehend much about the computer resources, training, and support that faculty and students need. They understand how students learn about, interact with, and use technology and what aspects of technology particularly challenge them. By working with faculty to integrate information literacy learning goals with course content, librarians also develop insight into faculty needs for training and support in the use of computer technology for their teaching and research. Whether or not they operate the server that operates the course management software, librarians can and should play an important role in introducing and providing support for faculty and students engaged in any kind of online learning. Participating in the development, implementation, and support of course management software, such as Blackboard, puts librarians and the library at the center of student learning and at the heart of the pedagogical work of the faculty. While they are supporting the work of classroom faculty, librarians can easily integrate their own information literacy learning goals into the courses delivered by this software and ensure that courses connect students with appropriate library resources. This considerable expertise can bring librarians to the forefront of the college's educational mission and also provides an opportunity to become essential to its success.

LIBRARY CULTURE

College library managers engaged in refocusing a library through the lens of information literacy learning need to take a careful look at the library organizational culture necessary to promote this effort. The library and its staff should model information-literate behavior in the management of the library, approaching challenges and problems with a spirit of inquiry, identifying when information is needed, and accessing, evaluating, analyzing, and presenting new knowledge in a public and intentional way. The library must also manage information ethically in compliance with copyright and intellectual property laws and free of plagiarism. For a college library focused on information literacy, learning is an important core value not only for its users but also for its staff. Risk taking, innovation, and inquiry are valued over stability, tradition, and certainty. All staff will need to think of themselves not only as learners but also as teachers and carry out job responsibilities with an eye to enhancing student learning outcomes. They should get excited about learning and ideas and think about and use information in useful ways. Additionally, they should have a healthy skepticism about information resources, acknowledge that there are many sides to every story, and recognize when it is appropriate and necessary to question and challenge traditional assumptions about library operations. These core values will result in a staff that collaborates frequently, that is cross trained, that eagerly embraces new challenges and ways of thinking, and that is rewarded for these ways of working. To foster this organizational culture, college library managers will need to ensure that there is a strong emphasis on staff development, reward for innovative thinking, and open communication about job roles and responsibilities.

CONCLUSION

So what kind of a learning experience can students expect in an information literacy–focused college library? When they come to the library, they will find a welcoming, comfortable environment where they can study and interact with peers and librarians. They will participate in formal information literacy instruction throughout their college experience in both introductory general education courses and more advanced, discipline specific study. As they pursue their studies, they will be able to access and choose among a wide range of information resources in multiple formats and to receive discipline specific assistance from expert librarians. They will interact with librarians and other library staff who believe in engaging collaboratively with students and in providing all library services as transparently as possible. They will find not only up-to-date, user-friendly computer technology but also assistance with using that technology that is readily and conveniently available. The research process will be an integrated experience from initial information need to final product creation and presentation. They will learn how to use information ethically and legally so that they may confidently engage in inquiry, make connections among seemingly disparate information, and create and present their new knowledge. In short, their experiences in the library will play an important role in their growth toward empowered, informed, responsible, and reflective learning.

Refocusing the college library through the lens of information literacy lays claim to the library's position at the center of the educational mission of the institution. Through this realignment, the library moves decisively from an institution that delivers resources and services in support of academic programs to one that fosters and indeed is critical to the successful student learning that is the hallmark of effective higher education.

REFERENCES

Association of College and Research Libraries. 2000. *Information Literacy Competency Standards for Higher Education*. Available at: http://www.ala.org/ala/acrl/acrlstandards/informationliteracycompetency.htm. Accessed November 28, 2006.

Association of College and Research Libraries. 2003. *Characteristics of Programs of Information Literacy That Illustrate Best Practices: A Guideline*. Available at: http://www.ala.org/ala/acrl/acrlstandards/characteristics.htm. Accessed November 28, 2006.

Bell, Steven. 2006. "The Great (?) Debate: Is Information Literacy a Fad and a Waste of Time." Available at: http://acrlblog.org/2006/07/04/the-great-debate-is-information-literacy-a-fad-and-a-waste-of-time. Accessed November 28, 2006.

Bennett, Scott. 2005. "Righting the Balance." In *Library as Place: Rethinking Roles, Rethinking Space*. CLIR Publication 129. Available at: http://www.clir.org/pubs/reports/pub129/bennett.html. Accessed November 28, 2006.

Radford, Gary. 2006. *Posted Remarks from the Great Information Literacy Debate*. Available at: http://acrlblog.org/special-features/posted-remarks-from-the-great-information-literacy-debate. Accessed November 28, 2006.

Steffen, Susan Swords, and Michael J. Bell. 2005. "Glass of Fashion: Librarianship for the 21st Century." In *Introduction to Reference Services in Academic Libraries*, ed. Elizabeth Connor, 159–66. New York: Haworth Press.

Wilder, Stanley. 2005. "Information Literacy Makes All the Wrong Assumptions." *Chronicle of Higher Education* 51 (18): B13.

IV

PROMOTING THE LIBRARY: COMPETITION AND COLLABORATION

9 CAMPUS PARTNERSHIP IN SMALL ACADEMIC LIBRARIES: CHALLENGES AND REWARDS

Patricia Hernas and Timothy Karas

Partnering has become the mantra and mania for many organizations over the past decade. Partnerships have flourished for many disparate reasons; however, two overarching themes become apparent: "to do more with less or to do something entirely different than their existing resource base permits" (Bergquist 1995, 11) and "to survive in these turbulent times, organizations must be nimble, adaptable, and. . . . People and organizations must recognize their deep interdependence" (Bergquist 1995, 12). Over traditional hierarchical structures, effective partnerships allow organizations to be responsive to the forces of change and to more efficiently use limited human and fiscal resources.

Within the overarching framework of forming strategic partnerships, academic libraries forge campus partnerships for several specific reasons: furthering institutional goals, building relationships with key client groups, and creating strategic opportunities to obtain additional funding. Often these reasons and subsequent activities overlap. For example, building a relationship with a specific department to increase use of the library might result in additional funding to purchase specialized material. Supporting the college's mission to reach out to a specific underserved community group by participating in events and activities might increase administration's support toward building library collections and services needed to enhance academic efforts for that targeted population.

While there are many commonalities among libraries, there are significant differences too. Being regionally located, private or public, or two- or four-year programs are important factors that shape the challenges and opportunities that influence the types of partnerships that can be formed. Much has been written about partnership and collaborative efforts in large academic libraries, and smaller academic libraries can learn from these examples. However, smaller public academic institutions have unique challenges, and this is especially true for community colleges.

Following is a brief summary of the colleges profiled in this chapter that describes partnership and collaborations between the library and faculty, administrators, and students at several colleges in the San Francisco Bay Area. Each of these institutions is briefly described to help better understand the institution's circumstances and the challenges of the particular small academic library. These statistics are from "California Library Statistics 2005" (B: 1–2).

College of San Mateo Library (FY2003/04)
San Mateo County Community College District

Number of Colleges in District:	3
Students:	24,067
Faculty (FTE):	3.1
Classified Staff (FTE):	6.3
Administrator:	1
Circulation:	34,909
Total Operating Budget:	$744,601

Evergreen Valley College Library (FY2003/04)
San Jose Evergreen Community College District

Number of Colleges in District:	2
Students:	14,432
Faculty (FTE):	4.3
Classified Staff (FTE):	6.0
Administrator:	1
Circulation:	30,057
Total Operating Budget:	$876,792

Menlo College Library (FY2003/04)
Private Academic (4 Year)

Students:	629
Faculty (FTE):	4.0
Classified Staff (FTE):	5.5
Administrator:	1
Circulation:	3,745
Total Operating Budget:	$427,864

Mission College Library (FY2003/04)
West Valley Mission Community College District

Number of Colleges in District:	2
Students:	11,093
Faculty (FTE):	4.0

Classified Staff (FTE):	6.0
Administrator:	1
Circulation:	20,737
Total Operating Budget:	$905,913

SMALL ACADEMIC LIBRARIES CAN PARTNER

With librarians and staff straining to provide standard services to faculty, students, and staff, how can a smaller academic library find the time and energy required to initiate and forge strong partnerships across campus? It is important to realize that without such partnerships the library is in danger of being marginalized—with collections unable to keep pace with the needs of the curriculum and outdated service delivery methodologies unable to support the needs of distance education students. Let us examine examples of what some small academic libraries are doing to forge collaboration and partnerships across the campus by building on already established activities or standard operating procedures.

Integrate with Existing Campus Activities

Partnerships are most often enjoined because each party is aware of the other and can identify mutual benefits through working cooperatively. Advertising the library and its services is important so that students and faculty are continually reminded of the benefits of the library; this keeps the library in the forefront when defining new potential partnering opportunities. Open houses, events, speakers' series, workshops, and fliers are some ways to advertise the library; however, with few staff and limited time, how can the library use events to advertise its value? Most easily the smaller library can take full advantage of existing campus activities sponsored by academic departments and student groups. Thus, the time to plan and implement a campuswide event is borne mainly by other groups.

Several times a year, various groups at colleges organize and host campuswide events. Some of these could be holiday related and sponsored by the student government or other groups. Often a student services department will organize events that highlight and advertise diverse offerings such as financial aid, student employment, health services, tutoring services, and the like. These provide an excellent opportunity for library collaboration. The library could provide host space where appropriate or simply help advertise the event through signs and fliers. These events also are excellent places for the library to advertise its services.

Student Services Events

At Mission College, the library was exploring various ways to encourage students to come into the library. As a commuter college, like many community colleges, students often come on campus for only a class or two. Early in the fall term, the student services department hosts a campuswide Student Success Fair in which the library decided to actively participate. To entice students to stop by the library's table, a drawing was held for prepaid print cards. The table was shared with the Extended Opportunity Program and Services (EOPS) and near the Counseling Center's table. Not only did students learn about the library and its services as they filled out the entry forms for the drawing, but librarians made contacts with counselors and staff at the EOPS group. These two programs touch a large percentage of students. Giving these departments an insight into the programs and services offered by the library to students allows them to in turn inform students and encourage them to "hit the library" while on campus.

Evergreen Valley College celebrates Kicks It Outside each semester in which all departments set up booths and activities across the entire campus. Academic departments, student groups, and the student government all participate in the full-day event. The library has a large presence at this event and uses it as a key method of communicating services to the student body. Fliers and bookmarks are handed out, and a large display is set up. Librarians are there to chat with students and faculty who stop by.

Articles

The library can take advantage of any ongoing campuswide communications. The Counseling Department at Mission College publishes a newsletter, *Counseling Connections*, twice a semester, and the library has an article in each issue. The library takes advantage of the Counseling Department's efforts to produce and publish an approximately six-page glossy newsletter. Often campuses have some sort of master calendar of events that the library can take advantage of to advertise any programming activity or other events, such as special hours during finals week.

Faculty Workshop

Kicking off each semester at Evergreen Valley College is Instructional Improvement Day, organized by the dean of instruction. Using this opportunity to reach specific faculty groups, the library hosts a workshop highlighting services and collection materials around a specific theme. Using the theme of teaching ethnically diverse students, the library showcases databases that help faculty find tips for working with these student groups, print collections that could be utilized in class assignments, and other specific materials that would be helpful. The library has been hosting such workshops for several semesters, and normally 30 to 40 faculty members attend. The dean of instruction's office organizes the entire day, and faculty members are expected to be on campus, so the overhead for the library to offer a workshop is very minimal for a large benefit.

Institutional Initiatives

Libraries need to identify large institutional initiatives that will be beneficial partners. Most of the time, these initiatives started without any formal participation from the library department and required the library to repackage its resources and services in a way meaningful to the initiative. Mission College has received a five-year U.S. Department of Education Title V grant. The grant's focus is "Improving Access and Success for Hispanic and Other Underserved Students." Key components of this grant include outreach, improving learning outcomes, and developing a more welcoming environment for Hispanic and underserved communities. The library's mission and goals easily dovetail with the components of this grant. By presenting a proposal to the campus advisory committee, the library has been able to secure funding to purchase two databases (*EthnicNews Watch* and *Enciclopedia Universal en Espanol*) and English-as-a-second-language books and textbooks. Additionally, the Title V project conducted a qualitative needs assessment for its Latino outreach efforts. One of the conclusions in the report was that "Mission College's library and science building are wonderful assets that could be shown off at Open House events for local high school students and their parents" (Mission College 2006, 16). Being investigated are ways to further integrate library resources, programs, and services under the Title V umbrella.

Community and Workforce Education

Mission College is one of eight regional health occupations resource centers (RHORCs) as part of the California Community College Health Care Initiative and represents the Bay Area. RHORCSs provide collaboration opportunities between health care employers and education providers from all segments. Services offered include needs assessments, job analyses, curricula and resource development, training, certification testing, and employee referrals to health care industry employers (California Community Colleges Health Occupations 2006, n.p.). Students enrolled in RHORC activities do not fall within the traditional college matriculation process and tuition structure. RHORC services are offered via workforce development. This program traditionally made resources available to its students through its own "resource library" located in the program offices. With the library being the information center for the entire campus community, it made practical sense to envelop these students' information needs into the library.

A pilot program was initiated between the library and RHORC for students enrolled in an NCLEX-RN course. RHORC is providing multiple copies of the textbooks that will be available in the library for checkout to students in this program. These students are not issued student body cards that double as library cards; rather, the library issues community cards to them. On the first day of class, a librarian gives the class a brief orientation regarding library services. In most cases, these students have not visited the library before. After receiving the orientation and being in the building, students can appreciate the full breadth of services offered to them and become active library users. Between May and June 2006, three classes averaging 20 students have participated in the pilot. Overall, the library adapted its existing model for course reserves, community cards, and library orientations.

Libraries should take every advantage to actively participate in campus events, programs, and publications. Keeping the library visible to students, faculty, and administration is a necessary foundation for future partnering opportunities, including large institutional partnerships begun by other academic departments.

ENCOURAGE STUDENT PARTICIPATION

Collaboration on campus is not limited to faculty and administration. Student groups also make excellent partners for the library. Students provide feedback on existing services and programs and so enable the library to better utilize limited resources. Knowing what to spend money and effort on and which things to discontinue can help the library make wise budgetary decisions. Both surveys and informal discussions are excellent ways to gather student feedback. Online surveys can be offered via the library's Web site.

Student Government

It does take an effort to reach out to students and student groups, but the rewards can be well worth finding the time. In small libraries, the limited resources and staff mean that time is usually a luxury, as there are literally not enough hours in the day to accomplish everything that needs to be done. However, making time to build bridges with the students can result in new and innovative services and offerings. One example is the collaboration between the Associated Student Body (ASB) and the library at Mission College. The cost and availability of textbooks provide ongoing challenges to college students everywhere, and Mission College is no different. A large percentage of students enrolled in community college are the first in their families to attend an institution of higher education. Mission also has a compressed academic calendar with semesters of only 15 weeks, meaning that courses start quickly and students need immediate access to textbooks for homework and study.

Librarians would periodically attend the ASB meetings. These visits might be used to advertise an event or new service or simply provide an opportunity to engage in a brief discussion about the library and hear the students' perspective. During these visits, the issue of textbooks often was discussed. According to a study in 2004 by the California Student Public Interest Research Group, the average cost of a new textbook was $102.44. The ASB and students in general wanted the library to purchase textbooks for the collection. This led the library to spend more effort to educate the ASB officers on the overall library budget, philosophy, and process of collection development and basically show them how little money could be used for this project.

Better understanding the situation, the ASB made a bold decision and initiated a program to fund textbook purchases by the library—a yearly $4,000 grant to purchase textbooks. The collection development librarian works with faculty to identify classes with high numbers of students and where new textbooks are being used. The library uses the ASB grant to purchase textbooks and place them on reserve for in-library use only. As newer editions of textbooks are eventually added, the older editions are placed in the circulating collection. Statistics show that this ASB-funded program of textbook reserves is one of the most highly used library services at Mission Library. In the fall of 2005, the reserve collection, which includes textbooks, accounted for 36 percent of total library circulation. As of December 2005, the library has a total of 768 textbooks on reserve for student use with a total circulation of 11,125 times.

Service-Learning Opportunities

Service learning is being incorporated into the campus culture across the United States. The report of the National Commission on Service Learning (2001) defines service learning as "a teaching and learning approach that integrates community service with academic study to enrich learning, teach civic responsibility and strengthen communities" (17). Two key components of service learning are the strong curricular connection and that the student learning is provided in a real-world context (Education Commission of the States 2002, n.p.).

Libraries can benefit from courses that incorporate service learning. By reaching out to the faculty and specifically the graphic arts and multimedia departments, the library at the College of San Mateo was able to provide service-learning opportunities. The college has a very small library staff, only two full-time library faculty, a director, and five staff members. Even with these few resources, the library provides programs and exhibits for the students, faculty, staff, and surrounding community.

Collaborating with the graphic art and multimedia departments, the library was able to offer a service-learning opportunity for several students. The students were presented with a real-world situation with the library in the role as clients—meeting with the students to provide a description of the program requirements (whether print or online), what the tone or feel of the resulting piece should be, style guidelines so that the material would reflect the look and feel of the college as well as the library, logos, and so forth. The students then returned a few days later with concept drawings that were then discussed, and a final selection was made. The students experienced the kinds of requirements a real-world client would make even before leaving school. Students created print and online products. In addition, the students could use the resulting promotional material in their portfolios to show prospective employers or future prospective clients. The library was able to receive professional-quality services without the need to hire additional personnel.

One example is the Web site, which utilizes the same graphics as the print pieces, to support National Library Week (http://www.smccd.net/accounts/csmlibrary/nlw.html). The professional look and functionality of the Web site is a reflection of the positive result of the library's collaboration with faculty to provide an opportunity for service learning in which all parties benefit.

HIGHLIGHT THE LIBRARY BUILDING AS PLACE

Providing services that encourage students and faculty to visit the library is necessary both to fulfill the institution's academic mission and to keep the library a vibrant campus entity. Highlighting the library building as a destination place can be accomplished with limited staff and resources, for example, establishing displays promoting campus activities, collaborating with the institution's information technology department to add computers and Internet access, and stressing friendly customer-centric behavior of staff and librarians.

Evergreen Valley College Library is incorporated into a learning resource center that includes not only the library but also counseling services, a computer laboratory, media services, a testing center, and other services focused on student learning. The library has a large display area, including glass display cases and a wall space designed for hanging art. Working with various departments across campus, the library provides an active exhibit calendar that draws in not only students and faculty but also local community members. The library advertises on its Web site (http://www.evc.edu/it/library/exhibits/index.htm) as well as through fliers and campus publications.

Mission College utilizes the entire library building to support a yearly Asian American speaker program. Supported by a grant from the Robert N. Chang Charitable Foundation, the author events have proven popular over the past several years. Faculty members encourage students to attend (sometimes for extra credit). Community members often visit campus for the first time to attend this speaker series. Last year the program was expanded to include a traveling exhibit, *Pioneering the Valley*, developed to highlight and celebrate the contributions of Chinese Americans to Silicon Valley by the Chinese Historical and Cultural Project (http://www.chcp.org).

Utilizing the library building as a destination does not have to be a resource-intensive endeavor for the library staff alone. Successful promotion can result in departments' competing for collaborative events, as with Evergreen Valley College Library's experience with displays. In addition, the library itself can be the draw. For example, Evergreen Valley College Library was one of the major locations for the college's thirtieth anniversary celebration, and Mission College Library is a key stop for campus tours.

TAKE FULL ADVANTAGE OF THE LIBRARY'S REPORTING STRUCTURE

In California's small academic institutions, the library most often reports organizationally to the dean of instruction/academic affairs or to the dean of student services/affairs. There are strengths in either organizational structure since the library straddles both the instructional and the service side of the college—whatever the reporting procedure, divisional and department meetings that naturally occur are excellent places to identify and create strong partnerships.

Instruction/Academic Affairs Reporting

The director of library and learning services at the College of San Mateo reports to the vice president of instruction, which means sitting at the same table with deans of the academic departments. This allows the director to easily keep informed of academic planning. It has also created partnerships between the library and specific departments for grant applications that have resulted in support for special programming and events, such as a speaker series to raise awareness of Banned Books Week—the departments included music and dance and literature.

The reporting structure at Mission College recognizes the important synergy between the library and information technology. One major partner for an academic library is the institution's information technology (IT) department. In today's information environment, access to online information is a vital service that the library offers to students and faculty; thus, a good working relationship and partner in the college's IT department is critical. However, in smaller academic institutions, this department is often as challenged for staff and time as the library is. By reporting to the dean of instructional technology, the library director is able to gain insight into the demands placed on the IT team by the institution at large and help negotiate support and prioritization of library needs. The dean of instructional technology also obtains an excellent understanding of the demands placed on the library by students and faculty and the challenges created in today's online world of information. This reporting relationship has resulted in an excellent partnering between the library, librarians, and members of the technology department. The very first implementation of wireless capability at Mission College was not the student-only computer lab managed by the IT department but the library. Today the dean of instructional technology and the library director are together exploring potential grant funding to purchase wireless-enabled laptops for the library instruction room.

Network beyond Report Structure

While the reporting structure of the college offers a natural opportunity for partnering, it is important to expand relationships (and the potential for partnerships) to all departments of the college. Even though the library at Mission College does not report to the student services department, the library director attends the student services departmental meeting as a visitor a few times per term. This small amount of time expense has proven to be time well spent and has allowed the library and the student services department to explore various partnership opportunities. For example, the dean of student services leads a campuswide outreach committee that identifies and targets potential student groups in the local community, and the library is included as a team member. The library has actively participated in the committee and is now included on all campus tours, enabling librarians to describe their services designed to help students achieve their learning/academic goals.

Aided by increased visibility because of its participation in the outreach committee, the library was awarded a portion of a large Title V grant the college obtained to improve services to local underserved populations. Both print and electronic resources were purchased with the grant money. It is important to acknowledge partnerships, and thus the electronic resources purchased with Title V money are noted on the library's database Web page (http://www.missioncollege. org/lib/dbs.html).

No matter the organizational structure of the institution, divisional and department meetings provide fertile ground for creating strong partnerships since meetings occur as a normal course of business. Finding a little time to occasionally drop into other department meetings can result in new opportunities to partner on campus.

BUILD ON SUBJECT SPECIALIST LIAISON RELATIONSHIPS

Similar to their larger academic brothers, the small libraries assign subject specialists to liaison with academic departments. A liaison is expected to build relationships to ensure the library collection, both print and electronic, and support the curricular needs of the institution. "Liaisons are on the 'front-line' for the library building relationships" (Tucker, Bullian, and Torrence 2003, 226). Often the resulting relationship with a department offers opportunities for strategic partnering to fund new services or programs.

Cooperative Funding

At Mission College, the art department had identified a specific database to better support their growing course offerings—*ARTstor,* an online collection including images representing a wide variety of civilizations, time periods, and media from museums, photo archives, and publishers of art reference. However, funding the database was a problem the department was struggling to overcome. The electronic resource librarian at Mission College is responsible for collection development of all online resources including subscription databases and marketing such resources to the faculty. As part of her normal liaison work with faculty, the librarian learned about the art department's interest in *ARTstor* and began a series of discussions with the department chair. Creative problem solving resulted in a joint purchase, with both the art department and the library providing 50 percent of the necessary funding. The joint partnership between this department and the library at Mission College was advertised through campuswide e-mail announcements as well as a description on the library's database Web page (http://www.missioncollege.org/lib/dbs.html), which will remain as long as the funding relationship endures. It is important to advertise partnerships. Not only does it positively reinforce the relationship, but it also provides a model for other departments, encouraging them to think creatively about working with the library to further their departmental goals.

BUILD ON THE LIBRARY'S EXPERTISE

At Menlo College, the career services department was approached by a vendor and reviewed the Vault Career Library, a collection of more than 80 career guides and employer profiles covering a wide range of industries. Menlo College is a small private undergraduate college of management that integrates programs in business, mass communication, and liberal arts. After review, career services was interested in purchasing the product but faced obstacles: funding, access, and infrastructure. Career services did not have enough funding to purchase the product, was opened limited hours to students, and in particular did not have the infrastructure or expertise to manage remote access to databases. Even if the department could fund the database, students and faculty would have to physically visit career services and access the information from the computers in the center. However, there was a department on campus that was the expert database provider—the library. Through the library's automated library system, the issues of on campus and remote access as well as infrastructure would be solved. In addition the library possessed the expertise to manage databases, and offered more hours of service to students than the career center, including 24/7 access through the library's Web site. After consultation between the departments, it was decided that the library and career services would split the cost of the database 50/50 and that access would be provided through the library. In the end, the library gained access to premium career information, maintained its campus leadership concerning access to information, and increased referrals to the library's online services. The library continues to be recognized as the campus gateway to information.

Faculty in the Library

It is not unusual for librarians to meet faculty who have not visited the campus library in quite a while. Enticing and encouraging these faculty to partner with the library is often a challenge, but the benefits of an engaged faculty in building the library's collection make the effort worthwhile. As Bullian described the challenge of being in a two-librarian library at the Brandon Campus of Hillsborough Community College in Tampa Florida, "There is only so much time to spend pouring over book reviews and selection materials. Trying to keep abreast of current materials required to represent the entire college curriculum has been a futile pursuit" (Tucker et al. 2003, 232). At the College of San Mateo, the liaisons brainstormed on how to reach out to faculty members and engage them in collaboration on collection development. A series of "Pizza Garden Parties" were planned. The purpose of these meetings was to have faculty help evaluate the collection in their subject area—color tags were used to denote what to keep, remove, or remove but purchase new on the topic. The faculty were provided a pizza lunch in recognition of the time they invested in the project. Two "Pizza Garden Parties" were organized the first semester as a trial and were such a success that the parties will become an often-held event. Faculty not only became better aware of what the library had in its collection but also began to actively partner with the library on building and managing titles that supported their academic programs—they are now sending donations and also purchase suggestions. Faculty who previously had not visited the library in a long time changed into active partners.

Building on the liaison relationship is a natural progression of what already occurs on most campuses. The library liaison networks with the departments and faculty they have been assigned, keeping in touch with the academic direction of the various programs. Using a little creative thinking and a small extra effort can result in rewarding partnerships for the smaller academic library.

BUILD ON SHARED GOVERNANCE ACTIVITIES/EXPECTATIONS

Academic faculty, including librarians, are expected to participate in shared governance activities, including the academic senate and its subcommittees. These committees offer the librarians an opportunity for networking with faculty with whom they might not otherwise connect. It also allows the library faculty to be seen in a different light. As Warner and Seamans (2004) describe, "An unexpected benefit has been a subtle shift in the way the librarians are viewed by their colleagues around the university. There is an increased sense of the librarians as peers" (39). Actively participating in shared governance can show faculty from around the institution that librarians provide more than document delivery and research services—that librarians are teaching faculty and play an important role in the academic purpose of the institution. Some institutions do not categorize librarians as faculty, and on these campuses it is even more important for the librarians to interact with faculty as peers on committees.

Even colleges with a small team of librarians can make the most of interacting with faculty by carefully selecting the committees on which to serve. Examine the college's strategic direction in order to focus librarians' efforts on where they can make the best impact and be most efficient advocates for the campus library. If the college is planning to enter or expand their distance education offerings, the technology committee might be an excellent group to join. To track discussion and planning for new or expanded programs, the curriculum committee is a good choice.

Active Partners

The library at the College of San Mateo worked with the Academic Senate to organize a new committee: the Library Advisory Committee. This committee includes one faculty from each discipline as well as representatives from student services and meets regularly to examine the library's impact on the academic progress of the institution and help the library director with strategic planning. The added benefit of this formal, Academic Senate–sanctioned committee is that an insight into the library's value and challenges is available by reading the committee meeting summaries as well as during the formal committee reports to the Senate. This helps keep the library in the minds of faculty.

Through active participation on the Academic Senate's Curriculum Committee, librarians at Evergreen Valley College have been able to formalize a library sign-off on all course development forms, which describe in detail new or significantly changed course offerings. This allows librarians to engage in a discussion and joint exploration of the existing library collection, both print and nonprint, and services related to the new course while identifying areas for improvement. If new material or services are identified, this opens up conversations concerning funding, enabling strong collaborations with specific departments as they expand their course offerings. When the automotive technology department was upgrading its certificate programs, the librarian on the curriculum committee alerted the library liaison, who in turn worked closely with the faculty to carefully review the collection. The department and library shared funding and made joint decisions about what material would be available to students through the library and what should be held in the department. For example, shelf space was freed for new books by giving the department older *Chilton Manuals*, which were then more immediately available to students as they worked in the automotive lab. This combination of librarian representation on the shared governance committees and strong liaison relationships shows how partnerships can be built while performing "normal" institutional duties.

Absent Partners

A few years ago, the director of library and learning services at the College of San Mateo found herself in the opposite situation. Mainly because of limited staffing (the library has only two full-time library faculty), the library had over the years stopped participating in the Academic Senate or its subcommittees. The Academic Senate's Committee on Instruction heard from faculty that the existing process for approving new courses or major revisions to existing courses was cumbersome and time consuming and had redundant steps. The process was seen as a barrier for innovation and also prevented faculty from meeting new educational needs of the community in a timely manner. The Committee on Instruction began reviewing the entire process, existing forms, and sign-off procedures with the intent to reduce redundancy and make the approval process as simple as possible while still ensuring that the resulting courses met the college's high academic standards. In the committee's recommendations for streamlining the process, several sign-off steps were to be eliminated—including the library.

It was only through reading the committee minutes in an effort to learn about her new institution that the library director discovered that the library was about to be dropped from the review process. By not actively participating in the shared governance process, the librarians were missing an opportunity to be visible on campus and to interact with department faculty; thus, the faculty were not fully aware of the value of the library review during the course review. "Active participation on the campus Faculty Senate, Faculty Senate Committees, and campus advisory groups brings a greater understanding by faculty of librarians and what they have to offer" (Dewey 2004, 10). The new library director and library faculty began to attend the Committee on Instruction and educate them on the library's key role in supporting the academic progress of the institution. A clearer understanding of the role and challenges of the library enabled the committee to see the value of continuing to include the library in the course review process. The new director and library faculty worked diligently over the following year to reinstate library faculty on both the Academic Senate and the Committee on Instruction.

Librarians may participate in shared governance activities; however, one of the most significant challenges for small academic libraries is the limited number of librarians. Examining campus priorities strategically and then deciding on which committees to spend time will allow libraries to meet institutional expectations, network with faculty in a cooperative setting, and provide insight on new areas for campus partnerships.

CONCLUSION

For many reasons, the academic library will benefit as it partners with other campus entities to further the institutional goals, create strategic opportunities, and obtain additional funding and support. For smaller institutions, the necessity to partner is great. Libraries need the fiscal resources and human support from other departments to carry out their mission. Partnerships also allow the library to free itself from the isolating hierarchal structure of the institution.

Before entering into a partnership, the library must look at its goals strategically. Partnerships are relationships. Any relationship needs committed time from each partner to be able to grow and thrive. The library's fiscal and human resources restrict the capacity to partner. Each opportunity must be evaluated against the library's mission and goals before going forward. Partnerships should be a net benefit for the library.

Examples from several institutions were highlighted in this chapter to illustrate the breadth of opportunities available to small and medium-sized libraries. Successful partnerships do not have to be grand schemes requiring large budgets. Many times, small-scale partnering with individuals and departments can have the greatest impact on student success.

Libraries are constantly making strategic decisions about where to expend limited resources. Partnering can facilitate our reaching the entire campus community and meeting information needs. Partnering is simply expanding on what the library already does.

REFERENCES

Bergquist, William H. 1995. *Building Strategic Relationships: How to Extend Your Organization's Reach through Partnerships, Alliances, and Joint Ventures*. San Francisco: Jossey-Bass.

California Community Colleges Health Occupations. 2006. *About Us*. Available at: http://www.healthoccupations.org/about.cfm. Accessed June 6, 2006.

California State Library. 2005. *California Library Statistics*. Sacramento: California Department of General Services.

Dewey, B. I. 2004. "The Embedded Librarian: Strategic Campus Collaborations." *Resources Sharing and Information Networks* 17 (1/2): 5–17.

Education Commission of the States. 2002. *Learning That Lasts: How Service Learning Can Become an Integral Part of Schools, States, and Communities*. Available at: http://www.ecs.org. Accessed May 29, 2002.

Mission College. 2006. *Qualitative Needs Assessment Report: Latino Outreach Efforts*. Santa Clara: Mission College.

National Commission on Service Learning. 2002. *Learning in Deed: The Power of Service Learning for American Schools*. Washington, D.C. Available at: http://servicelearning commission.org/slcommission/learningindeed.pdf. Accessed May 20, 2001.

Tucker, J. C., Jeremy Bullian, and Matthew C. Torrence. 2003. "Collaborate or Die! Collection Development in Today's Academic Library." In *Cooperative Reference: Social Interaction in the Workplace*, ed. Celia Hales Mabry, 219–36. Binghamton, N.Y.: Haworth Information Press.

Warner, J. E., and N. H. Seamans. 2004. "Teaching Centers, Libraries, and Benefits to Both." In *Libraries within Their Institutions: Creative Collaborations*, ed. W. Miller and R. M. Pellen, 29–42. Binghamton, N.Y.: Haworth Information Press.

10 COLLABORATION IN SMALL AND MEDIUM-SIZED ACADEMIC LIBRARIES

David P. Bunnell

Collaboration

1. United labour, co-operation; esp. in literary, artistic, or scientific work.
2. spec. Traitorous cooperation with the enemy.

—Oxford English Dictionary Online, 2nd edition, 1989

The *Oxford English Dictionary* shows two definitions for the word "collaboration." To many librarians, the second definition describes a collaborative relationship. This chapter takes the more optimistic first definition as its guide. No library can exist in a vacuum, and this is especially true for academic libraries. It is the mission of all academic libraries to serve the members of their institutions' communities above all other activities. In order to fulfill such a mission, libraries depend on the work of other departments at their institutions. Collaboration has the potential for extending the outreach of library service to students who otherwise would not even step into the library. The library also benefits politically from collaborating with other departments. Often libraries and librarians seem to be outside the regular processes of academic affairs, student services, or development. For the library to maintain its traditional position as the academic center of the institution, it is important to work with other departments to develop new services and improve existing services.

Small academic libraries have advantages and disadvantages when working on projects with other departments. One advantage is the opportunity to build closer relations with other departments. Often a small library staff gets to know the other faculty and staff more closely than at larger institutions. The disadvantage is that there are few staff members to develop and implement a project. In addition, the impact on student success as a result of a fruitful collaboration between the library and other departments is greater for smaller institutions, while the strain on resources may be more significant for a smaller staff and a smaller budget.

The key to any successful collaboration is to emphasize the strengths of being small while deemphasizing the weaknesses. To achieve this balance, it is important to learn to concentrate on the people who will be responsible for the outcomes of the project. This means that good team leadership must be practiced throughout the life of the project. Collaboration takes planning, patience, and negotiating skills that are not often taught in library and information science course work. The good news is that there is a wealth of information on managing teams in the business and management literature. No group can learn faster from a solid base of literature than librarians and library staff.

COLLABORATION AND LEADERSHIP

Developing collaborative efforts between libraries and other departments or outside agencies requires leadership skills and a strategic plan for leading the project to a successful conclusion. Leadership skills don't appear overnight. In the old Great Man theories of leadership, an individual was born a leader, and the best leaders came by their skills naturally. Leadership theory has evolved, and the field of leadership studies relies on the assumption that leadership can be learned. Studying different types of leadership styles and the theories behind them can help a librarian develop the basis for a successful collaboration with others.

There are many different theories of leadership that have been studied over the past century. Current leadership theory has been dominated by the difference between the transactional leader and the transformative leader as described by James MacGregor Burns. According to Burns (2003), the transactional leader is someone who leads by motivating followers with an appeal to their own self-interests. The transformational leader is one who motivates followers by appealing to shared values and their higher-order needs, aspirations, and expectations (22–27). The transformation takes place in the organizational culture and is more lasting, meaningful, and sustainable than a project driven by transactional leadership methods alone.

There are several different types of behavior that transactional leaders use. In the contingent-reward behavior, the leader clearly states the work to be done and then uses rewards when expectations are met. Transactional leaders employ passive management by exception. The leader will punish or correct unacceptable performance when the goal is not met. A variation on passive management by exception is an active management by exception in which the leader monitors the work in process and uses corrective action to keep the work within the boundaries of the project. Finally, in laissez-faire leadership, the leader takes a "hands-off" approach to the follower's performance, ignoring the needs of others, and does not respond to problems or monitor performance.

Most leaders implement transactional methodology and behavior at some point during the life of a project. The modern leader learns to judge the situation and know when to use transactional methods to their greatest effect. Transformational leaders will first develop the common mission and then work with individual needs. Recent research into leadership has identified the skills required to foster collaboration in a transformational way.

Kouzes and Posner researched leadership at all levels and have become two of the most quoted experts in the field of leadership studies. An entire section of their book *The Leadership Challenge* is devoted to the importance of collaboration (2002, 241–77). The authors give three essential skills for leaders who foster collaboration: create a climate of trust, facilitate positive interdependence, and support face-to-face interactions.

A climate of trust must exist right from the beginning. The department with which the library staff is collaborating should feel that it can trust that the project will succeed. Once the initial project idea is presented, library staff needs to make sure that they carefully listen and take note of all opinions and not summarily dismiss any ideas. If trust is established, a sense of interdependence will take root. The library staff must ensure that the collaboration will be balanced and that everyone will take an equal share of the work as well as an equal share of the credit.

Face-to-face interactions are vital to make sure that everyone understands the project's needs and expectations. E-mail and other electronic communications are great tools for transferring information, but without face-to-face contact, a lot of useful information is lost. Face-to-face communication is important for the participants in the project so that they can gather clues in body language and intonation that make e-mail have less meaning as a form of communication. Even within an academic institution, cultures can vary among departments.

The library culture can differ from the culture in student services, development, or even other academic units. Braskamp and Wergin (1998) point out that "collaboration does not occur without the partners spending time together to foster mutual trust" (72). The best partnerships are those in which the participants understand each other from their own individual perspectives. Consider activities that work with the strengths of your partners, utilizing their skills and spending time working with them in their environment. If it is appropriate, share office facilities or work space with other departments when working on the project.

Allow for informal communication to take place and make it easy to communicate. Ideas and solutions are more likely to develop when people meet informally and are in a relaxed situation. Use tools such as e-mail and message boards to keep all the members of the collaboration informed of the progress. Collaboration and communication are inseparable.

One requirement of any successful collaboration is to design assessment measures at the beginning. Assessment is important as a record of the effectiveness of the project and becomes part of the college's overall assessment strategy. Each college must determine not only what is needed as an individual institution but also what is required for others, such as state and federal governments and accrediting agencies. Collaborative projects that are well documented and assessed are a great asset when the next accreditation visit comes to the college.

Armed with these leadership skills and having a methodology for transforming the current culture, a librarian is ready to take the next step and look at the different constituencies that will be a part of the collaboration. Understanding the organizational background of the groups that will build the collaborative effort is important to ensuring success. Following is a look at some of the most important players in all colleges and some examples of successful collaborations.

WORKING WITH STUDENT SERVICES

Student services has been a part of collegiate life from the earliest institutions of higher education with a goal of developing the whole student. Student services traditionally includes programs for personal counseling, academic advising, career counseling, financial aid, residential life (including on- and off-campus housing), student activities, admissions, disability services, and academic support services (such as tutoring and study skills assessment). Student services at small and medium-sized colleges vary in the extent of services that they can provide because of the need to handle multiple tasks with a small number of people. The good news for library outreach is that small student services departments are always looking for ways to extend their services and will be open to collaboration and new ideas. There are a couple of areas in which libraries can develop collaborative efforts with student services departments by leveraging their collections. Both substance abuse awareness and career planning and placement are prime areas for joint effort with student services. Substance abuse awareness programs are required of every institution that receives financial aid monies from the U.S. Department of Education. (See the Drug-Free Schools and Campuses Act of 1989 at http://www.highercenter.org/dfsca/part86.htm.) Librarians can train staff in research methods and provide resources for students. Special collections can be developed that support substance abuse awareness especially in the areas of drugs, alcohol, and tobacco. In addition, librarians can be invaluable to student services personnel in developing Web sites, brochures, and training guides for students on substance abuse issues.

Career planning and placement services are one of the most important activities of any student services department. Librarians can provide staff training in locating resources, conduct workshops, and develop collections for student and staff use. Academic librarians have been helping with résumés and job searches for years. Working with career planning and placement, librarians can build more extensive services for students that help them find the right employer, perfect job interview skills, build Web-based résumés and portfolios, and generally market their skills and abilities.

Students with Disabilities

All colleges must have a disabilities compliance officer, and it is important that the library leadership develop a working relationship with their compliance officer. Libraries have been at the forefront of developing resources for students with disabilities, especially physical access to library and information resources. Projects can include development of assistive technology programs, faculty development workshops on Universal Design for Learning, and help with finding information resources on specific disabilities.

Small and medium-sized colleges often have only a single compliance officer on staff and depend on other staff and faculty to help fill in the gaps for service to disabled students. This was the case at Griffin Technical College in 2002, when the library staff developed a new plan to help disabled students get access to information resources and accommodate their needs in the classroom. The library staff designed a program funded by a grant from the Perkins Technical Education Innovation and Improvement Program that would improve access to information sources by purchasing specialized adaptive equipment and training faculty in how to use Universal Design for Learning methodology in their courses (Rose and Meyer 2002). This program to improve access for students with disabilities became a collaborative effort that drew on the personnel and resources of the library, the student services department, the academic affairs staff, and faculty. The most important lesson learned from this project was the need to develop a common vision among the various constituencies in the collaboration. There was a shared goal among all the participants to make it easier for students with all types of disabilities to take advantage of the college's educational programs. Turning a common goal into a vision was a matter of communication and planning. The representatives were able to plan the workshops and develop the new policies and procedures for accommodating disabled students. The philosophy of universal design became the central theme that helped pull all the different aspects of the project together.

International Students

International student admissions are constantly increasing at all types of institutions across the country. International students are a special case for library collaboration with student services. It is important to remember that international students come with little or no experience with American libraries. This makes library instruction very important to the success of these students.

International students often have their own orientation and advisers that are attuned to their cultural needs. Many colleges and universities have international student peer groups to help these students cope with their new environment. If your college does not have such a group, it might be a chance to work with student services staff to start one that meets at the library. A good place to look for the latest techniques in teaching international students is NAFSA: Association of International Educators (http://www.nafsa.org). NAFSA also has grant opportunities for innovative programs for training advisers, teachers, and counselors as well as grants for innovative international student programs.

The University of North Carolina at Chapel Hill has developed a Web site with an online tutorial for its international students (http://www.lib.unc.edu/instruct/international). The University of Wisconsin—Stout has audio tours as well as a virtual tour of the library (http://www.uwstout.edu/lib/services/intlstu.htm). The dual-use library at San Jose State University has collaborated with its public library partner to develop programs for international students (http://www.sjlibrary.org/gateways/academic/international.htm). This includes a self-tour handout especially designed for international students.

Small and medium-sized academic libraries can provide programming for international students as well as or better than the larger universities. The tools that are developed for traditional student instruction can be modified to fit the needs of international students. Using the help of international student advisers and some creative ideas from other colleges and universities, a smaller academic library with a limited staff can provide useful and creative service to its students from around the world.

WORKING WITH THE DEVELOPMENT OFFICE

Most development office staff and chief development officers build a comprehensive program that includes articulation of an academic plan, identification of prospects, cultivation of donor prospects, and solicitation and acceptance of gifts. The typical college will have a capital campaign (e.g., raising funds for construction, expansion, and endowments) and an annual campaign (raising funds for regular college expenses). In addition to the usual campaigns, there are special fund-raising campaigns for specific building projects, athletics, and even library collections.

There are many areas in which development offices can collaborate with libraries and use library resources to do a more effective job. This is especially true for small development offices that do not have time to do the kind of research that will lead to new fund-raising opportunities. The library can collaborate with the development office in identifying prospects and researching opportunities for other funds, such as grants.

Grants and Grant Writing

Grants are a significant part of every college's source of funding. There are grants from the federal and state governments for developing institutions, establishing new student services, and faculty development. There are private foundations that provide technology, funds for establishing new programs, and building projects. Libraries can work with development staff to create new projects for grant application or enhance existing projects.

New projects can be designed that will benefit library functions as well as contribute to better student services. Libraries can be instrumental in faculty development, especially in small institutions providing technical expertise and experience in media production to almost any project that utilizes technology.

Friends-of-the-Library Groups and Prospect Development

Friends-of-the-library groups are one of the most important collaboration projects for small and medium-sized academic libraries. A good friends group can significantly enhance the library's collections, programming, and outreach to the community.

At Spring Hill College in Mobile, Alabama, starting with the tenure of Library Director Dr. Alice Bahr, the friends of the Spring Hill College Library benefited the library and its parent institution. Many of Mobile's artists, scholars, and luminaries joined the friends and contributed money, effort, and time to the library and to Spring Hill College. The friends group at Spring Hill has funded new photocopiers, additions to the collection, and scholarships and awards and has even started a used bookstore for the students.

Spring Hill College's experience is not atypical. There are numerous examples of successful friends groups in small college libraries throughout the country. The key to starting a successful friends group is to work with the development department to establish a prospect list, marketing material, and an organizational system that channels the proceeds of the programs to the right funds. Friends groups can be a part of a larger campaign and help it succeed. Remember that no friends group will be successful without the support and advice of the development department at your institution. Attempts to start a friends group without this department may lead to turf issues and conflict. It may also interfere with other ongoing fund-raising and marketing campaigns.

Marketing

Marketing the college is another area where libraries can have successful collaborative efforts with development offices. Libraries have access to information that is useful to the community, and many have community services that go underused and need to be made known. These community services and information resources are valuable publicity for the college.

Librarians have always been good about celebrating special events and using them to promote the library within the college. Banned Book Week, National Poetry Month, and African-American History Month are all examples of events that can be used for marketing purposes. Inviting outside groups or speakers is a good way to work with the development office to show off the college and its facilities. Whether hosting a storytelling hour for an early childhood education class or sponsoring a chess tournament for local students, academic libraries can use their resources to help market the college.

There are several things to remember about working with those who promote the college. First, make sure you understand what the college is doing currently to market itself. That includes the themes of the publications, slogans, radio and television commercials, and the current target markets that are being used. Second, tailor your marketing to the college marketing efforts. Third, ask questions of the college marketing staff. What programs are being promoted? Is there a particular group of potential students that the college is trying to attract? These are all things you will need to know to coordinate a successful marketing event.

WORKING WITH ACADEMIC AFFAIRS

The primary mission of the academic library is to support academic programs, instruction, and faculty scholarship. An information literacy program and faculty liaison initiatives are the cornerstone of library collaborative ventures. Without these solidly in place, nothing else positions the library correctly. These are the subjects of more extensive chapters within this volume.

Tutoring, Testing, and Proctoring

Tutoring is one of the most often seen collaborations between libraries and academic affairs departments. Tutoring is a natural one for librarians. Where tutoring services are located and to whom they report varies greatly from college to college. The trend in small colleges is to have a tutoring or academic support center that is operated by the student services department. Despite this recent trend, tutoring has often started as a function of academic affairs and been initiated by faculty concerned with meeting student needs. For example, in Georgia, the technical colleges have developed tutoring and academic support services through both student services and academic services. At least two of these tutoring programs at Griffin Technical College and Augusta Technical College started in the library and were initiated by library administrators.

Testing centers and proctoring functions are often included with tutoring services. Testing and assessment is something that librarians are uniquely equipped to manage. Many academic librarians already offer proctoring services for their own students as well as others. Often the computer labs in a small or medium-sized academic library are the only places that are suitable for computer-based testing.

Writing Centers

There are many examples of successful collaboration between librarians and writing centers in English departments, online learning departments, and even technical communication programs. Elmborg and Hook (2005) describe several successful collaborative efforts between writing centers and academic libraries. Giglio and Strickland (2005, 138–47) describe an outstanding collaboration at Wesley College in Delaware. Lessons learned from this collaborative effort parallel those taught by Kouzes and Posner (2002). Individuals involved in the writing center–library collaboration built a shared commitment to student learning. The library and writing center found common ground. Each learned that they were using similar methods of providing service to students. The writing center tutors were employing the inquiry-guidance method, asking questions and build-ing on the answers to guide students to better papers. Librarians used the reference interview to clarify students' problems in depth and lead them to information rather than just retrieving information for them. What the staff at Wesley College found was that the mission, goals, and methods of the writing center and the library were a natural fit.

Randolph-Macon College in Virginia has a writing center located in the li-brary (http://www.rmc.edu/directory/offices/hac/WAC/index.asp). It is part of an academic support system that is a centerpiece of the library and library services. Fort Hays State University in Kansas houses a writing center in its library that is funded by the English department (http://www.fhsu.edu/english/writingcenter). This is an excellent example of how the academic faculty and the library can work together and build a sustainable service for their students.

Instructional Technology and Distance Learning

Instructional technology holds great possibilities for collaboration between aca-demic librarians and the college faculty and staff. Librarians in small colleges often are charged with media services and production among their many roles. Small colleges have limited funding, so sharing this instructional technology in a media laboratory environment is an efficient way to manage institutional resources.

Distance learning has grown exponentially over the past five years. Most col-leges, no matter what their size, have an online course management system. In Georgia, the Georgia Virtual Technical College (http://www.gvtc.org) provides a Blackboard system for all 34 technical colleges. Many colleges manage their own servers, but the situation is similar. Course management systems provide chat, threaded discussion, electronic whiteboards, and space for downloadable files.

One way to be a part of the college's distance learning effort is to work with faculty who teach online and see if online courses can have a librarian as a co-instructor. This gives the online students support when doing research at a dis-tance, allows the librarians to build their own skills at online course production, and gives the online faculty and librarians a chance to work together to build unique and innovative services.

WORKING WITH THE INFORMATION TECHNOLOGY DEPARTMENT

Relationships with the information technology department can be the most contentious and the most rewarding. This contention generally comes from mis-communication caused by differing terminology. A successful collaboration be-tween the library and the information technology department is dependent on the librarians' becoming familiar with the vocabulary of the computer technolo-gist. This takes research, reading, and working hands on with software.

The nonprofit association EDUCAUSE (http://www.educause.edu) is a great resource for building information technology and library collaborative efforts.

EDUCAUSE's mission is to promote the use of information technology in all levels of higher education. Collaboration between information technologists and other parts of academe is a keystone to the type of research and case studies that EDUCAUSE promotes. EDUCAUSE provides librarians with professional development, research, and connections to those that have carried out successful projects at their own institutions. Many institutions are members of EDUCAUSE, and librarians at these institutions should not miss out on a powerful resource for building collaborative projects.

Computer Laboratories

Computer laboratories are sometimes the first real collaboration between a college's information technology department and the college library. Small institutions have space constraints, and as new technology develops, it is difficult to find a place to physically locate equipment for student use. Libraries are a logical choice for establishing a publicly accessible computer laboratory. In addition to the use of computers and the Internet in the college library, the library has convenient hours and a willing staff for assisting students. Setting up a publicly accessible computer laboratory in a library has many challenges. Staff must be prepared to handle questions on computer usage along with their regular reference and informational queries. Preferably, information technicians should be on hand to help with computer questions, but often that's not possible in smaller colleges. If the space is available, a separate room in the library with its own part-time employees would be ideal. However, in many small libraries, the computers are placed in the public spaces.

Emerging Technologies

Collaboration with information technology departments in developing a publicly accessible computer laboratory can lead to adopting new technology to serve students in the future. Libraries have seen the growth of wireless networking in bookstores, cafés, and even fast-food restaurants. Setting up a wireless networking hub for students is the next step in successful information technology collaboration. Students can use their own equipment to work over the Internet, or the library can have wireless-capable laptops and other devices available for checkout and in-library use.

The past five or six years have seen a growth of the information commons concept. An information commons combines the resources of several different departments into a single area that offers "one-stop shopping" for meeting student information technology and research needs. An information commons is attractive to students and provides a great convenience to students and staff. Librarians and information technology personnel can work side by side with tutoring staff and student services staff. The management of an information commons can be difficult and complex, but the reward to the students and the college can be well worth the effort. MiraCosta College in California, a community college serving the northern San Diego area, developed a library and information hub that houses the library, writing center, tutoring center, math learning center, and computer laboratories (https://www.miracosta.edu/Instruction/Library/index.htm).

Web 2.0 is a set of technologies that are being developed to utilize the power of the Internet in a new way. The focus of Web 2.0 is the building of collaborative relationships. A Web 2.0 project will take full advantage of Web-based communication tools, such as discussion boards, chat, and podcasting. The learning environment is expanded through social interaction. Social Web sites such as MySpace (http://www.MySpace.com), Facebook (http://www.FaceBook.com), and YouTube (http://www.YouTube.com) provide individuals with their own Web space and a network of others with whom to socialize. Web 2.0 projects provide information in multiple formats and communicate that information to the student wherever he or she is located. Using these tools, the students become more engaged in the educational process.

Many colleges have implemented portal software systems that have features of course management software and also connect the student to campus resources such as e-mail, registration systems, and the business office. Portals have a potential to further connect students to the library and the library's resources. Working with the information technology department, the library's presence can go beyond a Web page and a link to the online catalog. Other tools that are available to build collaborative learning environments include wikis (cooperative authorship) and blogs (Langley 2006, 39–47).

COLLABORATION OUTSIDE THE COLLEGE

Collaboration outside the institution serves several different purposes. There is a need for higher education to reach out to its wider communities. This is done most often by academic departments that work with local schools, agencies, or government. Many colleges have student organizations that serve the community and support advocacy and charity groups. Libraries collaborating with local public libraries or school libraries may support the same purposes with mutual benefit.

Service learning projects are becoming increasingly common at small colleges, and librarians can work with students to develop service learning opportunities. One collaborative effort is combining with the local schools to promote literacy. Students and librarians act as tutors and mentors to elementary and middle schools. Another area that is underserved is outreach to health centers, hospitals, hospices, and retirement centers. Librarians can engage with students and faculty to reach out to these institutions to provide reading material, encourage mental activities, and help the facility staff.

CONCLUSION

There are definite advantages for small and medium-sized college libraries in collaborating with other departments and serving those outside the institution.

Collaborations can extend the reach of the small library staff, stretch scarce resources, provide improved service to students and faculty, and increase the library's presence on campus. Collaborative projects pay off in the goodwill established with faculty, staff, and students and show college administration that the library has an entrepreneurial spirit.

The library will also have an improved staff. Experience in team leadership will make new library projects move forward more smoothly. Staff will be able to work with new technology and methods that will increase their productivity. Research on burnout is a fixture in library science literature. Collaboration in the small and medium-sized college library helps stave off staff burnout. Entering into collaborative efforts increases any library's effectiveness and rewards all who participate.

REFERENCES

Braskamp, L. A., and J. F. Wergin. 1998. "Forming New Social Partnerships." In *The Responsive University: Restructuring for High Performance*, ed. W. G. Tierney, 62–91. Baltimore: Johns Hopkins University Press.

Burns, J. M. 2003. *Transforming Leadership: The Pursuit of Happiness*. New York: Atlantic Monthly Press.

Elmborg, J. K., and S. Hook. 2005. *Centers for Learning: Writing Centers and Libraries in Collaboration*. Chicago: Association of College and Research Libraries.

Giglio, M. R., and C.F. Strickland. 2005. "The Wesley College Library and Writing Center." In *Centers for Learning: Writing Centers and Libraries in Collaboration*, ed. J. K. Elmborg and S. Hook, 138–47. Chicago: Association of College and Research Libraries.

Kouzes, J. M., and B. Z. Posner. 2002. *The Leadership Challenge*. San Francisco: Jossey-Bass.

Langley, A. 2006. *Building Bridges: Collaboration within and beyond the Academic Library*. Oxford: Chandos Publishing.

Rose, D. H., and A. Meyer. 2002. *Teaching Every Student in the Digital Age: Universal Design for Learning*. Alexandria, Va.: Association for Supervision and Curriculum Development.

V

INTEGRATION OF STAFF, SERVICES, AND ASSESSMENT: WHAT IS NEEDED? HOW WILL WE KNOW? WHO WILL DO IT?

11 MANAGING TO KEEP ACADEMIC REFERENCE SERVICE

Christine Dettlaff

Reference service has changed mightily in the past few years. It has been altered by forces brought on by a wave of technology whose crest is the World Wide Web. Managing these changes has been no small feat. It has meant rethinking the entire service, from the ground up, and led to questioning whether reference service even has a future in academic libraries.

Why do we still offer reference service when students can find out the answers to questions so easily using the Web? This is the question college administrators will be asking the next time the budget needs to be cut. And we'd better have our answers ready:

1. The world of information is inherently confusing. Information comes in different formats, information providers have different biases, and the onslaught of information will not abate or organize itself for easy access. More now than ever, reference librarians are critically needed to identify the subset of information that will benefit their students and provide convenient access to it for them.
2. Students have differing abilities to find, select, and process information. Often, they don't even know what they need. Reference librarians help students define their information need and then connect them to the information that will best meet that need. By teaching students how to navigate through the information environment, reference librarians enable students to become lifelong learners.

Another thing we'd do well to explain is how reference service has changed recently. Reference librarians don't just sit behind a desk and wait for someone to ask them a question. They are reaching out to students in person and at a distance. They are anticipating student information needs and providing Web links so that students can help themselves. The rest of this chapter examines new ways of providing reference assistance that have emerged in academic libraries and explains how we can ensure the future of these essential services for our students.

HOW FAR WE'VE COME IN SUCH A SHORT TIME

In a way, we were better equipped to deal with these changes here in our small library than some of our larger cohorts. We didn't have to debate the need to combine the reference and circulation desks into a single-point information desk. Because of our small building size, we had only one desk to begin with, where all inquiries, from the technological to the research oriented, were handled.

We didn't have to seriously consider whether to staff our desk with nonprofessionals or student workers rather than professional librarians, with all its attendant angst over whether it was undermining our professionalism (probably) or whether it mattered to our users (probably not). In a library with only one professional librarian, this was done by necessity. The librarian could only hope that she had trained the staff well enough to refer questions they couldn't answer to her.

But like our counterparts, the medium and large-sized academic libraries, we also experienced a noticeable reduction in the number of reference questions due to the advent of the Internet. Gradually, our staff wasn't in demand anymore to help answer ready-reference questions. Instead, they helped people log in to their online classes and figure out why the printer wasn't printing.

This required a whole new shift, you might say almost a retooling, in the skills of library staff working at the desk. Job descriptions for part-time staff were rewritten, requiring familiarity with computer applications and online library resources. Additionally, one staff member was given the responsibility for updating the library Web site. In today's academic library, all staff, from librarians to student workers, need to have technology skills. And those skills need constant updating through training and professional reading.

THE NEW REFERENCE LIBRARIANS—NOT JUST ANSWERING QUESTIONS

So if well-trained nonprofessional or student workers are manning the reference desk, what are academic reference librarians doing with their time? Or, in other words, what would I be doing if I were a reference librarian more than 20 percent of the time?

- Librarians are designing some amazing Web sites and information services that are intuitive and seamless so that students can help themselves. Things like FAQs and "search this site" help promote user independence. They are integrating links to library resources into online courses and incorporating subscription databases into portals in order to reduce log-in requirements.
- Librarians are selecting new and better online reference tools. They are discovering Web resources with value for their students and placing links

to them on their library Web site. They are finding ways to make research databases easier to use.

- Librarians are teaching classes how to do research and talking with instructors to make sure that information literacy competencies are included in their assignments. They are creating online tutorials to teach information literacy as a supplement to or in place of formal instruction.
- Librarians are evaluating reference services and making changes on the basis of the results. They are doing original research on students' information-seeking behavior. And they are publishing those results in the professional literature so that other librarians may have the benefit of their research.

These are all things to bring up if you are asked by college administrators, "Why do we need reference librarians?" I think it is unfortunately true, as many have pointed out, that people outside the library profession have no idea what librarians do. It is also part of our job to educate them. We must promote our services, for no one else can or will.

IMPROVEMENTS IN SERVICE TO ON-CAMPUS STUDENTS

Like others in the library profession, we've realized that some people are afraid to approach the desk and ask for help. This was brought home to us by a user calling for help logging into library databases. The librarian checked the user's status to make sure this was a valid student in our system and then tried to talk the person through the log-in process. Ten minutes into the conversation, the user finally revealed that she was sitting at a library computer 15 feet from the desk. Logging in isn't required to use library resources on campus; it turned out that what she really needed was help navigating the databases.

As a result, we've reevaluated our information desk. Is the placement within the library right? Is it too imposing? Too cluttered? Are the staff members at the desk friendly and approachable? Do they appear too busy to be bothered? Since ours is an all-purpose desk, it doesn't have a sign above it that says "Reference" or "Circulation" or any of that other library lingo that no one outside the profession understands.

We've also made more of an effort to "rove"—getting out from behind the desk and offering service to those in our library who appear to be stumped but have not yet asked for help. The problem is that we can usually spot someone who needs help when they are wandering about the library—but it is a little more difficult to tell if they need help when they are sitting at the computer. Maybe we need a button on the screen that says "Click here if you need help" that sends an alert to the staff—a virtual desk bell.

On the other side of the technology coin is customer service, or what some like to call personalized service. In the small academic library, we have a chance to establish relationships with our users (somewhat like in a small public library but on a short-term basis). Some we nurture from the time they first learn to use a mouse (I'm talking nontraditional student here) until they graduate.

Personalized service means sitting down with the user at the computer and teaching them how to search a database—not just telling them about the database or showing them how to get to it on the library Web site. Sometimes we have to not only help students find resources but also, even more basic, help them choose and narrow a topic:

Librarian: What were you thinking of doing your paper on?
Student: I was thinking of something on health.
Librarian: That's a pretty big topic. What area of health are you interested in?
Student: Oh, I don't know. Maybe nutrition?
Librarian: [seeing that student's patience with questions was waning] Okay, then. Let's look for some articles on nutrition.

What businesses have known for a long time is that if someone gets bad service or really great service, they will tell others. If they get just okay service, then the business will disappear from people's minds. And that's what has been happening to reference service.

REACHING OUT: REFERENCE SERVICE FOR DISTANCE LEARNERS

Like many other libraries, the concept of online reference (or digital reference or virtual reference) has become an issue for us with the rise of distance education. Today a third or more of our students never set foot on our campus. They could be enrolled at another nearby college and taking one of our classes because it fits more conveniently into their schedule. Or they could be taking one of our classes while stationed at a military base halfway around the world. When our users are worldwide, we need to be available to them 24/7.

And it's not just distance that separates us from our users. Some have work and family commitments that leave them with only the middle of the night to work on school assignments. That's when they finally get the chance to sit down at the computer and do research. We want to be available to them on their schedules as well. But what does that mean? We know we don't have the budget to keep the library open 24 hours a day. Do we need to keep a BlackBerry on our bedside table to wake us at 3:00 A.M. with a question from a student working on a paper?

Libraries have tried to answer the call for round-the-clock service through consortia and other collaborative arrangements. These involve member libraries working together to answer each other's reference questions when the user's library is not open or short on staff. I believe this type of arrangement can work if the network is global, as in the case of the Online Computer Library Center's QuestionPoint. Regional consortia probably wouldn't work as well for collaborative reference because other libraries in the region are likely to be open the same hours you are, or all the off-hours reference questions would fall to the few who are open longer, with those libraries gaining little in return (perhaps being able to route phone calls to another library during a rush).

Another option might be to outsource reference service to a company like Tutor.com, which offers "Librarians by Request." If a library had the budget to hire out its after-hours reference service, there still might be concerns about the quality of help users would receive from the service and the image it would project in the minds of its users. On the other hand, these librarians would be more experienced in handling virtual reference and might give even better service in that environment than the library's own staff.

Mostly through lack of funding but also because our staff was still in the technology retooling phase, our library did not jump on the chat reference bandwagon that gained momentum in the late 1990s and early twenty-first century. Our only concession to chat reference was to provide a link on our Web site to the chat reference service offered by the state library. Now research by Janes (2003, n.p.) has shown that even the most easy-to-use, well-promoted library chat reference services receive only a few questions per day—far less than the numbers expected to justify the cost of implementing and staffing such a service.

Other libraries have added instant messaging and text messaging capabilities to their virtual reference offerings and had some success with them. Because of their low cost to implement, these might be viable options for a small academic library like ours. However, we would still have to ensure that staff was available to monitor these services during the hours we determined they should be available. And unless someone is willing to take their BlackBerry to bed with them, we still wouldn't be able to offer the service 24/7.

Virtual reference has its drawbacks. Unlike the traditional reference interview, we cannot infer meaning from visual cues and body language, leading to the possibility of miscommunication. Technological implications include the fact that the remote student may not have a computer readily available, may be using a dial-up service, or may encounter instant messaging service or chat software incompatibilities. However, there are also advantages. Virtual reference is more inclusive, allowing us to serve the deaf and hard of hearing as well as those who cannot or will not visit the library in person. It can be easier for someone to admit they need help when they don't have to do it face-to-face with a real person.

Coffman (2004) proposed that in reconsidering reference service, we ask ourselves, "How can I best serve my patrons wherever they happen to be?" (2). He suggests that we take another look at telephone reference since cell phones seem to be the preferred method of staying in contact these days. One of the best things we could do would be to offer our distance learners a toll-free number to contact us. Our college has one to the switchboard, which will connect callers to the library between 7:30 A.M. and 5:00 P.M. Even better would be to have a toll-free number directly to the library.

To give our telephone users even better service, what about employing call waiting and call forwarding so that callers never have to get a busy signal or no answer at all? When the library is closed, a voice mail system or answering service allows callers to leave messages and informs them of alternatives such as sending the library staff an e-mail message.

Let's not discount good old e-mail. If answered in a timely manner (say, within 24 hours), this is not a bad way to provide reference service. It can, however, take several e-mails back and forth to identify the question the user really meant to ask, as in the following example (original spellings retained):

Student: Hello, I am trying to use the college libuary and not finding what I am looking for. Can you asnwer a question for me. I was wondering if you can go maganize through this website. Please get back to me if you can help me. I am a student at redlands but live in California so can't get to the campus.

Librarian: To get magazine articles (if that is what you are asking for), follow the steps below:

Go to our library Web site: http://library.redlandscc.edu
Click on "Go to Log in Page" under "Distance Education"
Enter your student I.D. number, without the dash
Enter the PIN 1234 (same for everybody)

Then click on "SIRS" or "EBSCO". Once you are in the database, you will have to search for a topic which you want an article on. If this has not answered your question, please let me know.

Student: I can log on to the libuary Web site. But then trying to find maganizine articles i can't find anything. I talked to someone else at your libuary and she threw me to another person because I was an online student. I am looking for something in regards to Childhood Obesity and Childhood illness I need these in maganizine articles.

At this point the librarian sent the user persistent links to articles on the specified topics from our databases. As you can see from this example, the user tried contacting us via phone and was not successful in getting his question answered. He then fell back on e-mail and was eventually able to get the help he needed.

REFERENCE LIBRARIANS AS INSTRUCTORS

Instruction has taken on an increasingly important role in the academic reference librarian's duties. Some libraries have even broken off this traditional segment of reference work and created a separate instructional librarian position. And this is where we will have the least amount of trouble justifying the continuing need for reference librarians, provided that we tie our instruction to student learning outcomes and find meaningful ways of assessing what we are teaching.

I'm not going to take up a lot of space talking about instruction because I know it will be covered in depth in other chapters in this book. Instruction is fairly straightforward when dealing with on-campus students. We can have classes visit the library for instruction, we can go into smart classrooms and show students how to use our online resources, or we can do informal one-on-one instruction when we connect with students individually in the library. Some librarians have even set up research kiosks in student centers and dorms where at intervals they will set up with a laptop and show students individually or in groups what the library can do for them.

Instruction at a distance is a little more difficult, but there are many options. If we can go into a classroom that already has a distance component—for instance, the class is being broadcast—then our instruction reaches those students as a matter of course. We can create online tutorials describing how to use our resources. We can tape a video orientation to the online library and mount it on the Web site, hoping that the student will click on it and be able to view and hear the video. We can mount handouts that we use in our face-to-face library instruction sessions. And we can integrate library resources into course management software through electronic reserves and persistent links to recommended readings.

PROMOTING, MARKETING, AND ADVOCATING

Reference librarians not only assist users with questions and instruct them in how to use the library; they also have a traditional responsibility to promote their services among their users and potential user community. As Tyckoson (2002, n.p.) has so aptly recognized, the best way for reference librarians to build recognition in their community is to give the kind of personalized, superior service I described earlier. But first we must somehow get over the promotional hurdles of (1) letting people know that reference service is available and (2) getting them to use it.

For our on-campus students, we post fliers advertising our services and have our Web site address printed on pencils, which we give away liberally. We had mouse pads printed with an eye-catching logo and phrases reminding users that library staff members were available to help with research and finding resources in the library.

How can we let students who never come to campus know that they have access to library resources and services? We have tried mailing a flier with instructions for online students, putting out a bulletin on our course management software, and sending the information via e-mail to all instructors, with a request for them to let their students know about library services for remote students.

Ultimately, though, most students won't seek our help unless required to do so for a class assignment. That is why we need to meet with instructors and encourage them to require use of library resources in their students' papers. Remind them how much better papers will be when students know how to do research. Encourage them to direct students to ask for help at the reference desk.

Keep putting the need for reference service out there. Talk to anyone who will listen about how you helped a professor with a literature review or a student find the obituary of a cousin. Include reference statistics—including virtual reference—and survey results in your annual report. But also put a face on the need for reference service with anecdotes like the following:

"I noticed a student at one of the computers was becoming frustrated and approached her to ask if I could help. She said she had to find out what the 'Rule of Four' was, but her Internet search wasn't giving her what she thought it should be. I asked what class it was for, and she said Government. I said, 'Hmmm, it sounds like a law of some kind.' I walked to the reference shelves and pulled off *Black's Law Dictionary*, looked up Rule of Four, and handed her the book. She seemed confused that a book could quickly supply her with the answer when the Web could not. But finally she copied down the definition and the title of the reference book to complete her assignment."

PLANNING FOR THE FUTURE

So how can we manage to keep reference service in the academic library? First of all, I recommend that you find some way to relate reference service to your college's mission statement—and, of course, make sure it is an explicit part of your library's mission. The provision of reference service to students and faculty both in the library and from remote locations is one of our library's ongoing strategic goals, which are a part of the college's strategic plan.

Next, you should document the need for the service in every way you can. Collect testimonies from students and instructors regarding the usefulness of reference assistance. Conduct your own environmental scan. In library school we called this a community needs assessment. Are instructors advocating the use of library resources (not just Web resources) on papers and projects? Are they requiring real scholarship and research, or have they accepted the culture of copy and paste? What are the perceptions of your students? Do they know what reference librarians are for?

We need to rethink the terms "reference service" and "reference librarian." To the layperson, these terms mean nothing. Picture the information desk in a mall—the sign above it says "Information." In the online environment, people are used to looking for "Help." Yes, we do provide more than just information and help. But it is a way of drawing people in, of relating to them on their own comfort level, rather than alienating them with jargon.

Once you have documented the need for reference service, you should offer it where, when, and how it is needed. Determining ways to provide reference service to distance learners should be a priority, as the proportion of students using the library off campus will increase. Special problems to consider are how to provide an equivalent level of personalized service to remote learners that we offer to on-campus students, how to let remote students know the service is available, and how to evaluate the service to determine improvements that need to be made.

Your reference service (both within and outside the library walls) should be on a consistent cycle of evaluation and improvement. All staff working at the reference desk should have training and regular refreshers in customer service, online resources, reference techniques, and technology issues.

Most important, reference librarians have to ensure that there continues to be a need for their service by encouraging faculty to incorporate requirements for library research into their assignments. This may seem like we are merely drumming up business for ourselves, but I believe it to be essential. If faculty accept from their students only Web resources of questionable quality, then, truly, academic library reference service will not be needed.

CONCLUSION

I don't think any of us working in academic libraries have any doubts about the need to continue offering reference service. Students adrift in the ocean of information will continue to wash up on our shores, needing to be oriented to resources for completing their assignments. As Jassin (2005) puts it, "Librarians do a lot of hand-holding. That won't go away any time soon" (24).

With higher education's move to an increasingly online environment, the how and where of providing reference service will change—the why will not. We need to continue to emphasize the why to our entire community—students, faculty, administrators, and the larger community—lest academic library reference service become marginalized and one more budget item to be slashed.

REFERENCES

Coffman, Steve. 2004. "To Chat or Not to Chat—Taking Yet Another Look at Virtual Reference, Part 2." *Searcher* 12 (8). Available at: http://www.infotoday.com/searcher/sep04/arret_coffman.shtml. Accessed June 21, 2006.

Janes, Joseph. 2003. *The Global Census of Digital Reference*. Virtual Reference Desk 2003 Digital Reference Conference Proceedings. Available at: http://www.vrd.org/conferences/VRD2003/proceedings/presentation.cfm?PID = 162. Accessed June 21, 2006.

Jassin, Marjorie. 2005. "The Flat Track to New Career Options for Information Professionals." *Online* 29 (5). EBSCO Academic Search Elite database. Accessed June 21, 2006.

Tyckoson, David. 2002. "On the Desirableness of Personal Relations between Librarians and Readers: The Past and Future of Reference Service." *The Future of Reference Services Papers*. Reference and User Services Association. Available at: http://www.ala.org/rusa/forums/tyckoson_forum.html. Accessed June 21, 2006.

12 COMMUNITY COLLEGE LIBRARY STAFFING: EVOLUTION AND REVOLUTION

Sheila Beck and Barbara Bonous-Smit

The introduction of increasingly more cost-effective and powerful computers, beginning after World War II and continuing to this day, has affected the library no less than any other social institution. This chapter concentrates on the affects of technology and shifting economies on the staffing of small and medium-sized libraries. For the most part, these libraries are characterized as non-repository libraries, in which the primary mission is the assisting of users both in accessing information and in teaching what has become known as *information literacy*.

The new information technology is truly new—it is not simply a better means of doing what we used to do. It is, instead, a sea change in how we as a public deal with information and what tools librarians use to cope with this new information age.

Library holdings are no longer limited to what we have on our shelves physically but have expanded to what we can access when we need it. Computer experts say that information is round and that it spins—a reference to data stored on hard disks—and the information stored in books is no exception. As we shift from the shelf age to the database age, our staffing must shift in tandem. And our resources must be directed to make the most effective use of the new paradigm, even at the risk of being declared irrelevant.

TEACHING

Teaching pervades all aspects of academic librarianship. Teaching can consist of simply showing how to look up a call number in the online catalog or how to access electronic resources from home or a lengthy discussion on the best way to organize a research project. In each instance, the goal is to make the student or faculty member an independent learner. In other words, academic librarians are the providers of tools for their patrons to find what they need on their own. This distinguishes academic libraries from public libraries, where information is presented without any indication of how locating the information was accomplished.

Because of the explosive growth of the Internet, combined with decreasing costs and increasing power of personal computers (including laptops), the library is no longer the sole center of information. The vast majority of students believe they can go online to find out what they want. Many students come to the reference desk only when they have failed at using a popular search engine such as Google or Yahoo!. The Internet often appears to be the best source for ready-reference questions where a fact is needed rather than in-depth or background information.

The methods of providing reference service are continually evolving. Reference librarians still must conduct a reference interview, but the medium of the interview has undergone rapid change. Libraries offer reference services by e-mail ("Ask a Librarian"), various forms of instant messenger, chat, and text messaging. These services frequently are offered on a 24/7 basis to accommodate students' needs often by consortia of libraries or online commercial services.

At the library of Queensborough Community College (QCC), City University of New York (CUNY), the use of databases has increased dramatically over the past five years. There were 5,446 searches in EBSCO databases in 2001 and 17,415 searches in 2005. (The statistics are taken from QCC internal reports.) It is necessary to keep up to date with new databases and their coverage and interface. Another challenge for librarians is learning course management software such as E-Portfolio and Blackboard, as professors turn to these tools more and more. Again technology is determining how librarians refine their skills.

Information Literacy

In response to the changing nature of information, library instruction classes have changed from bibliographic instruction where students were taught to use catalogs, indexes, and reference books to information literacy classes where students are shown how to find, retrieve, analyze, and use information. The assumption is that no one can learn all the information they need in college. With information literacy skills training, people can locate what they need and evaluate its usefulness. Information literacy translates into skills for everyday life as individuals make informed decisions when buying a car, choosing a neighborhood, or voting in an election (http://www.ala.org). Both the American Library Association (ALA) and college accreditation agencies recognize the importance of information literacy.

The number of information literacy classes has increased at QCC and the subjects covered have broadened. In 2006, our librarians taught 108 library instruction classes compared to 84 in 2003. Subjects changed from primarily English and speech to art, business, health, physics, and education. Anecdotal evidence suggests that research papers are improved after the students receive instruction in information literacy. As information literacy becomes a mandated general education requirement (University at Albany, State University of New York) and satisfies the requirements for a college minor (Baruch College, CUNY), reference librarians are teaching more classes. This will remain true in the future. As demand increases, there will be a concurrent difficulty finding enough instructors, classrooms, and time slots to accommodate the need. Another method of delivering instruction is to train professors and graduate students. At the University of Arizona, librarians work with the English composition course to introduce the concepts of information literacy. Because of this collaboration, librarians trained the English instructors and graduate students (Reyes 2006, 304).

Plagiarism

Currently, reference librarians must discuss plagiarism in this age of cut and paste. As students use word processing on the same computer with which they located their citations, the temptation to plagiarize is strong. Librarians teach what plagiarism constitutes and how to cite accurately and honestly in information literacy classes. With the proliferation of electronic databases, this has become more difficult.

Changes in the role of academic reference librarians are driven by technology, the medium used to answer questions, the resources used, and what is taught. This process will continue because students, faculty, and staff prefer online resources, and the amount of information online increases constantly.

INTEGRATED LIBRARY SOFTWARE

The key to the new technology is the use of integrated library systems. Most extant systems use a standard Web browser on a personal computer. This type of access is itself a major component of the new technology—it is available to anyone anywhere through standard access means. There is no need to have special computer-specific software or to have learned an idiosyncratic interface. Users (patrons) can access records anywhere they have an Internet connection. This enables them to view the online catalog for books, journals, and electronic resources; check their library card; renew items; place reserves; and submit interlibrary loan requests. Consequently, there is less demand for support staff services at the circulation desk. In the future, this trend will continue as self-checkout of books, currently being introduced in the Queens Borough Public Library, expands.

Staffing functions have changed within technical services. The cataloging module integrates its function with other aspects of the system; newly cataloged records instantly become available in the online catalog. Records and data from vendors, bibliographic utilities (Online Computer Library Center, Library of Congress), and other libraries can be imported. Shortcut keys (itself a concept not available on a manual typewriter and a simple indicator of the shift from physical to logical services) minimize the number of keystrokes, resulting in rapid and accurate keyboarding.

Professional librarians supervise technical services divisions and handle original cataloging and issues requiring their training. Paraprofessional staff with a college education work as cataloging and ordering assistants. The acquisitions and serials modules make ordering, invoicing, and receipt of materials easy. The records are interrelated so that the ordering of any materials triggers an item record. Purchase order numbers link invoices to budget requests. A paraprofessional staff member places the orders, receives the materials, reviews the invoices, and requests missing items. The integrated software simplifies these tasks and serves as a check on keeping expenses within allocations. The twenty-first-century librarian needs systems understanding to make effective use of each system as it is introduced and evolves. As the software becomes more effective and more centralized, increasing the staff becomes less necessary.

Librarians select the materials appropriate for the specific audience of their library. This is made easier through utilizing and understanding the reports generated by the integrated software. For example, circulation statistics can help guide collection development decisions. The ALEPH Reporting Center generates 80 predefined reports and statistics.

The trend is toward fewer support staff positions as operations in the technical services and in circulation are further automated. Each system upgrade adds more functions, simplifying the manual tasks. But the support staff needs new knowledge and understanding beyond that of technical support staffing in the past. We can expect to see programmers and network engineers join our support staffs, replacing classically trained librarians as the technological shift continues.

Recently, both CUNY and SUNY (State University of New York) implemented ALEPH 500 for their integrated library software. This system generates Excel reports and has been customized for each university. Every new release ratchets up its utility, reducing the work of acquisitions librarians and support staff. Version 16 matches book orders and invoices by order number so that budgets accurately reflect expenditures.

NEW ROLES

In August 2006, the CUNY Libraries Intra-Campus Service (CLICS) was initiated. During the spring of 2005, CUNY conducted a Web-based survey, LibQUAL+, to assess and understand users' perceptions and opinions on the quality of library service and act on the results with the goal of improving services provided to users. (The LibQUAL+ survey was created by the Association of Research Libraries and Texas A&M. More information on LibQUAL can be found at http://www.libqual.org/About/Information/index.cfm.)

Comments from users indicated widespread discontent with the CUNY libraries collections. Interlibrary loan service is not offered to most undergraduates, and often it is too inconvenient for them to travel to other CUNY libraries. One result of the LibQUAL+ survey was a special task force created by the CUNY Council of Chief Librarians in March 2005 to study and analyze the possibility of a CUNY-wide patron initiated document delivery service. After a testing period,

CLICS began in August 2006. The service meant the realignment of two of the circulation and interlibrary loan support staff to process these CLICS requests, with the circulation and interlibrary loan librarians overseeing the operation. This is another example of a service that users can initiate themselves.

The availability of several good electronic reserve software programs that can be integrated with Blackboard and other course management systems has the advantage of providing reserve self-service 24 hours a day for all 365 days a year. The implementation of the electronic reserves and course management software such as Docutek ERes, which is used at QCC, resulted in realignment of the technical staff and reserve librarian. Queensborough students are able to download and print articles their professors selected to be placed on reserve. (For more on Docutek ERes, see http://www.docutek.com/products/eres/index.html.)

Another effect that technology has had is on the medium in which information is produced. Because information can be provided in a variety of formats, there is often an overlap of coverage of information between print, microfilm, and electronic resources. Electronic resources are growing at the expense of microfilm and print. Since electronic sources are preferred, print and microfilm subscriptions are being canceled. The library currently subscribes to approximately 184 print periodical titles, and the users have access to more than 900 print periodical titles at the library, plus remote access to hundreds more at the other CUNY libraries. Counteracting this, the users of the QCC Library have remote access to approximately 20,000 full-text periodicals. With the elimination of the physical component, there are fewer materials to handle; this can result in the reduction of support staff positions.

Catalogers are seeing major changes in their job responsibilities. Their expertise is needed for special collections; each unique item added requires original cataloging. As more special collections are digitized, catalogers use metadata to describe them. Special collections add prestige to the college and enhance its image. As special collections are put online, they are easier to find and view and so more accessible. This is another example of how technology has realigned staff functions.

Institutional repositories collect and archive the intellectual content of an institution. This would include faculty publications, theses, and dissertations in digital form. Institutional repositories are linked to the concept of open access because faculty publications are self-archived and available. Institutional repositories also preserve grey literature, such as technical reports that may not be published or indexed elsewhere. The principles are similar to the library—material is selected, classified, cataloged, preserved, and accessed in digital form. Librarians need to learn about publisher policies and recruit content.

At Auburn University Libraries (Alabama), technical services personnel work part time in reference to gain understandings of what students and faculty need from the library and what can be done to help facilitate their success. Benefits have been many and varied. First, there is better communication between the library departments. There are more joint projects. For example, a reference librarian collaborated with a member of the information technology department to produce a clickable map based on call numbers. Clicking on the link opens a map of the floor. This experiment worked because of the library administration's willingness to adjust staff work schedules (Olivas and McCurley 2006, 84).

At Virginia Tech, reference librarians work in the teaching departments outside the library. Over the 10-year period this has been in effect, librarians have become part of the departments and formed positive relationships with both students and faculty. The librarians act as reference librarians, instructors in information literacy classes, and collection development librarians and provide technology support. The reasons for decentralizing reference services were the number of databases available remotely from the library, a push by the university for increased collaboration, and on-site assistance for PC users (Seamans and Metz 2002, 324). Again technology is changing librarians' roles.

PROFESSIONAL TRAINING

The traditional approach to library training is the Masters in Library Science (MLS) course of study. This course of study is directed to library history and the theory behind day-to-day operation. The MLS degree places emphasis on professionalism. Libraries, however, are not staffed solely by MLS-degreed professionals. Actual day-to-day operation is frequently carried on by paraprofessionals lacking the MLS. Circulation service and shelving are the places at which the library patron encounters the support staff, but paraprofessional staff exist as well and are key to cataloging and technical services throughout other areas. With the introduction of digital assistance in so many areas of the library operation, from catalog maintenance to circulation operations, and the remote location of materials, the paraprofessional skilled in new technologies has become ever more important.

New trends are driving a reconsideration of the training requirements for library personnel. In one, the MLS or Information Studies (MIS) is the determining credential. It sets the individual apart from the support staff and paraprofessionals. On the other hand, support staff members and paraprofessionals argue that experience is as valuable and that they cannot advance without a professional degree. They assume greater responsibilities without a future (St. Lifer and Oder 1996, 30).

What type of professional is qualified to lead a library—an MLS or MIS librarian or someone from outside the field with Master of Public Administration training or even training in leading a data processing organization? A traditional argument is that training in an academic field such as a PhD is enough. Increasingly, college-educated paraprofessionals are viewed as being able to do the day-to-day work and are just as oriented to management in the digital future.

Training available in masters in library science programs is being actively evaluated. Pertaining to digital projects, there is a need "to improve access to hands-on learning, mentoring, and continuing education, as well as formal education of a new generation of creators and managers of digital assets" (Spinazze, Allen, and Bishoff 2004, 530). There appear to be a number of courses available in digital libraries that may or may not have enough training in digitalization projects. Updated skills are needed to preserve digital collections, audiovisual media, and visual materials. A survey by Gracy and Croft (2006) found that graduate schools in library and information studies programs are not offering enough courses in these topics and assume that continuing education is picking up the slack. Although they were encouraged by the enrollment in the courses offered, they speculated that schools may not have the laboratories, money, or current faculty necessary to provide advanced courses. Serialists also feel that their field is underrepresented in library and information science curriculums. Young (2005, 82) believes that it is impractical to expect more formal courses in LIS programs and that continuing education is the answer. Appropriate library education is the agenda of Michael Gorman, former president (in 2006) of ALA. Questions being considered are accreditation, new ways to educate library workers, the need for continuing education, and alternate routes to becoming a librarian (Gorman 2006, 3).

In the New York City area, continuing education is offered by the Metropolitan Library Council (Metro) to recent college graduates, librarians, support staff members, and library directors. There are special interest groups, classes, seminars, and online courses. Some events are free, such as presentations for the special interest groups. Many of the offerings are technologically oriented, such as *The What, Why and How of Wikis* and *PDAs and Handheld Devices* (Baruch College's text messaging system). Courses are also offered through NYLINK, a nonprofit organization consisting of all types of libraries throughout New York State. Theses courses focus on cataloging, metadata, accounting, digital preservation, information technology, and reference.

CONCLUSION

In the past 10 years, libraries have evolved into a digital environment. Librarians have given over the day-to-day operations to paraprofessionals and work instead on strategic planning. This will continue as each release of software makes routine jobs easier. Ultimately, librarians must continually re-create themselves through the redefinition of their roles and their relevance in the twenty-first-century library.

REFERENCES

Gorman, Michael. 2006. "President's Message." *American Libraries* 37 (5): 3. Academic Search Premier. Accessed November 24, 2006.

Gracy, Karen F., and Jean Ann Croft. 2006. "Quo Vadis, Preservation Education?" *Library Resources and Technical Services* 50 (4): 274–94. Academic Search Premier. Accessed November 24, 2006.

Olivas, Antonia, and Henry McCurley. 2006. "Working across Divisional Lines." *Library Administration and Management* 20 (2): 81–89.

Reyes, Veronica. 2006. "The Future Role of the Academic Librarians in Higher Education." *Portal: Libraries and the Academy* 6 (3): 301–9. Project Muse. Accessed October 23, 2006.

Seamans, Nancy H., and Paul Metz. 2002. "Virginia Tech's Innovative College Librarian Program." *College and Research Libraries* 63 (4): 325–32.

Spinazze, Angela, Nancy Allen, and Liz Bishoff. 2004. *Digital Resources for Cultural Heritage: A Strategic Assessment Workshop on Current Status and Future Needs*. Washington, DC: Institute of Museum and Library Services. Available at: http://www.imls.gov/pdf/ LibraryBrochure.pdf. Accessed September 11, 2007.

St. Lifer, Evan, and Norman Oder. 1996. "Net Work: New Roles, Same Mission." *Library Journal* 121 (19): 26–31. Academic Search Premier. Accessed November 24, 2006.

Young, Naomi Kietzke. 2005. "Formal Serials Education: A Problem We Can't Solve or a Solution We Can Live With?" *Serial Review* 31 (2): 82–89.

13 FROM SLIDE RULES TO SCORECARDS: SERVICE ENVIRONMENT FACTORS AFFECTING THE FUTURE OF ASSESSMENT IN ACADEMIC LIBRARIES

Larry Nash White

Reviewing the literature on the assessment of library service provides the reader with a sense of an uncertain journey. Assessment in libraries has a documented history, "beginning in 1876, with Cutter using cost benefit analysis in a study of cataloging effectiveness. The traditional techniques of performance measurement developed during the early history of performance measurement in libraries, which include interviews, input/output analysis, costs analysis, and activity analysis, are still the most popular forms of performance measurement today" (White 2002, 28–29).

Lubans (1975, 2) stated that Shaw and Rider were two of the early pioneers in performance assessment innovation as they introduced "scientific management" and a "total system approach" to the operation and evaluation of library service. "Rider was quoted (in the 1930s) as saying that if librarians did not use scientific management or cost benefit analysis to justify performance, non-librarians would come in and do it for us" (White 2002, 29).

The literature reveals that between the 1930s and the 1980s, the assessment of library services generally remained static in the types of processes and techniques employed, with little if any innovation. Because of this lack of innovation and increasing concerns and demands from stakeholders beginning in the late 1980s, libraries began to incorporate a limited number of assessment processes and techniques from outside the library profession (i.e., business and education). These techniques included a variety of methods, measurement styles, and processes to assess performance and service, including benchmarking, outcomes assessment, best practices, LibQUAL™, the Balanced Score Card, and other similar quantitative measurements. A continued review of the literature does not reveal any examples of major new processes and techniques originated and implemented from within the library profession during this time. Thus, it can be concluded that the limited, primary innovations that have been implemented were from outside the library profession. Rider's prediction of the future of library assessment has become truer than he or we may prefer.

White (2002) states that the absence of assessment innovation within libraries is based in large part on "the lack of consensus among members of the profession as to what performance measures should be used and the reasons for their use" (30). As a combined result of a lack of direction from within our profession and a lack of consensus as to future directions, the assessment of library services is experiencing little progress and has little support for the need for innovation in the future. These resulting conditions have left many libraries on their own to develop new methods or have left them dependent on their stakeholders and their service environments to provide them with assessment techniques.

OVERVIEW OF ASSESSMENT IN ACADEMIC LIBRARIES

Today's academic libraries operate in dynamic educational environments where providing services is constantly being reshaped by the settings in which they operate. Changes in customers, competitors, technologies, and stakeholders are creating powerful competitive forces. These forces are causing many educational institutions to innovate or transition their services, identities, capabilities, and missions in order to respond, better meet stakeholder needs, and compete. The impact on smaller and larger academic libraries is the same. The differences are in the scale and scope of the service environment–library interactions and the resources available in order to respond.

One of the strongest competitive service environment forces in education is assessment: assessment of quality, of value/impact, of efficiency and utilization, of mission support, and of meeting needs. An effective academic library is interwoven with its total environment, and the library shares many of the same service forces. (This may be even truer in the smaller academic library because of the increased blending of roles such a library often assumes.) Thus, assessment for academic libraries, just as for the whole of the educational setting, is becoming an increasingly difficult strategic challenge when it comes to providing evidence of accountability, efficiency, and the reporting of impact to stakeholders while maintaining alignment with their total surroundings. When this challenge is combined with a lack of innovation and consensus as to the future direction of assessment from within the library profession, academic libraries are left in the predicament of needing to be responsive and innovative yet are uncertain where this future lies.

OVERVIEW OF SERVICE ENVIRONMENT FORCES
AFFECTING THE FUTURE OF ASSESSMENT

In attempting to provide insight into the future of assessment in smaller academic libraries, one must first identify the variety of service environment forces

Figure 13.1
Service Environment Factors Affecting the Future of Assessment in Academic Libraries (design by Larry Nash White, PhD. Copyright 2006. All rights reserved)

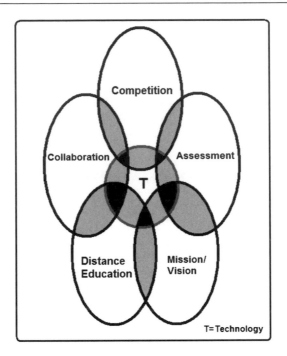

and then determine their effect. Through reviewing the literature, six factors were identified as primary indicators: collaboration, competition, distance education, mission/vision, technology, and assessment. These factors work independently and in combination with each other to directly affect the educational (and indirectly the academic library) context (see Figure 13.1). The following sections illustrate the theoretical interchanges between the six forces and provide the background for predicting possible future developments. Table 13.1 lists the specific impacts on assessment in academic libraries.

Technology

At the center of Figure 13.1 is technology. Technology serves as the hub of the service environment, as it is the only naturally neutral force. Technology facilitates and connects the other forces to allow for wider audience access and delivery. As a universal access point into the system, technology is frequently the common platform for innovation and implementation.

Table 13.1
Summary of Service Environment Force Impacts on Assessment

Service Environment Forces	Force Impacts on Academic Library Assessment
Assessment (general trends and developments) "The evolution will continue . . ."	➢ Array of assessment tools/capabilities vs. a "silver bullet." ➢ Continuous development of assessment tools and reporting capabilities. ➢ Culture of assessment will be required, not considered. ➢ Increased need by administrators for assessment data for data-driven decision making. ➢ Intangibles assessment (i.e., intellectual capital) will increase. ➢ Need to be less dependent on assessment innovations/methods/processes from outside fields. ➢ More patron-mediated/patron-involved assessment processes. ➢ Need for assessment results to be reported to a wider audience. ➢ Need for/ability to frequently conduct assessment. ➢ Proactive assessment vs. mandated assessment. ➢ Resources for conducting assessment and training staff in assessment will increase and become a fixed part of the budget. ➢ Training in assessment will increase in need and value. ➢ Transitioning from evaluating existing service/products to designing/valuing new services/products. ➢ Value assessment reporting will increase as output assessment reporting decreases.
Collaboration "More faces to reach more places"	➢ Creates new service/strategic partners with differing/new data types/assessment systems. ➢ Need for proactive assessment to identify new markets/new needs/new services. ➢ New assessments needed for diverse customers with dynamic needs. ➢ New participants in assessment data collection, analysis, and reporting processes. ➢ New stakeholders requiring new assessment reporting of addressing needs and effectiveness. ➢ Wider audience to effectively communicate assessment results.
Competition "Grow and go vs. stop and drop"	➢ Increased need of awareness of service environment and competitors. ➢ Increased offensive/proactive strategic response assessment information needed.

(continued)

Table 13.1 (*continued*)

Service Environment Forces	Force Impacts on Academic Library Assessment
Competition (*cont.*)	➤ Less defensive/reactive strategic response assessment information needed.
	➤ Wider array of assessment tools/processes needed to accomplish an effective result.
Distance Education	➤ Evolving service delivery will require evolving assessment processes.
"the new frontier"	➤ New/nontraditional customers with differing needs to effectively identify and address.
	➤ Ranges of assessment and impact reporting.
	➤ Transitioning from internal only assessment to inclusive assessment.
	➤ Wider area of service delivery/impact to collect data in and report assessment results.
Mission/vision	➤ Flexible assessment processes.
	➤ Frequent assessment retooling and innovations.
"new opportunities"	➤ Increase need and use of environmental SWOT; value and effectiveness assessment information.
	➤ Require assessment to serve more as a prognosticator of future needs/identifier of future missions.
Technology	➤ Assessment results available faster to wider audience.
	➤ Increased need of assessment of technical capability/services.
"innovate and integrate"	➤ Increased use of technology in conducting assessment processes.
	➤ Increased ability to assess intangible value.
	➤ Integrated assessment processes in all organizational functions.
	➤ More automated assessment processes.
	➤ Need for/ability to frequently conduct assessment.
	➤ Need to use assessment results faster to create strategic and other values.

Assessment

Impact from the general field of assessment on academic library evaluation will create multiple "paradigm shifts without a clutch" as it sparks innovations, questions, and opportunities. In Figure 13.1, the reader will note that assessment's impact on the academic service environment is interconnected between competition and mission/vision via technology. Using the wider access and integration of technology, assessment processes will become more utilized for outward, proactive-based assessments that will identify competitor activities (i.e., environmental scanning) while providing more frequent, faster access to a wider audience of the library's assessment processes and results. Technology will allow more participants from outside academic library facilities to participate in data collection, analysis, and dissemination while delivering proactive strategic information in real-time status for assessing, utilizing, and aligning the mission/vision of the library with its educational setting and its mission/vision.

As stated earlier, our profession adapted assessment procedures from outside the field of libraries. At present, the more frequently adapted ones focus on short-term quantitative data regarding customer impact or on the long-term affects of effort (i.e., outcomes), both of which are reactive in nature and not always aligned.

The nonlibrary evaluation processes and techniques often require the implementation of substantial adaptations within the library setting and may still not deliver the specific information academic libraries require to address stakeholder questions of accountability and effectiveness. Emphasis on academic libraries' ability to develop procedures for collecting and reporting strategic data to address accountability will be a priority from within the library profession.

Mission/Vision

The mission/vision impacts displayed in Figure 13.1 interconnect the general assessment forces and the "distance education" forces within the service environment. Having increased assessment information and access will provide proactive data and direction to a wider audience of stakeholders for developing, adjusting, and aligning the "mission/vision" of the educational (and library) service environment to address needs. As more educational providers use technology to deliver distance education to users in new markets as a component of their mission/vision via library services, academic libraries will be increasingly called on by stakeholders to proactively assess how these distance education library services promote, align, or generate the library's abilities to support institutional goals.

The dynamic nature and transformation of the academic organization's mission/vision will continue to demand assessment innovations. Flexible and quickly revised processes will be required by leaders and administrators to obtain critical information needed to develop effective strategic new missions/visions that support the overall institution.

Distance Education

Distance education forces interconnect mission/vision forces and collaboration forces in Figure 13.1, using technology to align and provide access of the mission/vision of the educational institution to potential and existing collaborators. Distance education is creating new markets, customers, and stakeholders and will cause library assessment processes and techniques to become more outwardly focused and self-mediated and will increase the numbers of customers, information requirement, and the geographic area to be assessed. This increase in participants, needs, and areas of assessment will also require more open/accessible evaluation processes with wider ranges of reporting abilities that address a larger audience for assessment results, a greater diversity of evaluative data to be collected in order to provide feedback on collaborators' impact and effectiveness in addressing the mission/vision of the education service environment, and identifying desired or unproductive collaborators to fill or correct strategic needs.

Collaboration

Collaboration is displayed in Figure 13.1 interconnecting the distance education and competition service environment force impacts. As the distance education technology force becomes more necessary and intertwined with the institution and library, collaboration will increase the scope, access, location, and capability of the resources, individuals, and groups required or available to adequately address service challenges.

The increased amounts of cooperation within and between service environments will create additional assessment challenges for academic libraries. Assessment processes and techniques will need to be highly flexible and customizable in order to adapt to a larger, dynamic set of collaborators (many being unfamiliar with library services and their evaluation) who will bring their own assessment processes and data needs into the service environment. Collaboration will also require academic library assessment to proactively expand outside the facility and into new settings that have their own forces and competitors. These will require accountability through proactive offensive (i.e., assessment that promotes or prevents) and defensive assessment (i.e., assessment that reaffirms and validates).

Competition

Competition is the final interconnecting service environment force depicted in Figure 13.1, connecting collaboration and assessment. By increasing the collaboration within the educational and library service environments, the amount of competitive forces is increased as well. Each new collaborator contributes new resources and opportunities while also bringing competitors into the service environment. Technology provides the competition force with a fast access point; this access is used to identify the service environment status and collaborators and to identify weaknesses and opportunities.

Therefore, the competition force will require assessment in academic libraries that efficiently creates proactive information about the environmental competitors and their potential impact on the service environment. Innovations must focus on developing a wide array of offensive assessment processes and techniques that will overlap in addressing stakeholder accountability and become less dependent on reactive defensive assessment processes and techniques.

CONCLUSIONS

The future of assessment in smaller academic libraries is foreboding for some because there is a lack of direction and a need for innovative processes and techniques, yet the future of assessment in smaller academic libraries is also golden for others, as there is an assessment research and application horizon waiting to be explored and utilized. In order to provide the innovations necessary to effectively respond and report pertinent evaluation to stakeholders, academic libraries will have to become more independent designers, implementers, and users of assessment than ever before.

The key to the future of effective appraisal in academic libraries will be the ability to overcome the lack of consensus in assessment directions, the lack of innovations in this area from within the library profession itself, and the need for developing processes to allow smaller academic libraries to closely identify with their institutions' need to dynamically transition into the future.

REFERENCES

Lubans, J. J., and Edward A. Chapman, eds. 1975. *Reader in Library Systems Analysis: Reader Series in Library and Information Science*. Englewood, Colo.: Microcard Edition Books.

White, Larry Nash. 2002. "Does Counting Count: An Evaluative Study of the Use and Impact of Performance Measurement in Florida Public Libraries." PhD diss., University of Florida.

14 BIG GROWTH IS NOT A SMALL STRATEGY

Michael A. Crumpton

Wake County, North Carolina, is one of the fastest-growing metropolitan areas in the country with projections for population growth in the double digits for years to come. Wake Technical Community College has served Wake County and surrounding areas since 1964 and has grown in accordance with the population. The recent accelerated growth in population is leading Wake Tech into another expansion of operations, and this includes providing library services to meet the increasing needs of the community and students.

The Wake County Board of Commissioners, in December 2005, established a Blue Ribbon Committee on the Future of Wake County and charged it with analyzing infrastructure plans and funding requirements needed for the next 20 to 30 years to support continued economic expansion. In its inaugural report, the committee projected the population of Wake County to increase 85 percent by 2030 and Wake Tech's student population to increase by 98 percent. The specific recommendations for Wake Tech include the following: continuing to seek public support on general obligation bonds for capital needs and encouraging public and private partnerships for funding other capital and equipment needs.

Given Wake Tech's present and projected growth, all divisions and departments are challenged to pursue their needs and compete for resources. As any organization grows, especially one that incorporates a library or learning resource/ information center as a component, strategic plans to include library facilities can vary. Organizational expansion within community colleges does not always provide immediate consideration for the growth of library services. Therefore, these smaller libraries must stretch available resources. Overall growth at Wake Tech is leading its library to develop strategic plans to provide library services to accommodate the additional students at new locations.

As students have become more electronic and Internet savvy, library expansion has come to include extending the library's influence beyond physical walls. Libraries with limited physical presence and with smaller collections also face competition from the Internet. The challenge is to find ways to identify resources and develop instruction that are appropriate for patrons without leaving them to seek Web-based options on their own. Facilitating growth both physically and virtually supports the accreditation standards to which the library and larger organization are bound. At Wake Tech, accreditation and accountability are assumed by the Southern Association of Colleges and Schools (SACS) as well as the North Carolina Community College System.

The economic impact of a community college on the community it serves can be significant. Earlier this year, William Green (2006, 22), chief executive officer of Accenture, called for support for community colleges, which he believes is vital to our competitive future as a nation. The economic impact of Wake Tech on Wake County was estimated for 2003 at $296 million by Omega Associates, LLC. This economic boost is a catalyst for continued growth. To respond to this growth, many community colleges, including Wake Tech, have added distance learning opportunities. Part of strategic planning must include offering resources and services for these distance learning classes. This strategy is supported by the American Association of Community Colleges in a position statement approved in November 2004 that calls for library resources for off-campus as well as on-campus needs.

The library must put strategic plans into place and provide justification to administrators that make a strong case for acquiring adequate resources to meet student needs. Without administrative forethought, community college library growth will be overshadowed by the entire expanding organization. Without attention, new library collections, resources, services, and facilities will lose out to other priorities. Library administrators and directors must find a way to become part of the process and help direct the outcome.

Because expansion can occur gradually, timing is a critical partner in creating a smooth plan of action for enhancing library resources, equipment, facilities, and ultimately the library's ability to serve its increasing population. This includes projecting long-term needs into strategic planning as well as addressing library attributes at the beginning of the process. Library operations and services will be impacted by changes that occur with continued development, and a strategic plan will be needed to control service outcomes. This presents an opportunity to review operational components, including an analysis of centralized versus decentralized functions. It also means looking at how future changes will affect present situations, including staff and their current responsibilities.

GROWTH LEVEL PLANNER

In order to facilitate the demand for library services at Wake Tech, a Growth Level Planner was designed to address needs at different levels of full-time equivalent (FTE) enrollment and unduplicated head count. As a point of reference, the chart given in Table 14.1 will serve as a blueprint for planning purposes. In a community college system that is experiencing tremendous growth, this planner identifies the elements within the library organization that necessitate action to meet required student and faculty service and to ensure that the library matches college quality goals, accreditation standards, as well as the expectations of related professional organizations. Other library types could follow similar steps.

Table 14.1
Growth Level Planner

Level	Designation	Up to FTE	Up to UHC	Library Services
Level 1	Site	50	269	
Services:				Library Web site available to public
				Basic services available virtually should include, portals to electronic resources, OPAC, and contact information for main library
Space Allocation:				None
Staff:				None
Resources:				All electronic through Web site
Equipment:				None
Level 2	Center	300	1,594	Level 1 plus
Services:				Outreach instruction available
				Remote access to databases available
				Distance learning amenities including circulation access, online tutorials, and virtual reference referrals
				Library published handouts available to direct users to resources
Space Allocation:				None
Staff:				1–1.5 full time as needed for instruction
Resources:				Contact point for obtaining material

Level	Designation	Up to FTE	Up to UHC	Library Services
Equipment:				Computers: shared access if available from partner departments
Level 3	Campus	1,000	5,304	Level 2 plus
Services:				Selected open instruction and reference services available by librarians
Space Allocation:				3,000–5,000 square feet
Staff:				1–3 staff (2 FTE)
Resources:				Basic reference collection
				Circulation collection up to 3,000 volumes
Equipment:				5–10 computers, shelving, journals on request
Level 4	Complete	5,000	26,504	Level 3 plus
Services:				Full instruction, reference and circulation services
Space Allocation:				6,000–10,000 square feet
				Spacing for staff work areas
Staff:				3–6 staff, basic cataloging and processing functions performed
				Lead librarian position to maintain administrative duties
Resources:				Reference collection broadened to include core basics
				Circulating collection expanded to support core
				Electronic resources purchased to support specific course offerings
				Audiovisual materials and equipment to support multiple teaching formats
				Collection: 11,000–25,000 volumes
Equipment:				10–50 computers, reference shelving, circulation collection shelving

(continued)

Table 14.1 (*continued*)

Level	Designation	Up to FTE	Up to UHC	Library Services
Level 5	Full	10,000	53,004	Level 4 plus
Services:				Full instruction, reference and circulation services
				Centralized operational functions that support levels 1–4
Space Allocation:				10,000–25,000+ square feet
				Spacing for staff work areas
Staff:				5+ staff (staffing levels adjusted to head count and traffic pattern)
Resources:				Collection: 20,000+ volumes
				Full range of reference and circulating materials
Equipment:				20+ computers, reference shelving, circulation collection shelving

To identify and manage the growth at Wake Tech, five levels have been developed, based on student admission numbers that will serve as a guideline for investment in library services, resources, and facilities. The investment in student-related services is tied financially and quantitatively to the number of FTEs being generated or other registration-generated numbers, such as unduplicated head count.

Services

One of the first steps in determining the direction growth should take is to make decisions on services offered. While it might seem that quantitative expansion of current services is assumed, this type of analysis is important for several reasons. First of all, this process might uncover duplicated or unused services that have continued unchallenged for some time. This is known as the "that's the way it's always been done" syndrome. Growth and the desire to increase the efficiency of resources, including staffing, is a powerful tool for eliminating outdated services or processes.

Underhill (1999, 11–39) created and discussed what he calls the science of shopping. Since libraries are considering many retail attributes in order to attract and keep patrons, a look at this methodology is useful. It will be especially helpful for small libraries that want to make every effort count. Concepts such as detail observation, written analysis of behavior patterns, and testing of new ideas and procedures before implementation can save time and money. This approach will also help determine library services both physically and virtually.

Another reason to analyze services in an expanded environment relates to communication and partnerships. Communication supports the resource (materials, equipment, and facilities) requests you are going to make as part of your growth activities. And partnerships ensure that services offered complement the curriculum. Costanzo (1992, 111–19) offers good insight into faculty members' views and suggestions for making a community college library an integral part of the learning experience.

Should smaller libraries whose purpose might be focused on current resource accessibility as opposed to historical, archival, or in-depth research materials worry about physical presence in the age of the Internet? With students and the Millennial generation already at ease with using the computer, can the library make a difference in how those resources are accessed and utilized? Of course they can, and this is a topic of discussion on many listservs, blogs, and professional literature in the world of librarians.

However, as an example of direct feedback from users, question number 1240 from the Online Computer Library Center's 2005 *Perceptions of Libraries and Information Resources* asked students what type of advice they would give the library. A 20-year-old undergrad replied, "Just remember that students are less informed about the resources of the library than ever before because they are competing heavily with the Internet." This statement reflects a big concern, namely, that students who are provided no guidance from the library will not learn to use information resources properly. It's part of the organization's mission as well as those who have chosen to be librarians not to let this happen.

In the Growth Level Planner, Wake Tech's library services begin with the basics available to anyone who can Google their way onto our Web site. However, the library's Web site is linked from the campus Web site and is intended to support and answer questions from the community at large. All students are provided with this link, and the library is a portal to a variety of resources. This includes study guides, tutorials, informational resources, policies and procedures, the Online Public Access Catalog, and links to electronic resources.

Another way to expand services is to think about how instruction makes a difference. For example, consider moving from traditional bibliography instruction formats to an information literacy approach. Grassian (2004, 51–53) discusses a comparison between bibliography instruction formats and the information literacy approach. For smaller libraries in particular, an information literacy emphasis to instruction will enable students to become better consumers without the dependence upon library staff, which is usually in short supply. Teaching the right skills up front provides a payback later in servicing users with stronger skills.

On the Growth Level Planner, as the number of potential patrons increases, other services, along with space, staffing, and additional resources, are added to match expansion. Level 5 would be the ultimate combination of services that could be offered to the entire user community with some room to expand over time. This includes the use of such features as wireless access, smart classrooms, and membership in library consortiums for resource sharing. The next level would be a significant upgrade of resources and facilities, and reaching that point would not be considered a small library anymore.

Space

Space is a common problem for small libraries sharing facility resources with other services. As areas compete for space, conflicts become more likely, complicating efforts to raise the level of service. For small organizations in particular, collaboration on space utilization is essential.

Once again, mimicking the science of shopping, paying attention to the science of a library user can tell a great deal about the effectiveness of the library. Combine that with the concept of "library as a place," and you have a formula for how to best use limited areas in a small environment where space is at a premium. This means finding out what is most important to potential users. Once the basics are met—room for equipment such as computers, materials such as books, and staff working area—what is the best use of anything that remains?

The use of space should appropriately match the intended services that are related to the physical attributes of resource materials and instruction available. In our Growth Level Planner, additional physical space is not required in levels 1 and 2. Library services begin as a virtual experience, an extension of the library's Web site and electronic resources. Add to that the physical presence of an outreach librarian who can provide the instruction needed to access and use those resources.

This concept can be critical to a small library because a virtual presence becomes the extension needed to market and provide substance for services at the basic level. Your Web site should be creative and understandable with links to tutorials and other easy-to-use resources. This is also where virtual reference or consortium collaborative experiences would be helpful. Such a step could also satisfy the accreditation need for providing materials and instruction at the primary level.

As FTE grows along with natural traffic patterns for students and staff, the need for space becomes clear. Books and other physical materials still have a place in a library as well as access to electronic information in a controlled environment. Group instruction will also require space, and more patrons mean more questions. A level-three library space could provide the minimum accommodation for physical service points and be supplemented by level 1 and 2 activities.

Level 4 should be considered a "full-service" facility with equipment, resources, and staff. Space considerations include elements that are aesthetically pleasing, comfortable, and easily accessible. At this level, staff members are still decentralized, meaning sharing similar job functions, so work space should be conducive to a shared environment.

Level 5 includes a main campus library or head branch. This level offers full service and operating hours that have been determined appropriate for all. This becomes a primary location for patrons by centralizing important functions, but it also supports satellite branches. Ideally, this facility would also have room to expand.

Considering the demographics of users is also important. For example, once FTE reaches a certain level, secondary space takes on added importance. Will students require a place to study, meet in groups, have access to word processing or other programs, or simply have a shelter? Will these other requirements conflict with the intended use of the space?

Part of this answer at Wake Tech comes in the form of shared space. A variety of service areas and/or individuals assist with the effort to provide library services by allowing their space to be made available when not in use. The library takes advantage of these opportunities by presenting itself and its resources in a format that encourages users to come forth.

Facilities

At Wake Tech, growth in recent years has lead to a variety of facility types. Additional off-site classroom locations have been added, as have facilities directed at specific curriculums. Typically, these are supported by the library at level 1 or 2 from the Growth Level Planner perspective. But expansion is now toward facilities with campus status, and this creates the opportunity for the library to add branch locations.

Branch locations are usually an extension of service points, based on need, from main campus or main library facilities. In the community college system in North Carolina, this covers a wide range of sizes and operating attributes. If you are fortunate enough to be part of the planning for new construction, you then have a great opportunity to make some decisions that can affect operations for years to come.

With small libraries, new construction usually indicates that the library is included within a larger building that will also house classrooms, offices, labs, or other functions. And, as in the case at Wake Tech, this means that a senior administration official and library staff members are responsible for basic construction issues. However, since the library will have specific requirements that are important to its function, it is important that the library director and library staff members take responsibility for construction attributes that make a difference to the library.

A great resource for this is Woodward's (2000) *Countdown to a New Library: Managing the Building Project*. While you might not have the responsibility for the entire building, this book can be broken down into aspects of the library that others might not recognize. This includes issues such as placement of equipment, shelving, furniture, or even doors. The librarian must see these spaces as they are to be occupied, not simply drawn on a blueprint.

The beginning of new construction can also represent an opportunity to anticipate growth beyond the initial opening. Once again, it becomes the librarian's responsibility to point out that the space for computers should be expandable or that shelving to hold VHS tapes must be adaptable to DVD cases at some point in the future. This type of thinking and planning is critical for small libraries that can take longer to upgrade resources.

Staffing

The key to success is your staff and their support for all these other actions. In a small library environment, it is already typical that job responsibilities are shared and that the same services are provided by all staff. Multitasking could already be working nicely. But as services stretch, so can the resilience and patience of staff members who may feel that there wasn't enough staff to begin with.

Keep staff informed early and consistently. The growth of an organization is a wonderful experience, but there is also the potential for stress and anxiety. Staff buy-in to an expanding operation is essential in order to maintain smooth service flow. Keep the mission in the forefront: providing library service for your patrons is more important than individual comforts, but keep staff assured that, with a little teamwork, you can have both.

A consideration in the expansion process should be how changes made as a result of growth might affect each staff member's job description. A job analysis of each position would be appropriate as changes occur in order to ensure that each position's requirements are aligned with a person's skills and qualifications. This work should be done in partnership with the college's human resources department and is an investment in building staff relations. Rue and Byars (2000, 242–65) discuss this in detail.

Once the ground rules are established, the next task is related to training. Small library organizations do not usually have many funds related specifically to training. But given a situation where staff members will be expanding their duties, reeducation is necessary to provide good service, good morale, and confidence in their actions. A recommendation regarding training comes from the Brick and Click Libraries conference. Glover (2005, 56–60) delivered a presentation emphasizing participant-centered training that focused on the needs of the individual rather than directly on the topic. This is appropriate for the small library to ensure that individual staff members have the skill set needed. At Wake Tech, a variety of low-cost options are selected on an individual basis in order to maximize training. Planning ahead to ensure that everyone has appropriate skills for an expanded role is a great investment not only for staff knowledge but also to better meet user expectations.

Cross training is also an important aspect of staff development. While basic service points might already be shared, a small library can maximize its efficiency with a formal cross-training program. This is also useful for staffs that rotate between locations or use shared work space. When asked to wear many hats or serve multiple functions, staff members need the outfit to go with it or the training to achieve a sense of accomplishment. Cross training also helps eliminate territorial boundaries that staff members might have developed before growth stretched their activities. Make sure that the benefits of cross training are understood by all. More information about cross training and the benefits to team development can be found in Noe (1999, 181).

Multitasking is also worth a mention because in a small library environment this becomes necessary, especially in peak traffic times. While some people do this naturally, recognition of the effort and resulting benefit can also be a boost to morale. Formally, you can address multitasking in the job description by acknowledging the need, but informally it is an individual effort that takes motivation and recognition.

In the Growth Level Planner, the number of staff at each level changes, and this is a guideline or goal to achieve on the basis of circumstances. At the beginning of a new level or the opening of a new facility, staff might be stretched until funding or operational growth provides the monies needed to hire additional staff. Hours of operation, services provided, and detailed processes can all be affected by spreading out the existing staff. While there is no magic answer, recognize that each situation is different, and changes made to the operation should be purposeful, as part of the intended strategy. For example, if a decision is made to reduce the number of hours a branch library is open, justify this strategy with how those hours are redistributed and why this particular decision was made.

Materials and Resources

Small libraries must spend dollars on resources very carefully. Every dollar counts when requests for materials outnumber dollars to buy. Expanding collections can have some advantages in terms of duplicated curriculum. Duplicate monographs can easily be split up. Data are available to determine high-usage items or classifications, and this justifies multiple purchasing for other locations.

Books don't stretch, but they can walk around. As single-unit libraries become multiunit systems, the best course of action is to create an interbranch loan system that provides the conduit for helping materials get to users at different locations. Although this sounds obvious, many things can go wrong that can create the possibility of losing control of where materials are located. Forethought will ensure that materials are used efficiently and wisely.

There are other methods of providing appropriate materials, including short-listing requests from patrons, which means writing down requests for materials that cannot be filled. When it is time to place orders, these short lists provide documentation of student requests needed in the collection. In addition, it is important to ally with neighbor library systems (in Wake Tech's case, it would be Wake County) and make appropriate referrals to students needing resources.

Growth can also become a reason to start considering more electronic resources over print, for the level 1 and 2 advantage. Electronic resources cover a wider audience of users but are more expensive and, in the case of subscription services, temporary. In a community college environment, this proves to be appropriate, as teaching methods are also changing.

The Internet offers many free, open-access resources that can stretch resource dollars. Vendors are starting to recognize that smaller libraries should have special packages of resources that are streamlined and more affordable. This can make electronic resources desirable, but a conscious effort must be made to strike the right balance between print and electronic.

APPLYING ACCREDITATION AND ACRL STANDARDS

In addition to the Growth Level Planner, other factors to consider in the methodology to develop a growth strategy are accreditation standards, in this case set forth by SACS and the Association of College and Research Libraries (ACRL 2004). These standards will govern the future success of growth and should be used at the onset as a tool for decision making.

The SACS standards are titled "The Principles of Accreditation: Foundations for Quality Enhancement" and are less prescriptive than previous compliance statements (SACS 2001). Much is left to interpretation and proper support of items related to collections, staff, instruction, and other services. Nelson and Fernekes (2002) developed a workbook for the American Library Association that provides exercises and guidance on developing assessment techniques and compliance strategies. These factors should be considered in developing a growth strategy that will endure time and prepare the organization for accreditation.

The ACRL standards approved in June 2004 provide guidelines for analyzing library operations using outcome assessments as a means to measure the success of goals developed for each institution. These standards allow individual libraries to assess themselves within the context of their own larger organization. A good use of this in developing a growth strategy is to review a range of libraries, suggesting points of comparison to establish criteria and goals to achieve. This method of analysis creates comparisons and establishes baseline ratios to compare services with similar-sized library operations and is considered much more equitable for community colleges and smaller libraries.

A resource that is available to help establish these comparisons is from the National Center for Education Statistics at http://nces.ed.gov/surveys/libraries/academic.asp. On this site is a tool to compare academic libraries that can provide the data needed to develop baseline comparisons with resulting ratios used as a standard or goal. Libraries that have gone through the accreditation process recently have probably created this comparison.

Table 14.2 compares ratios for input measures and the levels of growth identified in the planner. At Wake Tech, this provides a planning tool for the library services identified in the table measured against the growing number of students at the levels previously discussed. Addressed in ratio format, this establishes guidelines when developing budget requests for materials and equipment, planning space, and projecting staffing needs. This can also be used when addressing needs for either a new campus under construction or an off-site facility not yet

Table 14.2
Input Measures for Growth Level Planner

Ratios per FTE	Volumes to Students	Resource Dollars to Students	Library Staff to Students	Library Space to Students	Instructional Sessions to Students	Computer Workstation to Students
Level 1	N/A	2:1	N/A	N/A	N/A	N/A
Level 2	N/A	10:1	1:300	N/A	1:300	1:50
Level 3	3:1	1,000:1	1:500	1.5:1	1:200	1:50
Level 4	5:1	3,000:1	1:800	2:1	1:100	1:40
Level 5	10:1	10,000:1	1:1,000	2:1	1:50	1:40

identified as a full campus but with the number of students that could have an impact on services.

These numbers are not absolute in the sense of direct comparisons across the board. A comparison of similar-sized libraries at each level produces more realistic results at each level of service. Other factors must be considered as well, but an investment in creating this type of formula for managing growth lends credibility to arguments for resources.

Another concept to consider in this formula is the law of diminishing returns or the opposite. The ratios can change at different levels because the output measures are not equal across a standard set of numbers. For example, consider the volumes-to-students ratio: at the top of level 3, with 1,000 FTE, the anticipated number of volumes needed would be 3,000. However, at the top of level 5, with 10,000 FTE, the ratio of volumes should increase because of other factors involved, such as range of curriculums to be covered or because of the larger overall size and greater use of the facility by noncurriculum patrons.

SUMMARY

Institutional growth is an exciting but sometimes stressful activity that can really challenge the stamina of the people involved. In smaller organizations, fewer people are available to address critical issues related to the needs driven by the growth of services. This can also create competition between service areas for resources, and the library should be prepared to present sound, valid arguments for enlarging its services.

At Wake Tech, the library system has already expanded over the years by adding a health sciences library branch, upgrading the main library to a new and larger facility, and developing a Web site that supports basic student needs for information. But in this case, growth is continuous and is projected to be so for many years. In an electronic age, processes for expansion have changed, so tools like the Growth Level Planner and the table for input measures have been developed to provide guidelines for directing the growth of library services.

Table 14.3
Summary Actions

Standards for Libraries in Higher Education	Suggested Actions
Planning	Review mission statement and goals as they apply to your growth.
Outcomes assessment	Establish benchmarks of current operation with surveys (i.e., LibQUAL+).
Facilities	Comparison of campus reports for space at each growth level for library services vs. other.
Administration	During periods of growth, gather advice from users groups and advisory committees and be a part of overall planning.
Assessment	Evaluation of information literacy, bench-marked at current levels as a guide for directing growth.
Instruction	Projecting future needs with regard to changes in technology or methods of delivery.
Communication and cooperation	Flowcharts, time lines, and responsibilities should be developed and shared by all.
Services	Compare reference transactions (NCES) for different-size libraries and establish focus groups to prioritize access and service activities.
Access	Determine specific points of access or service affected by growth, use gate count comparisons (NCES) and create action plan for changes.
Staff	Develop a program for cross training and compare staffing levels (NCES) for librarian support as well as total needs at different levels.
Resources	Determine content need for growth areas and compare size of print collections (NCES) and Circ transactions (NCES) to create a level to plan for.
Budget	Review comparison of expenditures (NCES) for staff and collections to make a case for needs.

The Growth Level Planner provides five levels of student population and the affected areas of library services. Services, space, staffing, resources, and equipment are addressed at each level. This furnishes administration with a preview of expectations, in terms of investment, for growing into each level. These levels can include off-site locations for classroom use to full campus services that incorporate a library within the larger facility.

In addition to the planner, the data in Table 14.2 help guide resources for growth in an appropriate path to ensure that standards are met for accreditation. These ratios should be customized to address other concerns or considerations for library services but can also be compared to other institutions at similar levels for compliance.

Table 14.3 provides a summarized view of actions to be taken as an organization grows and classifies these actions with each of the ACRL standards. This includes collecting the information needed to justify expenditures, changes to work environment, and services offered. Keeping and documenting actions in line with these standards, as well as your accreditation standards, will save time and effort in the future.

All these tools provide a small library with the needed construct to manage and control library services during periods of growth.

REFERENCES

Association of College and Research Libraries. 2004. *Standards for Libraries in Higher Education*. Chicago: Association of College and Research Libraries.

Costanzo, William. 1992. "The Community College Library: A Faculty Perspective." In *Community College Libraries Centers for Lifelong Learning*, ed. Rosanne Kalick, 111–19. Metuchen, N.J.: Scarecrow Press.

Glover, Kim. 2005. "Engaging Library Staff through Dynamic Training." In *Brick and Click Libraries: Proceedings of an Academic Library Symposium*, 56–60. Maryville: Northwest Missouri State University.

Grassian, Esther. 2004. "Building on Bibliographic Instruction." *American Libraries* 35 (9): 51–53.

Green, William. 2006. "We've Overlooked One of Our Greatest Assets." *Newsweek* 147 (18): 22.

Nelson, William, and Robert W. Fernekes. 2002. *Standards and Assessment for Academic Libraries: A Workbook*. Chicago: Association of College and Research Libraries.

Noe, Raymond A. 1999. *Employee Training and Development*. Boston: Irwin/McGraw-Hill.

Rue, Leslie W., and Lloyd L. Byars. 2000. *Management, Skills and Application*. Boston: Irwin/McGraw-Hill.

Southern Association of Colleges and Schools. 2001. *Principles of Accreditation: Foundations for Quality Enhancement*. Available at: http://www.sacscoc.org. Accessed May 29, 2007.

Underhill, Paco. 1999. *Why We Buy: The Science of Shopping*. New York: Simon & Schuster.

Woodward, Jeannette. 2000. *Countdown to a New Library: Managing the Building Project*. Chicago: American Library Association.

15 FROM PREDICTABILITY TO MANAGED CHAOS: THE CHANGE FROM PRINT SERIALS TO ELECTRONIC RESOURCE MANAGEMENT—INDIANA UNIVERSITY, KOKOMO CAMPUS

Kirsten Leonard

The Indiana University system is comprised of eight campuses with 37 libraries, including the residential campus at Bloomington with 27 libraries, the urban campus at Indianapolis with four libraries, and six regional campuses each with a library. Librarians have faculty status. Combined, the campuses serve more than 92,600 students and have more than 4,700 faculty. The administration of each library is independent and campus based, with library directors/deans reporting to a vice chancellor or vice president of academic affairs on each campus. The Council of Head Librarians, comprised of the 37 library directors led by the Ruth Lilly Dean of University Libraries at Bloomington, fosters communication and cooperation between the libraries. This council reviews and advises on major initiatives such as automation upgrades and large cooperative purchases. Other cooperative bodies exist in the Indiana University system, such as the Indiana University Online Cataloging Congress and the Acquisitions/Serials Congress. Indiana University libraries purchase resources individually using Indiana University systemwide agreements through the Committee on Institutional Cooperation and the Indiana Cooperative Library Services Authority. The eight campus libraries share a SirsiDynix Integrated Library System (ILS).

Indiana University Kokomo (IU Kokomo) is a regional commuter campus in the Indiana University system located in north-central Indiana. IU Kokomo serves 3,300 students and faculty. Approximately 80 percent of the students work full or part time. Because the students live and work off campus, providing online access to resources is essential. In 2002, library management recognized a need to enable online access for print subscriptions with a free online component. Although the library provided online access to journals through databases, direct access to individual journals was limited to a handful of titles. The library personnel at the time consisted of five full-time tenure-track librarians: the director, the head of public services, an instruction librarian, a government documents/Web librarian, and the head of technical services. A half-time public service librarian and three full-time support staff members completed the staff. Although recognizing the demand for online access to electronic journals, the limited number of librarians made it difficult to devote the time needed to investigate and develop the procedures for enabling online access, let alone implement access for a large number of titles.

Changes and advancements in library technology and automation have been transforming libraries for decades. The shifting of collections from print to electronic, begun a little more than a decade ago, has now reached a critical mass where many libraries have more electronic serials than print serials through database collections and individual electronic subscriptions. Librarians often argue that electronic information will never completely replace print. Some academic libraries have already converted all content to electronic in certain collections. In 1998, Drexel University began ordering serials in electronic format rather than print (Montgomery and King 2002, n.p.). In 2003, the University of Arizona "Virtual Depository" project investigated moving to electronic-only selection of government documents through the Federal Depository Library Program (FDLP). After assessing user satisfaction and savings in space needs and staff time, the library determined the pilot project successful and continued selecting only online documents (with the exception of maps and data sets) (Rawan 2003, slides 25–31). In August 2006, Indiana University conducted a Digital Futures Study to assess the ways that Indiana University will respond to a shift in mission "from supporting the creation, management and navigation of information in physical form to supporting its creation, management and navigation in digital form" (McRobbie 2006, n.p.). This chapter examines the positioning of small and medium-sized academic libraries in the transition to electronic information through an examination of the immediate requirements and challenges of managing electronic resources at the IU Kokomo Library with recommendations for areas to develop further in managing the transformation from print to electronic journals.

In 2002, IU Kokomo Library management created a part-time position focused on electronic resource management that was filled by a candidate with the required skill set (this author). The immediate challenge was identifying journals with free online access for which the library had a print subscription, activating the online access, adding the uniform resource locators (URLs) to the catalog record, and developing a system for managing administrative information. The state of online access to individual journal titles was evolving rapidly. Most publishers did not have their own online journal archive and relied on intermediaries such as Ingenta to host their individual journal titles on the Web. IU Kokomo purchased the majority of its subscriptions through one agent, but the agent did not include online access registration as part of its services for the majority of publishers. In fact, the agent often did not provide the library with the information required by the publisher to register for online access. This lack of service is most likely indicative of the rapid transformation that causes growing pains for the publishing industry.

The process of activation is completely unlike the process of ordering, renewing, and receiving print subscriptions. Each publisher has different purchasing policies, registration requirements, and Web interfaces for registration that have to be discovered, deciphered, and completed. This was a painstakingly slow process for only a couple of hundred journal titles, growing more burdensome as the number of titles increased. In addition, this process was far from static. Servers and interfaces were upgraded, publisher subscription policies changed, publications moved from one host to another, or the publisher developed a platform of its own. These changes often resulted in journals that had been carefully registered one month becoming inaccessible in a matter of weeks. In order to address these registration and access difficulties, the IU Kokomo Library began to centralize data on a shared server to allow for easier reference but retained multiple paper and electronic files for consultation when problems arose.

Online access proved popular with students, faculty, and librarians. IU Bloomington purchased the link resolver SFX and offered each of the IU regional campuses their own instance of SFX. The Council of Head Librarians approved the creation of a position based in Bloomington to foster more systemwide licenses of electronic resources. A team at IU Bloomington was investigating federated searching products. In addition, the Government Printing Office was positioning the FDLP to provide more electronic access to government information as a result of President Bush's E-Government Act. The need for electronic resources management at IU Kokomo Library was imminent and inescapable.

As early as 2002, Duranceau and Hepner (2002) identified that "the problem of staffing for e-resources has reached a crisis level in our profession that demands data, attention, and action" (316). In 2004, IU Kokomo Library management reorganized to create a full-time Electronic Resources/Documents Librarian tenure-track position within technical services from the part-time technical services position and an open full-time public services position. I was offered the newly created full-time position. Because of my skill set and experience in the IU system and strong support from public services, we were able to implement SFX on the Kokomo campus in less than six weeks from my start date.

The duties of the new position were divided half time between electronic resources management and managing participation in the FDLP, which includes the supervision of one staff person and one student handling print materials receiving. IU Kokomo Library management coupled these responsibilities in anticipation of the transformation of the FDLP to electronic format. Electronic resource management responsibilities were handled differently across the IU libraries. Bloomington had created an Electronic Resources Unit in 1999. Some libraries added electronic resource management to the duties of existing positions rather than creating a separate electronic resources librarian position. Wherever assigned, electronic resource management needs are considerable, and libraries often do not have the necessary staffing (Duranceau and Hepner 2002, 319).

IMPACT OF ELECTRONIC RESOURCES

Most discussions of the benefits of an electronic collection include the following:

- User demand for 24/7 availability of resources
- Competition with online information providers
- Economic concerns, such as reducing staffing and storage needs
- Simultaneous multiuser access
- Protection from loss, damage, or theft

Montgomery and King's (2002) study comparing the cost of print journals to electronic journals shows that total costs are less for an electronic collection because of storage savings but that staff costs increase. Their study found that at Drexel University, staff costs were three times greater for electronic collections in both collection development and acquisitions (2002, 6).

Managing print resources differs considerably from that of electronic resources. The processes used to manage current and archived print journals are controlled largely by the library. Print subscription processes are predictable and straightforward and do not vary from publisher to publisher. Fair use alone determines interlibrary loan permissions. By contrast, subscription processes for electronic resources differ from publisher to publisher, and the process is outside the control of the library. Once electronic access is enabled, it must be verified frequently because it can be modified or eliminated without notice. Access to archival content may be available only through a separate purchase or a higher subscription level, or access is subject to change without notice. Interlibrary loan permissions must be interpreted for each purchase.

ELECTRONIC RESOURCES WORKFLOW

The workflow of electronic resources often is described using the term "life cycle" with the following stages: selection, acquisition, receiving/activation, ongoing access verification, and renewal assessment. However, the implication of a single repeating cyclic pathway that is the same for every product is an oversimplification. Instead, the process is recursive in some stages, repeating in multiple loops, with multiple communication points involving differing personnel. The activation stage is recursive depending on which resource discovery and access products, such as an A–Z list, proxy server, link resolver, or federated search product, are used by the library. Upgrades and changes by information providers can tangle the entire process. Geller (2006) concurs that, "for better or worse, the cyclical nature of electronic resources management is wrong. At best it is a helix, spirally upward and hopefully implying progress; at worst it brings to mind images of Medusa's hair" (6).

Selection

Selection is a recursive stage that requires communication within the library, with patrons, with the vendors, with the institutional information technology (IT) group, and with other libraries and consortia. The selection process must assess interest, package options, pricing, trial access and analysis, and collection and budget analysis. Pricing models and options may vary from year to year, such as the option to subscribe to the print copy plus the online, print only, the print with free online access, or an online-only subscription. Additionally, the type of access authentication and the number of allowable simultaneous users may affect the final cost. An analysis of the product overlap with the currently held collections must be conducted. There may be a choice in platform or vendor availability, and evaluations of the vendor's stability, customer service, and platform reliability must be made. Resources need to be evaluated for usage statistics availability and COUNTER compliance status, compatibility, or availability with MARC record services, proxy servers, link resolvers, A–Z list management systems, and federated searching products. Because of the level of complexity and the coordination required, the process of selecting an electronic resource may take more than a year and require facilitating extensive communication among all interested parties. Furthermore, products may go through this process and not be selected as new offers arise with different details.

Acquisition

Acquisition includes price negotiation, license analysis, ordering, and payments. Negotiation can benefit both the library and the vendor by improving a library's buying power while also increasing a vendor's customer base. The key is developing strong avenues of communication with as many libraries as possible and being willing to float ideas that have no precedent. License analysis has no parallel in print acquisitions. The industry as a whole has yet to develop standardized language or best practices. Negotiation and analysis of the license include institutional obligations, terms-of-use restrictions (off-campus access, interlibrary loan permission level, walk-in access), administrative information, pricing terms, and archival or perpetual access rights.

Receiving/Activation

For print subscriptions, libraries must ensure receipt of issues and initiate claims if not received. For electronic resources, the process is more substantial. The receipt and activation of an electronic resources product requires performing the technical setup of the resource, configuring the user interface, and verifying access to the entire purchased content. Access verification is particularly important given the number of purchase options and content hosted on the same Web site. Do not assume that the entire range of purchased content is accessible.

The resource must be cataloged or MARC records added to the catalog. It must be added to the proxy server to allow access from off campus and to other resource discovery tools like the library A–Z list Web page, the link resolver, and the federated searching product. Each step must be tested to verify that access is established properly. All data concerning the resource purchase and activation must be added to the appropriate files, ILS, or electronic resource management (ERM) system, including the means of administrative and statistics access, user names, and passwords.

At IU Kokomo, the electronic resources librarian is also responsible for managing the proxy server, the A–Z list, the link resolver, and the federated searching product. Thoroughly understanding the resource makes it easier to activate the resource correctly in the link resolver and the federated search product. Consolidating responsibility in one position speeds the process with all the work going into one work queue rather than waiting for it to come to the top of multiple work queues. Managing the entire process of a complication-free activation has taken less than two hours. However, as the library moves further toward replacing individual print subscriptions with electronic ones, the print serials assistant will take over some receiving and ongoing access verification duties. In addition, with the recent retirement of the government documents assistant, that position was reconfigured to include electronic resources duties. While it is essential that information is shared among those responsible for managing electronic resources, the implementation and maintenance needs are far larger than one person can manage on her own. Instead of proactively managing access and organizational issues, too much time is spent putting out fires to regain access.

Small and medium-sized libraries should take the time to activate connectivity of acquired resources to other information providers, such as Google Scholar and Windows Academic Live. Libraries will remain relevant as long as they are known by their users to be an easier or more effective means of getting information. Integrating these competing tools into library resources absorbs their functionality and publicity into the library. Millennial generation users who may begin their search at Google are brought into the library when the library's link resolver is registered with Google. These competitors become potential gateways into the library.

Ongoing Access Management

Publishers and vendors are transforming their organizations in response to the demand for electronic versions of their products. Faced with a highly competitive environment, vendors frequently upgrade online delivery platforms to meet increasing server demands and standards requirements resulting from greater usage through link resolvers and federated searching products. These changes, combined with a complex information delivery pathway and issues with subscription account maintenance, cause frequent outages of service to the information content. The vendor changes often require maintenance to the library catalog, A–Z list, link resolver, federated searching product, ERM system, or other administrative data storage files to restore access.

Often libraries of all sizes do not monitor deeply enough to discover these outages and rely on students and patrons to report problems. IU Kokomo's large collections of resources offer alternative content should a certain article or resource not be accessible. Very few report problems. The complexity of the catalog, link resolvers, and databases can confuse students who do not recognize that an access problem has occurred. Therefore, some method of ongoing access verification is strongly encouraged.

Renewal Assessment/Statistics

Evaluations for renewals include comments from users and librarians, usage statistics compared to cost, budget data, product ease of use and reliability, and comparison to other resources covering the same subject area. The contract terms and price may be renegotiated. Gathering statistics presents a challenge. New standards such as Standardized Usage Statistics Harvesting Initiative, a National Information Standards Organization (NISO) standard for delivering usage statistics and new products such as ScholarlyStats from MPS technologies, uses the library's user name and password to gather usage statistics from different vendors providing significant time savings. Comparing statistics presents a further challenge. Although more vendors are indicating that they have COUNTER compliant statistics, these are not always complete or accurate in their compliancy. Davis and Price (2006, 1243) showed that the number of downloads is inflated when the vendor requires a user to access the HTML version before being able to download the PDF version. Statistics of varying levels of usefulness can be gathered from link resolvers, catalogs, Web pages, A–Z lists, and federated searching products.

MANAGING STAFFING AND STAFF COMPETENCY CHANGES

Dureanceau and Hepfer (2002) noted few "routine" tasks in electronic resource management in their survey but instead identified "many complex and interdependent tasks that require a broad knowledge of library systems, the campus network, and our proxy server, as well as broad and deep knowledge of the particular products we have purchased" (6–7). Managing proxy servers, link resolvers, and federated searching products requires some knowledge of the OpenURL standard, the electronic delivery of journals, Web interfaces, searching syntax, the NISO MetaSearch Initiative standard, and Web services, standards, and syntax, such as XML, Z39.50, HTML, and others. The electronic resources librarian must understand how these products and services interact. Development of enhancements and plug-ins for additional services may require programming expertise. Along with technical expertise, the electronic resources librarian must have strong communication skills and should develop a network of contacts and communication channels within the library, the library system, other similar libraries, larger libraries, vendors, and consortia. New electronic resources librarians should be strongly encouraged to seek mentors among other such librarians and to partner for training and joint purchases.

Geller (2006, 22–23) outlines three options for reorganizing the library to handle electronic resources. The first is to develop a separate unit devoted to electronic resources that capitalizes on selecting and training staff with the skill set to manage complex, Web-based, intertwined systems. As a separate entity, the unit is organized to work and effectively communicate information sharing among areas of responsibility. Zhang and Haslam (2005, 88) at the University of Nevada—Las Vegas (UNLV) planned to use this method to handle a subset of electronic resources responsibilities within the serials unit. UNLV created three new staff positions, one each to manage the proxy server, Serials Solutions and Web links, and the link resolver. Not only was this unit created to work together, but each staff person is cross trained to handle the other two areas of responsibility. This is a very effective means of communicating the deeply intertwined nature of these services and the need for continuous communication within the unit. Cross training—or at least an introduction to the other areas—is recommended for the entire scope of electronic resources management to foster more effective communication and ultimately better maintenance and performance.

The second option is to distribute electronic resources activities. In this model, electronic resources activities are assigned to the staff member with the most related print responsibilities. One benefit to this approach is that staff members are already repurposed should the decision be made to eliminate print altogether. However, the time for training, ongoing education, and maintenance needed to manage electronic resources is considerable, and unless there is a dramatic decrease in the print responsibilities, the workload may be unmanageable. In addition, the need for communication must be clearly delineated, and strong and effortless means of communication must be developed. A unit that is territorial, noncommunicative, or isolated by organizational silos will struggle to manage electronic resources effectively.

The third option is a hybrid of the two previous approaches: repurpose or create some positions with only electronic resources responsibilities and add some electronic responsibility to those with print responsibilities. Some areas allow for easier overlap between print and electronic than others. Budget management is one area that has similar workflows for print and electronic formats. At the First Electronic Resources and Libraries Conference (http://electroniclibrarian.org/moodle) in 2006, the challenge of distributing electronic resource management tasks to staff without technical expertise was a frequent topic of discussion (Carlson 2006, 6). The challenge of providing training is considerable given the fast pace of change and the high level of technical expertise required. The electronic resources librarian may be unable to both manage the considerable workload and create and continuously update training for staff.

Joan Conger (2004) calls for a team approach for both responsibility and leadership: "The pervasive effects of electronic resources in a typical library require a different kind of management. Turbulent change disrupts stable efficiency, with the insistent voices of new situations and daily requires unprecedented, creative solutions from professionals throughout a library. Competence becomes less about static knowledge and the application of rules and more about daily, adroit innovation and the use of pooled talent through collaboration. Management becomes less about planning and direction and more about collaborative management and adaptive learning" (2).

We must reinvent the process of creating workflows and procedures to create an innovative, iterative, open, collaborative process with involvement from an expanding and fluctuating number of subordinates, colleagues in technical and public services, IT, other libraries, consortia, vendors, and beyond. Decision making should not and cannot be done in isolation because too many areas are interconnected. Changes in one area will most certainly have some consequence in another.

FOR THE FUTURE: AMPLIFIED COLLABORATION AND COMMUNICATION

Within the Library

With only five full-time librarians in the IU Kokomo Library, the communication challenge is somewhat easier. Consolidating the management responsibilities of all electronic products under one person increased the awareness of how vendor changes, upgrades, policy changes, or report of a problem from a listserv for one electronic resource product affect the other products. The smallest change that appears limited to the proxy server or catalog, for example, may also cause access problems for the link resolver and federated search product. When responsibilities are distributed among several staff members, vigilance is critical in communicating every change to everyone with electronic resource responsibilities and to public service librarians. The creation of an automated means of notification of changes to all personnel would ensure that stakeholders get the needed information and reduces the workload of the electronic resources librarian.

With Other Libraries and Consortia

All libraries can benefit from sharing management tools, checklists, training guides, problem reporting, and product enhancements. Listservs for electronic resources, proxy servers, link resolvers, and federated searching products are invaluable for identifying problems and sharing solutions, but participation is still limited considering the number of libraries that use the products. Even the smallest library is able to benefit all libraries by reporting problems since it is very likely that others will have the same situation. Training is a substantial challenge given rapid change in the industry and the varying levels of technical knowledge held by staff. Libraries should look to form partnerships and take advantage of training offers from vendors, consortia, and professional organizations. With the number of product upgrades done in any given year, the main challenge then becomes focusing on training for the most long-term direct benefit to the library user.

With Subscription Agents and Multipublisher Vendors

Lugg and Fischer (2003) assert that "agents have realized the need to innovate, to re-invent themselves as trackers, licensors, and brokers of electronic content" (3). Agents are increasing their support but haven't reached the phase where all online access to subscribed content is enabled automatically. Agents are much more likely now to provide swift troubleshooting assistance and resolving access problems than in the past, a significant improvement of which libraries should take advantage. The IU Kokomo Library purposely limits the number of individual online journal subscriptions to content unavailable in a collection because of the extensive amount of maintenance required and the greater likelihood of access problems. As more publishers move content from database aggregates, as has been done by the University of Chicago most recently, we may not have this option much longer. Publishers must be able to provide easy and accurate activation to individual subscriptions before forcing libraries to subscribe individually.

ERMS AND OTHER TECHNOLOGICAL SOLUTIONS

The demand for an ERM system to address the challenges of electronic resources is high considering the inability of current ILS systems to handle the selection, acquisition, maintenance, and presentation of electronic resources. Libraries look to the ERM systems for centralizing and standardizing electronic resource management information and presenting that information to library users as well as to staff. ERM functions include tracking access problems and troubleshooting efforts and the ability to generate notification messages on Web pages and in e-mails. Other functions include centralized statistics management and license restrictions that affect interlibrary loan. Some libraries and library consortia have created their own systems. There are many existing, new, and forthcoming products, but they are often expensive. ILS vendors are beginning to partner with ERM system vendors, such as SirsiDynix's new partnership with Serials Solutions to create an ERM module to interface with Sirsi Unicorn. The advantage is that the cost might be subsumed within the ILS budget. Open-source options exist, and while there are no costs associated with the product, there are IT costs to install and maintain the software.

A product to verify access to an entire full-text article and that all subscribed content is accessible, perhaps operating in conjunction with an ERM system, is a critical area for development. Some progress has been made to speed the verification process. In January 2007, the Online Computer Library Center's Openly Informatics released Link Evaluator, a free add-on for the Firefox Web browser that functions as an advanced link checker. Given the level of competition with other information providers, libraries must provide accurate and trouble-free information products to patrons to remain relevant and viable.

Another possibility for taming electronic maintenance is moving to an Applications Service Provider (ASP) model product in which the software company provides the hardware, hosting, maintenance, upgrades, and support for the software and delivers the product to the library through the Internet. The library need only manage its list of purchased resources and customizations. The software vendors handle upgrades and software, knowledge base, and server maintenance. No local IT staff is needed to install and manage software and hardware, and knowledge base updates can be done more often. Serials Solutions updates the knowledge base for its Article Linker (link resolver) daily. The Software as a Service (SaaS) product model takes the ASP model one step further with complete Web integration and the ability to quickly take advantage of emerging Web technologies and standards with faster product development cycles. The disadvantage to purchasing an ASP or SaaS product is that the library doesn't retain control over the content or software, it doesn't control the timing of upgrades, and the price may be higher. The shorter development cycle means changes in procedures or training material may be needed more frequently.

Another means of reducing maintenance and increasing interoperability between information products is selecting one vendor to provide multiple products to ensure that the patron is seamlessly connected to the information being sought. In some cases, this may have the added benefit of requiring the maintenance of only one configuration file and one set of Web page customizations. Examples are Ex Libris with SFX (link resolver), MetaLib (federated search product), Verde (ERM system), and ALEPH (ILS) and Serials Solutions with Article Linker (link resolver), Central Search (federated search product), ERMS(ERM system), and the interface to SirsiDynix's ILS. Other vendors, such as EBSCO, Innovative, and Endeavor, offer multiple products. Maintaining information in one location creates a more efficient workflow and provides more powerful holdings and usage reporting and analysis.

CONCLUSION

While the electronic resources world is still quite chaotic, the library world has responded and begun to find the solutions to manage the chaos. Small and medium-sized academic libraries should focus their efforts on the following.

First, staffing and organization changes and realignments must be made to accommodate the extensive demands of electronic resources. Staff assigned to electronic resources must have problem-solving, technical, and Web services competencies; an understanding of licensing and contract negotiation; and a commitment to continued professional development. In a library unable to add staffing, processes and services must be streamlined and an electronic resources transition plan developed to methodically downsize print and increase electronic resources. The processes for change in libraries must be reengineered to speed adaptability.

Second, communication among library electronic resources, print, and public services personnel as well as users must increase and not be isolated or delayed by restrictive organizational limitations within the library. An environment of active and open communication and education among all parties involved in electronic resource management is essential. Select electronic resource systems and structures for interoperability and faster but more quality-controlled development cycles to remain relevant in the face of global competition among information providers.

Finally, cooperation and communication among libraries with similar ILSs, proxy servers, link resolvers, ERM systems, and other products must increase for the betterment of all. The Electronic Resources and Libraries Conference is one major avenue for sharing strategies between libraries in both formal presentations as well as more informal wikis and blogs that facilitate the sharing of checklists, implementation guides, and quick fixes. The very fluid and fast product development cycle of electronic resources means that our responses must also increase in speed and fluidity.

GLOSSARY

Collaborative management. Term used by Joan Conger (2006): "Responsibility for organization success is shared among members. These members have authority over their own work, contribute through teams to the work of others, and contribute through leadership to the decision making and overall purpose of the organization" (231–32).

COUNTER. Counting Online Usage of Networked Electronic Resources, an international initiative providing guidance on usage statistics identifying and defining data elements and usage report content and formats.

Electronic resources. All information content and service products delivered online, such as e-books, journal databases, citation databases, e-journals, link resolvers, ERM systems, and federated searching products.

Federated searching product. Software product that simultaneously searches multiple databases from multiple vendors from one location.

Interoperable. The ability of one system to communicate or work with another.

Link resolver. A Web-based application that uses citation data formatted according to the OpenURL standard to construct links to the content.

NISO Metadata Initiative. NISO-sponsored move toward industry standards to enable metasearch service providers to offer more effective and responsive services, content providers to deliver enhanced content and protect their intellectual property, and libraries to deliver services that distinguish their services from free Web services.

Open source. Software source code that can be freely used, modified, and distributed.

OpenURL. A definition and syntax for describing elements in a URL.

Recursive. A process, procedure, or mathematical function that calls itself either indefinitely or until a specified point is reached. A computer program that calls itself into operation or calls other programs that in turn recall the original. *SMUG*. SFX/MetaLib Users Group (http://www.smugnet.org).

REFERENCES

Carlson, Jake. 2006. "The First Electronic Resources and Libraries Conference: A Supplemental Report." *Library Hi Tech News* 23 (6): 6–11.

Conger, Joan E. 2004. *Collaborative Electronic Resource Management: From Acquisitions to Assessment.* Englewood, Colo.: Libraries Unlimited.

Davis, Philip M., and Jason S. Price. 2006. "eJournal Interface Can Influence Usage Statistics: Implications for Libraries, Publishers, and Project COUNTER." *Journal of the American Society for Information Science and Technology* 57 (9): 1243–48.

Dureanceau, Ellen Finnie, and Cindy Hepner. 2002. "Staffing for Electronic Resource Management: The Results of a Survey." *Serials Review* 28 (4): 316–20.

Geller, Marilyn. 2006. "ERM Staffing, Services, and Systems." *Library Technology Reports* 42 (2): 4–27.

Lugg, Rick, and Ruth Fischer. 2003. *Agents in Place: Intermediaries in E-Journal Management.* Available at: http://www.ebookmap.net/pdfs/AgentsInPlace.pdf. Accessed July 22, 2006.

McRobbie, Michael. 2006. E-mail announcing Indiana University Libraries Digital Futures Study. July 18.

Montgomery, Carol Hansen, and Donald W. King. 2002. "Comparing Library and User Related Costs of Print and Electronic Journal Collections." *D-Lib Magazine* 8 (10). Available at: http://dlib.org/dlib/october02/montgomery/10montgomery.html. Accessed July 20, 2006.

Rawan, Atifa. 2003. *Virtual Depository: Arizona Project Final Report and Recommendations.* Available at: http://www.access.gpo.gov/su_docs/fdlp/pubs/proceedings/03pro_rawan. ppt. Accessed July 31, 2006.

Zhang, Xiaoyin, and Michaelyn Haslam. 2005. "Movement toward a Predominantly Electronic Journal Collection." *Library Hi Tech* 23 (1): 82–89.

16 IS THERE A FUTURE FOR TECHNICAL SERVICES?

Amy E. Badertscher

There are many angles from which to view the future of technical services in academic libraries, and all of them have the potential to be right. Without a crystal ball and the wisdom to properly use such a tool, it is impossible to predict this future with any certainty. There are many things happening within the technical services realm that demonstrate a future can and should exist. Here we look at literature on the topic as well as the current experience of two liberal arts colleges in the Midwest.

THE RECENT PAST

In Freedman's (1984) article, he begins with this statement: "The demise of technical services has so often been predicted that our continuing discussions of that part of librarianship could be called a tribute to heartiness, or perhaps, in a darker light, a manifestation of its die hardiness" (1197). Freedman continues his argument: "So, despite the wisdom and prognostication of our best thinkers and qualified success of our latest technology, I submit that technical services has a future, at least for a while." Given that more than two decades have passed since these words were printed, one might think either that technical services no longer exist or that radical changes have occurred within technical services units. My observation is that neither is true today and that the last line of the quote remains accurate.

There are many professionals who believe that the role of technical services is obsolete and that it exists only because of the tenacity of the remaining catalogers and acquisitions personnel. The notion that changes do not happen because of staffing challenges and inertia may be partly responsible for this belief. On the other hand, many who work in the technical services areas of academic libraries consider themselves dedicated, detail-oriented employees.

ANOTHER VIEW

Another view of the past provides a look into what to consider when reevaluating technical service organization and work flow. Gorman (1979) describes in his writing on the subject a library split into two distinct areas with little or no middle ground—technical processing departments and public service departments. "One finds catalogers who have a tremendous knowledge of the subject field in which they work, yet that knowledge is seldom or never used in reference work" (435). Gorman's statement implies that libraries are not utilizing the talent within to expand services. There is clearly opportunity for the two groups to interact on a different level. Technology is moving in a direction with electronic resource management tools that focus on the common ground between user access and user services. User focus is becoming more prominent and easier to define across the library and not just as a public service function.

Gorman (1979, 436) envisioned a library grouped around services, subjects or languages, or a combination of both rather than an emphasis on the services provided—social science services or language services versus public services or technical services. This vision of the academic library is just now gaining momentum within the more traditional reference and instruction areas and has not trickled down into the technical services areas. Automation is changing the role that technical services plays in the library arena but has not reached the point of moving functions out of the back room and into the public area. What happens in technical services departments still seems to be a mystery to reference librarians. According to Stephan (2006), "Several times I have told my colleagues in technical services, 'I don't know what y'all do; as far as I am concerned it's all magic.' Of course, I know it's complicated, in-depth, and a necessity to every library. Some people refer to reference librarians as public service, but when it comes down to it, everyone in a library is part of public service" (21). Given these scenarios, the possibilities of sharing skills and ideas between the technical service groups and the public service area is logical, but making it happen is challenging.

This brings us to the future of technical services within academic libraries. The notion that this area is obsolete is not true; however, there are many changes in the library field that necessitate modifications. The past few decades brought more and more automation to acquisitions and cataloging, and over time the roles changed. This is not complete because the transformation continues to be an evolving process. First, there was basic copy cataloging, then the Online Computer Library Center (OCLC) with continuously updated catalog records, and then shelf-ready books and Promptcat. All of these, along with the Online Public Access Catalog (OPAC), Web sites and Internet access, and the explosion of electronic resources, transformed the technical services function. The very nature of the work itself is changing, and where it will stop is unclear. There is a possibility that the end result may look very different from the organizations currently in place.

The notion that the future of technical services is an automated process and that people are no longer part of the equation is foreign. It may be that the acquisitions and cataloging functions are completely outsourced and that technical services departments at academic institutions will be only a fragment of the size they are today. In many areas in the corporate world, outsourcing to remote locations is the norm for entire functions. Is this the future of acquisitions and copy-cataloging?

WHAT IS THE FUTURE?

Many different ideas come to mind when this question is asked, and there is no way to know which answer is correct. The possibilities are varied and include some of the following options. Acquisitions and cataloging will be outsourced completely with a few paper materials still received; all serials and periodicals will be electronic as well as many of the monographs. Daily newspapers will be available only in electronic formats that are fed to your cell phone, palm, MP3 player, or future versions of these handheld tools. Behind the vision for the future, there are issues and obstacles facing technical services departments in small and medium-sized academic institutions. These issues include the following:

- Increased availability of shelf-ready material (outsourcing)
- Aging workforce
- Need for additional technology skills
- Space and storage issues

In order to address these points, let's take a deeper look at several from this list. Outsourcing, at least for the cataloging functions, will become more prominent over the next decade. There are a number of vendors today that will customize shelf-ready material, and the options should continue to expand. While these services are available, they cannot replace the human touch. Even the most practiced vendor process will not be perfect. Each institution would like to have the library catalog as accurate as possible without duplicating the work of the vendor, and there are times when it is necessary to reprocess material. Tracking the accuracy of a vendor providing materials does help build confidence that the processing is correct. Librarians need to understand their comfort level with regard to perfection. Is 80/20 good enough for your constituents?

Another of the issues facing most technical service and cataloging departments in colleges and universities today is the average age of the employees. They are closer to retirement than college graduation, and this has the potential to be a benefit or a determent depending on how you manage the changes this group will face over the next 5 to 10 years. There are the continuing trends of automation, outsourcing, and technology versus an aging workforce. This combination leads to benefits in the next decade if you manage the process and consider the preparation of a different type of employee to replace workers as they retire. What skills should be required of someone entering the technical services area in 2010?

In a review of technical service organizations and their functions, Branton, Green, and Martin (2006) present some forward-thinking ideas that are overlooked in other areas of library organizations. For example, "acquisitions personnel are also most familiar with the publishing world and trends in publications. They often work closely with vendor sales representatives and negotiate the discounts and services" (22–25). This is important as librarians move beyond traditional thinking toward streamlined work flows and efficient ordering processes.

Acquisitions staff or serials catalogers enjoy the role played in solving the mystery of "where is that issue" when pulling together the issues for binding and filling out the necessary paperwork. Yet they understand that the future for serials is moving toward electronic journals with lease-to-use options rather than ownership of bound journals for decades. Changes will affect the roles that technical service personnel play in the next five years. However, they will still have a role. Access to the material is required, and control of the collection necessary, and therefore fewer people with slightly different job descriptions will be needed. If we agree on what is "good enough" for our standards, are there some members of our constituencies who would question the decision-making process that arrived at the abbreviated version of a catalog record? Is it the place of the technical services department to decide what should and should not be included in a catalog record?

In order to understand the future of technical services, one needs only to review the literature of the past. When considering the question "what is the future of technical services at academic institutions?" many ideas come to mind and not all of them are positive. The most difficult aspect of the future of anything is the idea or change versus the reality of change. Change in and of itself is often difficult to grasp; however, it is something that occurs in most lives on a regular basis. Many people view little changes in their personal lives to be a good thing—getting a new haircut, buying new shoes or a new golf club, or even a new car or house. When it comes to the daily processes that occur in the workplace, the emotions are somehow different. The first reaction seems to be negative. The challenge is to have the employee gain confidence early to build momentum, enabling negative concerns to turn into positive action. This is not simple.

COOPERATION OR COLLABORATION AS AN ALTERNATIVE

There is potential for additional cooperation within the area of technical services that utilizes the talents of the current workforce in different ways. The challenge here is to truly separate the work from the person. Many of these roles have gone unchanged for long periods of time. It is difficult to sort out the necessary processes from those that are just nice to have or those that are no longer working. It takes time, patience, and a good deal of evaluation. Denison University and Kenyon College are currently cooperating on a work redesign process with their technical services operation. This is not the first nor will it be the last cooperative venture between these two establishments. Finding ways to cooperate in a somewhat competitive environment, like small liberal arts colleges, is not always easy but is in many ways necessary in order to continue offering high-quality services in a rapidly changing environment.

Is it possible to combine the technical services departments of two or more institutions—to have a team that works well together, reorganizes the work flow, and manages, troubleshoots, but somehow maintains the uniqueness of each institution and does not become a call center organization? The goals of the merged organization are to have a streamlined, efficient work flow with a joint processing plan while maintaining individual institutional personality.

Here are some of the issues and ideas we struggled with in the Kenyon College and Denison University cooperative project:

- Future—what is our goal or our mission?
- Change—the ability to embrace change
- Challenges—view the challenges as opportunities to grow
- Rethinking the organization
- Arranging work and tasks
- Considering the people as well as the functions
- Reviewing outsourcing options
- Professional development
- Cooperation—critical to the success of the project
- Team thinking/team action
- Compromise
- Be proactive
- Be interactive
- Take initiative
- What can change, and what needs to remain the same?
- What things are traditional, and how do you handle tradition?
- What things are flexible and open to change?
- Finding methods to analyze the results
- Reevaluate the processes on a periodic basis

Right now, people are the most affected for the reasons already discussed. Some seem to enjoy complaining but also enjoy accomplishment—getting to the accomplishment is not always easy. Working in technical services differs from public service roles. The skill sets aren't the same, and there is a level of detail to most of the roles. The most intriguing factor as I get to know the staff of Kenyon College and Denison University is that employees are interested in accomplishing goals, enjoy much of what they do, care about the customer, and are dedicated. This seems to be true even when the pay is not exceptional, and the tasks are detail oriented and repetitive. Yet staff persist and pursue and enjoy the nature of their work. However, they understand that the serials future is moving toward electronic journals with lease-to-use options rather than owning copies of bound journals for decades. They will still have a role. Access to and control of material is still required; therefore, we may need fewer people with slightly different job descriptions in the next decade, but they will be necessary.

A major area to consider is keeping control and access of electronic resources. This is a growing function that requires its own work flow for a variety if reasons. For example, when new databases or electronic journals are added to the collection, they should be cataloged in order to appear in the OPAC. They may also appear in subject pages or in a course folder and therefore need a work flow to cover that aspect of the process.

Keeping the big picture in mind is not always easy. The attraction to acquisitions and cataloging is often the focused attention to detail, and following routines is more the norm than the exception. Moving toward a vague goal or image of what might be is not simple. Facts, information, and tradition are easy; concepts, ideas, and future vision are hard. Rethinking the way we process everything gives an opportunity to make changes, but it is not the only way. Many of the things that occur in a technical services area will continue in some format at least for the next five years. Nevertheless, the focus of the functions and tasks has shifted—people now need to think about why they are doing the different steps in a process. Some questions are more straightforward than others. Do we really need two printed copies of an OCLC record, or can we use one online? More difficult is consolidating our work processes, but we are not eliminating positions. When we have an opening on our new combined technical services organization, we review the work carefully and may hire someone with an entirely different skill set from the previous employee.

Rethinking, redesigning, and reorganizing any group will present challenges. I have found that the redesign Kenyon and Denison are undertaking is not unique in that sense. What makes this project interesting is that we are combining the technical service areas from two different institutions, each with is own goals and objectives. Even the basic structure is different at the two schools. The Kenyon team reports to one leader; however, the Denison group reports to a variety of people. The cataloging assistants report to the catalog librarian, the acquisitions team reports to the collection development librarian, and the government documents assistants report to the government documents librarian. Therefore, the integration and discussions about changes are complex. In order for the integration to be complete, there needs to be one leader with the authority to make decisions and changes.

What qualities must you have to take on a challenge like redesigning and combining the technical services departments for more than one school? There are a number of sources on the early stages of this process available on the Kenyon College LBIS (http://lbis/about/Kenyon-Denison%20Technical%20Servic es%20Work%20Redesign%20Project) and Denison University Library and the Five Colleges of Ohio (http://www.denison.edu/collaborations/ohio5/libres/lwrtf/ lwrtf.html) Web sites. In addition, there are several recent reports and articles that review the history of the project, including a Council on Library and Information Resources report at http://www.clir.org/pubs/abstract/pub139abst.html titled *Library Workflow Redesign: Six Case Studies the Chapter Titled Cooperative*

Work Redesign in Library Technical Services at Denison University and Kenyon College, by Andreadis, Barth, Cochrane, and Greever.

Here are some of the skills that may be necessary to be a strong team leader in such a work process redesign project:

- Listening skills
- Negotiation skills
- Team player
- Ability to comprehend the overall aims and goals
- Lots of planning time
- Understanding of the different roles and responsibilities
- Understanding of the people involved in the project with a realistic understanding of abilities, desires, and interests

CONCLUSION

The collaboration project between Kenyon College and Denison University focuses on the acquisitions and cataloging functions. Although my role is project manager and overseer, this project requires input and support from two institutions and two administrations and the involvement of the workers themselves. The endeavor, while challenging, is starting to have positive results. It is sometimes difficult to measure the changes in a quantitative manner, as the tasks are more nebulous. There are qualitative measures that seem to be logical, like time for special projects, eliminating backlog of materials, time to perform original cataloging providing access with only a very brief record, time to work on enhancing electronic tools, and targeted conversations about collaboration in the future.

Looking forward, we are focused on rethinking the roles of people within technical services and redefining positions as individuals retire. Jobs that cross traditional lines of cataloging and acquisitions will not be as clear in the future as they are today. The knowledge base of workers entering the academic library market as paraprofessionals is different than it was 20 years ago, and we, as academic librarians, need to adjust our thinking to expand these positions.

Talking points for this project as we analyze what might be detrimental to progress:

- Separate locations
- Experience
- Trust
- Forces outside of technical services (circulation, vendors, cost, and so on)
- Our own fears
- Procedural differences that seem too vast to change or reformat into one unit

- Lack of documentation
- Lack of information
- Too many possible choices

Things we plan to see happen in the next two years:

- Shared government documents collection
- Shared classification method for all audiovisual material
- One bindery source used by both schools
- Reduced number of "paper" periodicals and a "shared" collection of the remaining items
- Forward movement towards a shared collection development plan
- Stronger bond between the two schools
- Continued outreach to our other CONSORT partners
- Less confusion about what our roles are and who does what

Things to think about:

- More shelf-ready material from a variety of vendors
- Better methods of sharing information and communicating changes
- Eliminating overlap in our roles
- Increased time for special projects, database cleanup, training, and other "back-burner" things
- Continual process improvement that moves beyond the technical services staff to those in the collection development, circulation, and stacks management roles

REFERENCES

Branton, Ann, Carol Green, and Malachi Martin. 2006. "Technical Services: General Overview of Its Organization and Functions." *Mississippi Libraries* 70 (2): 22–25.

Freedman, Maurice J. 1984. "Automation and the Future of Technical Services." *Library Journal* 109 (11): 1197–203.

Gorman, Michael. 1979. "On Doing Away with Technical Services Departments." *American Libraries* 10 (7): 435–37.

Stephan, Elizabeth. 2006. "What Actually Happens in Technical Services?" *Mississippi Libraries* 70 (2): 21.

VI

CONNECTIONS FOR COLLEGE ARCHIVES: TAKING ON NEW MISSIONS

17 OPPORTUNITIES FOR SMALL AND MEDIUM-SIZED COLLEGE ARCHIVES IN THE DIGITAL AGE

Carol P. Johnson and Ann M. Kenne

From an administrative point of view, if we look at the majority of small and medium-sized academic libraries and the archives of these same institutions, the story is one of limited staff, technology, technological expertise, and financial resources. However, there is also creativity in overcoming these obstacles when a project or service is considered an important goal. Libraries and archives are used to doing more with less and making creative alliances to get their work done. All libraries are deep into the digital shift, increasingly moving to electronic journals and experimenting with electronic books. Students are voting with their fingers, overwhelmingly preferring digital resources to print or other formats. This preference is now having an impact on archives and special collections.

BACKGROUND

As defined in the *Guidelines for College and University Archives*, the purpose of an archives is to serve "as the institutional memory of the college or university and play an integral role in the management of the institution's information resources in all media and formats. To fulfill the responsibilities of that role, the archives identifies, acquires, and maintains records of enduring value that chronicle the development of the institution and ensure its continued existence. The archives documents the process of institutional evolution by retaining both the evidence which shapes decisions and the decisions themselves" (Society of American Archivists 1998, 22).

At most small to medium-sized colleges and universities, the management of the archival collections falls under the auspices of the library system. This arrangement is often convenient for the school, placing the management of all of an institution's information resources under one roof. The employment of only one staff member with the responsibility for managing the archival collections is quite common at the bachelor's- and master's-level academic institutions. Often this individual is assigned the additional duty of managing the library's collections of rare books and manuscripts and/or holding a split appointment with additional duties in the wider library setting (e.g., reference and cataloging). In other cases, there is no one specifically assigned to manage the archival collections. In these instances, a reference librarian or the library director aids administrators, faculty, or students in the use of such collections on an as-needed basis.

An archivist who works alone in a repository, rather than as part of a team, is often known as a "lone arranger." This one individual has the responsibility for all aspects of archives management, including appraising, accessioning, processing, arrangement and description, reference, and outreach. While student workers and volunteers can be utilized to great effect with some of the more basic tasks in the archives, the more complex and confidential work with institutional records must be undertaken by a professional.

The collections managed by the archives are often as varied as the faculty, staff, and students of the institution. Administrative records and minutes mingle with student-produced newspapers and yearbooks. Still and moving images developed by the institution's news service and development offices are housed with faculty research. The process of collecting such a broad scope of records can be a challenge for a small staff to identify and acquire for the institutional archive.

Unlike many of their colleagues in the broader college and university library setting, the primary clientele of the archives is not students. Institutional administrators, news service, alumni, and development professionals rely heavily on the archives specialized collections to serve their information needs. The accrued institutional memory is frequently tapped for such varied efforts as strategic planning, fund-raising, and promotion of the school.

WHAT HAS BEEN CHANGING?

Archivists have traditionally dealt with records at the end of their life cycle. Boxes of noncurrent administrative records were sent to the archives on a change in administration or a move to a new building. Files of photographs and audiovisual materials migrated to the department when they were out of date for the purposes of the news service or the development office. Primarily paper based, these records would generally arrive in the archives arranged with some context intact (e.g., file names listed on file folders) and with some semblance of their original order. The archivist could derive from the available information the nature of the records and how the office used them.

The shift to electronic records has made the process of preserving the documentary heritage of an institution a much more complex venture. In dealing with electronic records, the archivist can no longer rely on accompanying evidence to provide the necessary information to identify, describe, and preserve the records. As Samuels (1998) notes, archivists have "had to face the necessity of intervening at the creation of electronic records to assure that they will exist and continue to be useful" (13). Institutional archivists now have an important role to play within the organization to assist those creating the records to be aware of documentary problems and strategies to mitigate them. Potentially, certain records important to the history of an institution might never transfer to the custody of the archives. The archivist in this case must play a role in ensuring that the records created and presented only in an electronic form are migrated and maintained as technologies change and the staff and interests of departments evolve.

The creation and distribution of digital collections on the Web is another phenomenon with implications for the archives. While digital collections can provide greater access and knowledge of an archival collection's existence, their creation can cause some pitfalls for the smaller institution. This work can direct staff time way from other integral responsibilities in the department and is labor intensive (Schina and Wells 2002, 43).

For those institutions with valuable yet little-known collections, digitizing content can lead to increases in research requests for information and content from around the world. Providing research assistance remotely adds complexity to the response process. Patrons expect quick responses to their requests, preferably online. These expectations, however, can run into the barrier of a staff unprepared technologically to respond speedily.

Additionally, the content of the collections held in archives and special collections is often a mystery to most students and faculty. Potential users of these collections are unfamiliar with the structure of primary sources and the finding aids and indexes created to provide access to the collections. While reference interview skills are a part of the archivist's tool set, the digital environment requires the ability to communicate the complexities of special collection research to those not experienced in research using primary sources. This difficulty is compounded if they are accessing the collections remotely. Larger universities are incorporating this type of research as a core information literacy skill and providing online tutorials (Yakel 2004, 63).

Archives staff can sometimes experience difficulties defining their role in accommodating electronic record systems because managing electronic records is considered the province of another profession: records managers. These professions are now converging, and archivists need some of the records manager's training and skills. For archives in smaller colleges that rely on part-time employees, student employees, and volunteers, this is a problem. Archivists need new KSAs (knowledge, skills, and abilities) that include the records manager's skills, or they need to develop ways to collaborate with those who have the skills already. They need to blend their organizational and descriptive skills with newer technology skills, for example, understanding Web page design and maintenance, USMARC and SGML/EAD (Standard General Markup Language/Encoded Archival Description) standards, and the design and operation of campus networks and servers. They need to be open to training opportunities and able to work in a team environment with library, administrative and academic departments, and computing staff. If there is a campus committee to oversee records retention, then the archivist should be a member. The library director and archivist must identify the priorities and muster all their persuasive skills to work with campus administration to plan for the future. Communication, collaboration, and team-work are essential.

The issue of rights management plays a significant role in the development of digital collections as well. For example, oral histories recorded in the past may have donor agreements that allow them to be listened to and permit the duplication of copies for use. The distribution of these over the Web may not be covered by these agreements. To do so would require renegotiation with the individuals or their estates. Additionally, many academic institutions are making the move to digital repositories to house institutional documents (e.g., official reports and meeting minutes) as well as student honors papers, theses, and dissertations. While digital repositories provide easier access to certain materials, several areas of concern for the archivist arise. For official institutional documents, the need to migrate subsequent versions of these documents is paramount for historical and sometimes legal purposes. In mounting materials like honors papers, theses, and dissertations to such systems, the strictures of the Family Educational Rights and Privacy Act (FERPA) relating to the confidentiality of student work products must be followed.

OPPORTUNITIES

Colleges are enthusiastic about the Web, and most are participating in the broader trend to integrate campus administrative and academic computer systems into portals. The Web is used as a public relations tool, not just to recruit students but to make the institution known to a wider audience, advertise the unique character of the college, communicate with alumni, and attract donors. Additionally, there is the realization among administrators that increasingly the business of the college is done via electronic media. There is a growing awareness of the potential loss of important electronic records that will be needed in the future. These same colleges are beginning to think strategically of how to retain these records electronically, and they consider libraries, the archives, and the computing center as logical collaborators in providing solutions for their records dilemma. The result is that archives and special collections are enjoying renewed attention.

One way for the small archives to make an impact in the digital age is the creation of digital collections. In addition to photographs, yearbooks, and student newspapers, there are many collections of unique and rare primary resources located in small college libraries whose existence is unknown to scholars. Highlighting these collections by mounting Web pages and/or digitizing collections on the Web makes them more visible to the outside world. Art works, drawings, prints, maps, manuscripts, and print texts are all suitable candidates for such a project. Digitization serves to preserve rare materials from too much handling and, by placing a digital copy on the Web, decreases the physical use of the item itself. Staff time can also be saved if popular and frequently called for images and content are placed in the digital collection for easy access by researchers.

Hughes (2004, 104–5) notes that faculty and students can be resources for the digital project—faculty members as collaborators and selectors and students as assistants working on the actual digitizing processes. In addition to faculty and students adding information gleaned through their own research to the digital collections, there may be opportunities for the creation of digital collections to support curriculum. For example, the Oberlin College Archives (http://www.oberlin.edu/archive) is developing a "Teaching Resources" space on its Web site to support the use of primary source materials from its collections in the classroom. Additionally, information on digital collections housed across the country and world can be brought together in subject portals. An example of this is the collaboration between Emory University and Boston College in the Irish Literary Collections Portal (http://irishliterature.library.emory.edu).

Testing and investigation by the large research institutions is starting to pay off in shared expertise, best practices, rubrics, and models for the creation of digital collections by smaller institutions. Digital cameras and scanners are more common in homes and offices, making college employees at all levels familiar with their use and management. For institutions with limited budgets, some vendors now offer the option of digitizing and maintaining collections on off-site servers. Additionally, a variety of consortium projects provide digitization services for materials to be included in particular projects. One such example is the Minnesota's Digital Library's Minnesota Reflections project (Minnesota Digital Library: Minnesota Reflections, http://reflections.mndigital.org). This is designed to unite historical images from academic institutions, historical societies, museums, and other organizations in one digital collection.

Another arena in which small to medium-sized colleges may wish to participate is in the creation of institutional repositories. In a recent interview in *Educause Review*, Lynch noted that there was very little implementation or testing of institutional depositories among liberal arts colleges as of early 2005. He noted that "most of these will get institutional repository services through various kinds of consortial and commercial approaches" (quoted in Hawkins 2006, 48).

While research institutions have been experimenting for the past 10 years using open-source software (e.g., DSpace, Fedora, or Eprints), these open-source software products require the resources of a large university to sustain them. However, in the past few years, the technology has evolved, and more options are available that require less support and are easier to use. For colleges with master's degree programs requiring theses, Proquest's Digital Commons or a similar package provides another option to binding and circulating theses. Institutional repositories also provide a place for faculty and student research to be highlighted.

The character of institutional repositories will differ by college, depending on college culture, mission, and goals. Institutional repositories are a bigger stretch for smaller colleges unless the same software can be used to manage other digital collections. Deciding what will be included in an institutional repository will depend on ownership and copyright and privacy laws. Lynch noted that, in his view, they "are services deployed and supported to offer dissemination, management, stewardship, and where appropriate, long term preservation of both the intellectual work created by the intellectual community and the records of the intellectual and cultural life of the institutional community" (quoted in Hawkins 2006, 6). This is a very broad definition that has a dynamic, inclusive quality.

Small colleges need to be very specific in determining what will be included in their institutional repository. Defining what has "long-term" value requires planning since it has future financial implications for the institutions, as these materials will need to migrate to new electronic formats as technology changes. To the best of their ability, library/archives must invest in vendors/products that have some guarantee of handling the inevitable transition of formats into the future. Collections of images, teaching aids, and masters theses are relatively traditional formats to be included in the institutional repository. Student portfolios, media, and musical performances are just the beginning of an unknown array of content that could be included in the future.

STRATEGIES FOR ACHIEVING YOUR PRIORITIES

At present, there is no one-sized model for the campus archives in the digital age, as each archives situation is unique to its campus. From an administrative point of view, maintaining current archive operations, managing digital projects, and taking responsibility for centralized electronic records retention with the usual minimal staffing level is not possible at small to medium-sized institutions. There are some basic strategies, however, that archives and libraries can employ to move strategically into the digital age.

The implementation (or potential) of a digital program is an opportunity to organize, review, and assess materials that have long been housed in the archives collection, resulting in better analysis and control of the collections. This review is a chance to weed items that do not fit into the scope of the collection. If there is no formal policy in place, the development of one, preferably in concert with a campuswide records retention policy, is advisable. The archivist brings experience in evaluating record series that are important for the long-term history of the campus, and a campus records policy is becoming essential as records continue to shift from print to electronic. The archivist is an essential member and adviser on a campuswide committee convened to examine ways to identify important records that should be retained and the methods to do so.

Prioritizing service goals is the basis for action and budget plans, and best practices identified by the professional organizations and colleagues in the larger research institutions can serve as learning models for smaller organizations. Cornell University's Digital Preservation Manual online (http://www.library.cornell.edu/iris/tutorial/dpm/index.html) and the Collaborative Digitization Project (http://www.cdpheritage.org) provide useful documents on technical standards and best practices. Hughes's (2002) book *Digitizing Collections: Strategic Issues for the Information Manager* is an excellent source providing guidelines for the selection of materials for digitization projects, project management, the process of digitizing, and funding opportunities.

Implementation of identified priorities will require skills not possessed by individuals on the archives or library staff. Assembling a team that includes the archivist, public and technical services librarians, Web site developers, and appropriate information technology professionals will bring together the knowledge and skill sets necessary to complete a successful project. The expertise of this diverse set of individuals will allow for the appropriate selection of the software and hardware required, the creation of appropriate metadata, as well as an interface that will be useful and appealing to users. This collaboration should ease future integration with other systems such as the OPAC and in future migration to new software or other electronic formats.

Parallel to the planning for the implementation of digital collections is the need to identify allies who might have a future stake or interest in such projects. Within your campus community, faculty, administrators, and art curators are likely allies. The purchase of software and hardware for an archives project may fulfill the needs of others on campus or inspire creative uses of the digital collection products. For example, sharing a server and/or hardware with faculty with image collections or other research projects will help them make their research or teaching materials available to their students and the wider research community. Outside the institution, allies may be found in consortiums of libraries, local and state, that are working together to build digital libraries with particular subject matter and scope. Training opportunities, demonstrations of model projects, and vendor recommendations and contacts will result from networking with peers in other institutions.

The administrative wing of the college or university may be an unexpected resource. Centralized electronic records management and retention systems are probably already a long-term goal for the campus. While there is no guaranteed electronic long-term storage medium that can replace print today, this will not be true in the future. Small colleges can plan ahead by developing a standing campuswide committee assigned the charge of preparing a records retention policy identifying important record series that must be retained for accreditation, legal or historical purposes, and setting destruction dates for others. The records retention policy will provide information on where important records are stored and can be consulted and permit the disposition of those not needed. Those records identified as necessary for the history of the college will necessarily be retained in print for the indefinite future until an affordable alternative that can be relied on exists.

Once projects and costs are identified, the library/archives must determine how to fund the project. Small colleges are likely to absorb indirect costs into the current staffing budget and enlist campus colleagues (the team) to help cover skill deficits. The costs of outsourcing projects or the purchase of new equipment and software, however, will require funding in some way. Previous cooperation and interaction with institutional colleagues (on both the academic and the administrative front) on digital collection issues will develop strong allies for an application for funding in the institution's budget process. By documenting how these resources support the college's strategic plan and teaching and learning at the institution, a budget allocation is more certain.

Another potential source of funding is through external sources. If the library has an established friends-of-the-library group, they may be willing to fund a project or part of one. The development and alumni office staff may be able to assist you in targeting alums who might be interested in supporting a project to promote the history of the institution (e.g., digitization of collections of archival photos, yearbooks, and newspapers).

Your institution's development office should be able to assist you in identifying federal and state granting agencies, private organizations, and local foundations interested in funding digital projects. Several federal agencies provide grants for digitization projects, including the Institute for Museum and Library Services (IMLS; http://www.imls.gov), the National Historical Publications and Records Commission (NHPRC; http://www.archives.gov/nhprc), and the National Endowment for the Humanities—Digital Humanities Initiative (http://www.neh.gov/GRANTS/digitalhumanities.html). In a number of states (including Illinois, Indiana, and Pennsylvania), state library or archives agencies provide grants for digitizing projects. If you have interesting collections in a particular subject area, look for collaborative opportunities with other libraries that gather resources into a Web site or portal. One example is the American Theological Library Association's Cooperative Digital Resources Initiative (http://www.atla.com/digitalresources), which provides grants to member libraries to create a Web site and central repository of digital resources related to religion.

When thinking of applying for a grant, there are several issues to consider. First, review the purpose and requirements of the grant carefully to see if your project meets the criteria for support. Second, keep in mind that grants do require staff time and energy to prepare, submit, and administer. Typically, staffing is one of the most limited resources in the small academic library/archives, and preparing and implementing a grant should not be allowed to interfere with the library's primary purpose, namely, providing support for the academic program. Grants permitting employment of additional staff and/or student workers to do project tasks such as scanning or that support the purchase of software and hardware could be of real benefit and worth the effort. Additionally, if the project requires institutional matching funds, those projects that support the college's strategic plan are more likely to gain your institution's support of the grant application. Finally, you should also consider if your organization has the commitment, personnel, and the physical infrastructure to continue to sustain, maintain, and enhance projects initiated with grant funding over the long term.

CONCLUSION

The small and medium-sized college archive is challenged by changing formats, higher service, and digital expectations that may be overwhelming to a "lone arranger." However, the archivist, as a member of the academic community and a team of library and instructional technology/computing staff, can work with colleagues to assess the college community's needs, define priorities, and generate strategies. Communication and collaboration are keys to success, and, taken one priority or project at a time, much can be achieved.

In the next 10 years, most small and medium-sized college and university libraries and archives will invest in digital projects beyond a Web page. The size and scope of these projects will vary according to each organization's strategic goals. However, by investing in digital projects, archives and libraries can glean greater visibility for unknown local collections for research and scholarship, strengthen support of local curriculum, create opportunities to help the college tell its story to donors and alums, and ensure that the historical record will be maintained.

SELECTED ORGANIZATIONS AND VENDORS OF INTEREST

Readers may find the following list of organizations/vendors useful in identifying publications and journals as well as workshops and conferences on topics related to the challenges faced in managing and maintaining archival collections.

Organizations

Society of American Archivists (SAA)
527 S. Wells St.
5th Floor
Chicago, IL 60607
http://archivists.org. Accessed June 15, 2006.
SAA also maintains a directory of regional archival organization:
Directory of Archival Organizations in the United States and Canada
http://www.archivists.org/assoc-orgs/directory/index.asp. Accessed June 15, 2006.

ARMA International
13725 W. 109th St., Suite 101
Lenexa, KS 66215
http://www.arma.org/index.cfm. Accessed June 15, 2006.

American Association for State and Local History (AASLH)
1717 Church St.
Nashville, TN 37203-2991
http://www.aaslh.org. Accessed June 15, 2006.

Council of State Archivists (CoSA)
308 E Burlington St. #189
Iowa City, IA 52240
http://www.statearchivists.org/index.htm. Accessed June 15, 2006.

Coalition for Networked Information (CNI)
21 DuPont Cir., Suite 800
Washington, DC 20036
http://www.cni.org. Accessed June 15, 2006.

Council on Library and Information Resources (CLIR)
1755 Massachusetts Ave. NW, Suite 500
Washington, DC 20036
http://www.clir.org. Accessed June 15, 2006.

Northeast Document Conservation Center (NEDCC)
100 Brickstone Sq.
Andover, MA 01810-1494
http://www.nedcc.org. Accessed June 15, 2006.

Vendors
OCLC
6565 Frantz Rd.
Dublin, OH 43017-3395
http://www.oclc.org. Accessed June 15, 2006.

ContentDM—Digital Collection Management Software
DiMeMa Inc.
100 W. Harrison St.
North Tower, Suite 480
Seattle, WA 98119
http://www.dimema.com. Accessed June 15, 2006.

Luna Insight—Digital Collection Management Software
Luna Imaging, Inc.
2702 Media Center Dr.
Los Angeles, CA 90065-1733
http://www.luna-imaging.com/index.html. Accessed June 15, 2006.

DSpace Institutional Repository Software
http://dspace.org/index.html. Accessed June 15, 2006.
DigitalCommons Institutional Repository Software
http://www.bepress.com/digitalcommons.html. Accessed June 15, 2006.

The following Web sites might be useful for identifying best practices as related to preserving electronic records and developing/maintaining digital collections:

Collaborative Digitization Project
http://www.cdpheritage.org. Accessed June 15, 2006.

Digital Preservation Management Tutorial (Cornell University)
http://www.library.cornell.edu/iris/tutorial/dpm/index.html. Accessed June 15, 2006.

ABBREVIATIONS

AARMA—Association of Records Managers and Administrators
FERPA—Family/Educational Rights and Privacy Act

IMLS—Institute of Museum and Library Services
KSAs—Knowledge, skills, and abilities
NHPRC—National Historical Publications and Records Commission
OCLC—Online Computer Library Center
OPAC—Online Public Access Catalog
SAA—Society of American Archivists
SGML/EAD—Standard General Markup Language/Encoded Archival Description
USMARC—United States MARC format

REFERENCES

Hawkins, Brian L. 2006. "Advancing Scholarship and Intellectual Productivity: An Interview with Clifford A. Lynch." *Educause Review* 41 (3): 44–56.

Hughes, Lorna M. 2004. *Digitizing Collections: Strategic Issues for the Information Manager.* London: Facet Publishing.

Samuels, Helen Willa. 1998. *Varsity Letters: Documenting Modern Colleges and Universities.* Lanham, Md.: Scarecrow Press.

Schina, Bessie, and Garron Wells. 2002. "University Archives and Records Programs in the United States and Canada." *Archival Issues* 27 (1): 35–51.

Society of American Archivists. College and University Archives Section. 1998. *Guidelines for College and University Archives.* Available at: http://www.archivists.org/governance/guidelines/cu_guidelines.asp. Accessed May 4, 2006.

Yakel, Elizabeth. 2004. "Archives and Manuscripts: Information Literacy Skills for Primary Sources: Creating a New Paradigm for Archival Researcher Education." *OCLC Systems and Services: International Digital Library Perspectives* 20 (2): 61–64.

SELECTED BIBLIOGRAPHY

Bicknese, Douglass. 2003–2004. "Institutional Repositories and the Institution's Repository: What Is the Role of University Archives with an Institution's On-Line Repository?" *Archival Issues* 28 (2): 81–93.

Dearstyne, Bruce W. 2001. *Leadership and Administration of Successful Archival Programs.* Westport, Conn.: Greenwood Press.

Ghetu, Magia. 2004. "Two Professions, One Goal." *The Information Management Journal* 38 (3): 62–66.

Maher, William J. 1992. *The Management of College and University Archives.* Metuchen, N.J.: Society of American Archivists and Scarecrow Press.

Samuels, Helen Willa. 1998. *Varsity Letters: Documenting Modern Colleges and Universities.* Lanham, Md.: Scarecrow Press.

VII

ISSUES AND CHALLENGES FOR THE FUTURE: A BIBLIOGRAPHIC ESSAY

18 THE ACADEMIC LIBRARY: ISSUES AND CHALLENGES FOR THE FUTURE

Susan Naylor and Rashelle Karp

The academic environment evolves rapidly, influenced by dramatic changes in knowledge, technology, economics, student demographics, and consumer behaviors (Goldstein 2006). Among the challenges identified for academic libraries in today's turbulent world are information literacy instruction, the recruitment and retention of academic librarians, ensuring that the educational preparation of academic librarians is adequate, managing the impact of distance education and distant students, controlling and influencing the impact of digital resources, selecting and organizing e-books and e-journals, demonstrating accountability, and redefining the concept of a library as a "place" (Hisle 2002; Stoffle, Allen, Morden, and Maloney 2003).

INFORMATION LITERACY INSTRUCTION

Information literacy instruction has evolved from a resource-centered to a user-centered focus, with student education transitioning from an emphasis on learning just the "nature and use of devices for finding what students seek" (Echavarria Robinson 2006) to fostering the critical analysis and skillful selection of multimedia resources. These changes have created a need for concurrent growth in the role of the librarian as an instructor. In response to this need, the Association of College and Research Libraries (ACRL) has developed literacy immersion institutes geared toward expanding librarians' understanding of the best strategies for delivering bibliographic and information literacy instruction (Springer 2005).

Paramount to the delivery of information literacy instruction has been librarians' attempts to "promote collaboration with faculty and campus units in an effort to integrate information literacy into the curriculum" (Lindstrom and Shonrock 2006) by making all instructional staff and faculty members stakeholders in information literacy. This push, which is still being met with resistance by nonlibrarian instructors, is driven by the need to provide information literacy instruction to a larger number of students simultaneously within the contexts of the general curriculum. The concept has led to an extensive amount of outreach work for librarians who are increasingly becoming information literacy managers who must create long-term plans for holistic information literacy education across the sponsoring institution (O'Brien, Libutti, and Zlatos 2006).

Effective planning for campuswide literacy instructional services begins and ends with assessment. To broaden the understanding of the information literacy needs of new undergraduates, assessment devices are currently being used to evaluate students' information literacy levels on entering higher education, as opposed to evaluating the effectiveness of programs only after implementation. The result has been a significant amount of literature that reveals that students are entering college with a wide and inconsistent range of lower-level information skills, making advanced literacy instruction sessions ineffective for a large number of undergraduates (Islam and Murno 2006). This trend is forcing librarians to scaffold their preplanned literacy curriculum, often preventing them from reaching a point at which they are working with students on the types of information literacy skills that all graduates should possess. In spite of this, academic libraries are receiving positive reinforcement via postinstruction assessments that reveal that students are highly satisfied with their instruction and retain new literacy skills at a very high rate (Wong, Chan, and Chu 2006).

It is also critical that librarians meet the information literacy needs of the many students who attend classes online by creating online information literacy instruction tutorials. The tutorials meet the needs of students at all levels, making it possible for them to learn at their own pace and skill levels, reinforce existing skills, and develop a knowledge base prior to in-person instructional sessions (Kowalczyk and Jackson 2005). Librarians are also delivering instruction through the use of online modules that are embedded within the media through which a course is delivered (e.g., Blackboard-driven courses).

Increasing emphasis on information literacy instruction is coming not just from end users and the profession of librarianship. It is being fueled by requirements from regional accrediting agencies, most of which now identify information literacy as a core skill for all students at the institution. For example, the Middle States Commission on Higher Education (2002) specifically states that an institution's curricula should be "designed so that students acquire and demonstrate college-level proficiency in general education and essential skills, including . . . information literacy" (37). Similarly, the Commission on Institutions of Higher Education (2005) states that institutions must demonstrate "that students use information resources and technology as an integral part of their education, attaining levels of proficiency appropriate to their degree and subject or professional field of study" and that "the institution ensures that . . . throughout their program students gain increasingly sophisticated skills in evaluating the quality of information sources" (20).

RECRUITMENT AND RETENTION OF LIBRARIANS

The recruitment of new librarians is a pressing issue in the field of academic librarianship. While retention is thought to be more preferable and less costly than recruitment, a higher than average rate of retirement in the field of librarianship argues against an exclusive focus on retention. It is estimated that more than 45 percent of all librarians will leave the workforce by 2008 and that 41,000 job openings from new job creation and retirement replacements will occur between 2000 and 2010 (Griffiths and Latham 2006). With librarianship ranked seventh among occupations demonstrating the highest percentage of workers aged 45 years and older in 1998 (Dohm 2000), it is estimated that the field of librarianship may lose as many as 61,000 librarians (Davis 2004) and as much as 58 percent of its professional workforce by 2019 (American Library Association 2002). Of this number, about half will be academic librarians (Wilder 1996).

However, "new librarians are turning with more frequency to high tech jobs in private industry that pay significantly higher salaries and could be construed as being more glamorous than library jobs. Libraries are facing a shortage of people both interested in and qualified to form the 21st century information professional workforce" (Bothmer and LaCroix 2004, 11). These trends have led some academic libraries to broaden their scope of hiring to include candidates who possess a subject PhD but not a graduate library degree. These PhD job seekers are deemed qualified for librarianship because of their expertise in a specific subject area. While significant subject expertise is a tremendous benefit to a library's professional staff, it is thought by some that this hiring practice strikes a painful blow to the professionalism of the field as well as the accreditation process that gives the field credibility as a profession with its own clearly defined culture, value system, and educational core (Crowley 2004; Neal 2006).

While the PhD without a library graduate degree may be problematic for some librarians, many academic librarians recognize the need for both library and subject degrees as they support the trend for academic librarians to pursue an additional master's degree as "vital to creating the scholar librarian." Supporters of second master's degrees for academic librarians report that a second masters is important for career advancement, credibility, and increased status and that it enhances a librarians' skills in reference, bibliographic instruction, cataloging, collection development, distance education, electronic resources, and research (Mayer and Terrill 2005).

Regardless of the degrees held by librarians, job descriptions for academic librarians often list a wide variety of knowledge, skills, and attitudes. Exner (2004) provides a list of broad categories that includes (1) administrative and interdisciplinary skills, such as evaluation of electronic resources, programming experience, and negotiation of licensing agreements; (2) digital libraries, metadata, and archiving skills, such as digital rights management, scanning and imaging, and digitization processes; (3) ability to provide instruction in an electronic classroom; (4) technical support and networking skills, such as PC support and using data communications protocols; and (5) Web authoring skills, such as HTML authoring, form creation, database design, and Web usability testing. Other employers add to this list competencies such as (1) general management knowledge and skills; (2) knowledge of planning and budgeting principles; (3) knowledge of statistical and evaluation principles; (4) knowledge of legal, financial, and funding issues; (5) public relations and marketing skills; (6) leadership skills; (7) ability to communicate effectively in writing and orally; (8) knowledge of subject specialties; (9) knowledge of foreign languages; (10) behavior management skills; (11) project management skills; and (12) portal management skills (Griffiths and Latham 2006; Jackson 2004; Winston and Hoffman 2005).

As academic libraries work to fill vacated positions because of retirements, they are also working to recruit librarians that represent the existing diversity of the academic population. In 1998, the Association of Research Libraries (ARL) Salary Survey reported that minorities accounted for less than 12 percent of the academic library staff, with fewer than 10 percent in administrative positions (Edwards and Fisher 2003). In 2006, the ARL Salary Survey reported similar numbers: "only 13.1 percent of the professional staff in U.S. ARL libraries belongs to one of the four non-Caucasian categories for which the ARL keeps records" (Kyrillidou and Young 2006). Contributing to the lack of diversity among librarians is the lower number of minorities who have (1) achieved higher education and (2) chosen to attain that education in the area of librarianship. For example, a study by Lance (2005) found that while Hispanics represent one of the largest and most rapidly growing groups in the American population, they are the most underrepresented group among librarians. Other minority groups on this list include African Americans and Asians, Pacific Islanders, and American Indians/Alaskan Natives.

Even in libraries where minority *recruitment* is successful, administrators often fail to *retain* minority employees on a long-term basis. Long-term retention depends, in part, on how well the institution can avoid common pitfalls such as "tokenism" or a commitment to "minority residency programs" rather than "diversity initiatives." Hankins, Saunders, and Situ (2003) describe minority residency programs as "short-term and quota-driven to raise affirmative action statistics . . . often in response to accreditation threats. They take newly graduated students, insert them into often hostile environments, and expect them to address all the problems of diversity that continue to simmer and stew among faculty." A short-term residency approach to retention can lead to "tokenism," a phenomenon where the actions of minority librarians "take on symbolic consequences, since they act, in the eyes of the dominants in the group, not as individuals but as representatives of the social type/underrepresented class they belong to" (Edwards and Fisher 2003). Tokenism often leads to overcommitment for minority librarians, who are placed on too many projects and committees because they are minorities. Trying to serve on so many committees and in many cases trying to provide advising for too many minority students and faculty takes up so much time that minority librarians do not have the resources to engage in professional development or to work on projects that will help them earn tenure and promotion. Hankins et al. (2003) describe "diversity initiatives" as attempts to "address systemic problems within the university as a whole . . . that involve long-term solutions, including defining the problems, offering concrete steps to resolving barriers, [and] devising a plan of action, follow-up, and accountability."

A promising strategy for retaining librarians of color is the provision of mentoring programs (Bonnette 2004). Supported by national organizations including the American Library Association's (ALA) Black Caucus Mentoring Program, REFORMA's Mentoring Project, the ACRL's New Member Mentoring Program, ALA's New Member Round Table Mentoring Program, and the Government Document Round Table Mentoring Program, academic libraries are increasingly working to increase the longevity of minority librarians by pairing them with senior faculty members who will advise them on issues of process, organizational and cultural values, and expectations for promotion and tenure (Lee, Hayden, and MacMillan 2004; Trejo and Norlin 2001).

EDUCATIONAL PREPARATION OF ACADEMIC LIBRARIANS

As the world of academic librarianship has changed, so have library and information science (LIS) curricula and the faculty that teach them. The KALIPER Project, which studied LIS curricula across the United States and Canada from 1998 to 2000, concluded that "while LIS curricula continue to incorporate perspectives from other disciplines, a distinct core has taken shape that is predominately user-centered. The LIS core is consolidating and clearly delineating what makes LIS distinct—as a knowledge domain—from other disciplines" (Kaliper Advisory Committee 2000, 2). Recent surveys of library employers seem to reinforce the need for library education to focus on fostering a service orientation among librarians (Bajjaly 2005). However, there is concern among practicing librarians that the curriculum wrapped around the user-centered core is leaving gaps in preparation for new librarians.

Of particular concern is the need to prepare librarians to provide effective information literacy instruction (Forys 2004) using "pedagogical approaches that support Web-based learning (Tempelman-Kluit 2006) and go beyond the traditional classroom or library (Galvin 2005; Westbrook 2006). Surveys of students find that they tend to depend on simplistic but responsive search engines such as Google rather than using the more complex but less responsive library Web pages, catalogs, and databases (Hiller 2004). Students report that they find that "digital library resources often reside outside the environment that is frequently the digital home of students' coursework, namely, the course management system, or CMS. In spite of this, however, library services are often presented in the library organization context rather than in a user-centered mode" (Lippincott 2005). And analysis of library school curricula as recently as 2004 found that less than half of all library schools offered a course on information literacy instruction (Julien 2005). The importance attached to a librarian's ability to provide information literacy instruction is reinforced by job advertisements for new librarians that, as early as 1998, demonstrated that academic library positions routinely included instruction as an integral part of reference work (Lynch and Smith 2001).

There are also increasing needs for academic librarians to be prepared to instruct students about Internet plagiarism (Jackson 2006). A survey of almost 50,000 undergraduates on more than 60 college campuses revealed that the students believed "that 'cut & paste' plagiarism—using a sentence or two (or more) from different sources on the Internet and weaving this information together into a paper without appropriate citation—is not a serious issue" (McCabe 2005). Additionally, almost 60 percent of the surveyed students indicated that they were using cut-and-paste plagiarism from the Internet (McCabe 2005).

According to employers, cataloging and classification is another area of concern. While cataloging functions are critical to the efficient access of information, employers report that they cannot find new or experienced librarians with enough practical experience or education to provide cataloging services. Studies have found that practitioners and library school educators tend to agree on a detailed set of at least 25 core cataloging competencies that all entry-level academic librarians should possess (Letarte, Turvey, Borneman, and Adams 2002; Turvey 2002). A study by Hall-Ellis (2006) found that, in particular, "potential employers expect entry-level catalog librarians to be familiar with each of the MARC 21 bibliographic formats for eight types of materials (books, continuing resources, computer files, maps, music, sound recordings, visual materials, and mixed materials), especially monographs, electronic resources, and continuing resources, . . . projected media, and monographs." This same study found, however, that only a limited number of ALA-accredited programs required all students to take a cataloging course and that "the number of full-time LIS faculty members who focus on cataloging, classification, metadata schema, and related courses may be insufficient to meet teaching demands."

Leadership is a final area of preparation that is often identified as necessary for librarians. Leadership has been defined as the ability to act "in advance to deal with an expected or observed difficulty. It [leadership] requires followers to be engaged and concerned with what is happening [and] to be intelligent about the big picture" (Lubans 2006). Librarians who are leaders embrace concepts of teamwork, fairness, and loyalty (Young, Hernon, and Powell 2006), and they realize that leadership is not exclusively the province of library directors; it should be encouraged in all employees (Hernon and Rossiter 2006; Hernon and Schwartz 2006; Stephens and Russell 2004). Institutes such as the ACRL/Harvard Institute and the Frye Institute attempt to address librarians' preparation for leadership through immersion experiences where participants engage in one to two weeks of concentrated learning activities. However, unlike the Harvard Institute, which enrolls only librarians, the Frye Institute enrolls university presidents and other administrators, faculty, researchers, and technology staff (Gjelten and Fishel

2006), thus providing a more holistic approach to learning about leadership. This holistic approach may be more realistic for librarians in an environment where new technologies have blurred the distinctions between departments, making it imperative that librarians "work at the interface of cultures" (Dewey 2005). A holistic approach to leadership training is also most appropriate at a time when libraries are experiencing increasing competition from commercial companies that provide entire digital libraries with the search engines and online help needed to effectively access contents. These pressures, along with an increasing recognition of the interdisciplinary responsibilities for the university's chief information officer, require a sense of personal and organizational leadership among librarians who must be able to "calibrate their own vision with that of the organization, the institution, and key individuals" (Wittenborg, Ferguson, and Keller 2003, 20). The blurring of the lines between departments necessitates that academic librarians be prepared to collaborate with information technology, institutional research, development, and student affairs professionals whose values, certifications, and skills are much different from their own (Cervone 2005; Dewey 2006; Stoffle et al. 2003; Vaughan 2004). Academic librarians are becoming "more deeply engaged in the creation and dissemination of knowledge . . . [as] essential collaborators with the other stakeholders in these activities" (Lougee 2002, 1).

DISTANCE EDUCATION AND DISTANT STUDENTS

Although distance education has brought convenience and opportunity to students and faculty, it has also ushered in a host of new problems and issues for academic libraries, not the least of which has been the task of defining "a scalable and viable strategy for making information resources available to distant learners" (Thompson 2002). The complexity of providing library services to a "virtual" student body has necessitated librarians' creation of new ways to deliver much-needed information and assistance to users who may *never* set foot inside the physical library.

Among the difficulties are issues of communication and collaboration among teaching faculty and librarians. In *Guidelines for Distance Learning Library Services* (Distance Learning Section Guidelines Committee 2004), it is stated that "the originating institution is responsible for involving the library administration and other personnel in the detailed analysis of planning, developing, evaluating, and adding or changing of the distance learning program from the earliest stages onward" and that the "requirements and desired outcomes of academic programs should guide the library's responses to defined needs." In contrast, however, an ACRL survey of distance learning at college and research libraries found that 90 percent of the universities surveyed reported either minimal or no involvement by library staff in the development of course content (Thompson 2002).

Librarians at college and research libraries often do not know "who their registered distance education students are or who teaches distance education courses" (Yang 2005). They also indicate that "only students of above-average self-motivation will recognize the worth of using libraries and will use them voluntarily and independently. For the rest of the student body, it is the librarian's and the instructor's responsibility to create this necessity" (Maness 2005). Further, it has been demonstrated that students' use of information sources is most often "governed by the principle of least effort" (Liu and Ye Yang 2004), thus leading students to use online sources of information that are accessible because they have been integrated into course Web sites and courseware (Cervone and Brown 2001). In spite of this, more than 75 percent of the libraries in the ACRL 2000 Academic Library Trends and Statistics survey reported using only "face-to face methods of delivering library instruction" (Thompson 2002).

Distance education students must "know how to connect remotely to databases, how to use the file transfer protocol to access information on remote servers, how to download, cut and paste, understand the difference between an index and Web search engines, the differences among the databases, how to select appropriate databases, apply the principles of Boolean logic, identify and narrow a topic, and evaluate information" (Sittler 2005). They must also be able to navigate technological failings, commercial restrictions on free access to online resources, and difficulties with the mechanics of searching, defining key words, and accurately evaluating the results of queries (Boyd-Byrnes and Rosenthal 2005). Faced with these obstacles and, in some instances, not being able to receive online library instruction, many distance education students opt to limit the resources they use to instructor-provided materials or their local library (Antell 2004), bypassing the academic library altogether (Webb 2006). Conversely, issues are "faced by academic research libraries in providing virtual reference services to unaffiliated users. These libraries generally welcome visitors who use on-site collections and reference services, but are these altruistic policies feasible in a virtual environment?" (Kibbee 2006).

Online real-time reference services, online database tutorials, online research instruction, e-mail reference services, 800 reference telephone services, online learning communities for librarians, and live chat reference services are being used most effectively and positively to provide the quick and convenient service and to provide virtual support and exchange of ideas among library professionals (Bell 2005; Gandhi 2003; Mariner and Harrison, 2004; Mizzy 2003). Some academic librarians, however, express concerns that online services for patrons place "most of the burden of answering the question squarely on the librarian" (Coffman 2001) rather than engaging students and librarians in a collaborative learning activity.

Another aspect of distance education is the almost exclusive reliance by patrons and librarians on electronic resources. Electronic resources and the Internet have brought with them a myriad of legislation aimed at protecting authors, publishers, and aggregators of digital information. Academic librarians are responsible for maintaining their levels of knowledge about these laws, in addition to defending, understanding, and teaching them to others. While the copyright and protection laws of the past were relatively static in nature, digital protection legislation is constantly evolving to keep pace with the rapid evolution of the medium. Of particular concern for academic librarians are the limitations that licensing and copyright place on fair use, the ambiguous nature of the laws governing licensing and copyright, and the weight of responsibility that these laws place on teaching faculty and librarians to comply while still providing high-quality distance education services for students. In the past, "people took notice of fair use only when someone blatantly disregarded another's intellectual property through outright plagiarism, or 'pirated' copies through illicit copying and sold them as if they were from the original creators or publishers" (Schuler 2003). Instructors and librarians were largely held innocent for copyright violations, as their activities were related to education rather than profit.

The Digital Millennium Copyright Act created a set of remedies for cases of pirated online materials and required diligent awareness as it placed the responsibility for deviation squarely on the shoulders of the institution delivering instruction. However, the act, aimed at protecting the rights of investors by creating "better tools to fight digital piracy," restricts the use of digitized information in the electronic classroom (Crawford 2002; Dames 2006) and, in the minds of many, impedes "free expression and scientific research, fair use, competition and innovation" (Electronic Frontier Foundation 2006). Even though the Technology, Education, and Copyright Harmonization Act (TEACH) significantly relaxed digital legislation in the interests of allowing greater use of digital media for "accredited, nonprofit educational institutions" (Lipinski 2003), distance education librarians are still generally held responsible for knowing and informing others of copyright legislation, in part because librarians are often the source of the digital materials being protected and used.

DIGITAL RESOURCES

With more than 1,000 digitization projects underway at more than 80 percent of Association of Research Libraries member libraries (Kahl and Williams 2006), the conversion of print collections to digital forms is a challenging arena for academic libraries. Without generally agreed-on standards for best practices and without a history of "effective collaborative mechanisms to leverage resources and expertise" (Lefurgy 2005), numerous policies and processes are used, depending on the intended audience (De Stefano 2001; Jerrido, Cotilla, and Whitehead 2001; Phillips 2005). In addition, numerous access mechanisms for digital materials are being used, with special attention often paid to metadata schemes whose purpose is "to link and integrate heterogeneous, multi-platform, massive digital information collections that are contributed by different institutions into a single, unified resource so these digital repositories are accessible by anyone, from anyplace, at anytime" (Alamneh, Hastings, and Hartman 2002). Metadata schemes foster intuitive use, often through techniques such as information visualization (Wan 2006). Academic librarians have recognized the importance of meeting user expectations for unmediated access while at the same time creating systems that are robust enough to handle scholarly inquiry and allow for cooperative activity "even when cooperating institutions ha[ve] different archival practices and staffing" (Parker 2005). The Northeast Document Conservation Center

(Conway 1999) identifies traditional core principles of preservation practice that should be applied to digital preservation including longevity (extending the life of various media), choice (selecting what needs to be preserved), quality (specifying standards for faithful reproduction of an item), integrity (maintaining high standards for physical and intellectual preservation), and access (ensuring access over time). Equally important in the field of digitization are the concepts of provenance, "providing access to archival documents grouped together in collections according to the circumstances of their creation" (Zanish-Belcher, Christian, and Daly 2001, 44); authenticity, or making sure that the content of a document remains unchanged over time (Romano 2002); and "preservation of the apparatus needed to locate, retrieve and represent the material" (Chapman 2001).

Other issues that must be addressed as libraries digitize resources revolve around the concept of ownership. "Although the Web is popularly regarded as a public domain resource, it is copyrighted; thus, archivists have no legal right to copy the Web" (Lyman 2002, 39). In the past, "libraries could base their preservation activities on the sure knowledge that they owned the material they preserved and could therefore, set the terms of reader access to it" (Bennett 2001). In today's libraries however, archivists who wish to preserve items that include the contributions of multiple authors, artists, or publishers have to locate and receive permission from all contributors before digitizing their works (Shincovich 2004). In the case of digital periodicals, ownership of a scholarly journal might include authors, copyright owners of materials in the article such as photographs and drawings, the scholarly society that owns the journal, the publisher of the journal, the distributor of the journal, and an aggregator who might own the article in an electronic compilation (Flecker 2002). When items are on the Web, the process of identifying ownership is "complicated by the fact that only part of it [the Web] is publicly accessible. . . . It is not clear, for example, that a Web site may be 'harvested' for purposes of preservation without the knowledge and permission of the various stakeholders" (Freidlander 2002). Additionally, there may be disagreement regarding what version of a Web page can be saved or how the information should be used. In some cases, the creator may no longer maintain ownership of a work, having sold it to a third party who cannot be located or even identified (Tyser 2006). No less complicated than the issues discussed above is the variety of digital formats that exist, ranging from "rather straightforward transcriptions of traditional documents, such as books, reports, correspondence, and lists . . . [to] forms of digital information [that] cannot be expressed in traditional hard-copy or analog media; for example, interactive Web pages, geographic information systems, . . . [and] virtual reality models" (Thibodeau 2002). Other types of digital formats include course material, digital images from scientific instruments, scientific and statistical data sets (Smith 2005), and social software that supports group interactions through various mechanisms including Web logs (blogs), wikis, podcasts, and instant messaging (Huwe 2006; Shirky 2003; Stephens 2006).

The digitization of video and sound recordings presents additional unique complications that include the need for "adequate storage facilities and bandwidth . . . to store and deliver large amounts of AV materials online" (Choi 2005) as well as needs for "high-end workstations and software to capture, edit, compress, and manage the files; servers and high-speed network connectivity to distribute the files; backup and storage systems (offline and/or online) to ensure sustainability and longevity of the files; and media playing/viewing hardware and software to use the files" (Thomas 2004). Adding to the complexity of digitizing media is the need for archivists to move beyond their traditional roles as archivists into new roles as "digital asset managers" who work cooperatively to save a completed work as well as the "wide body of material that contextualizes a work" through value-added components that may include "interviews, scripts, correspondence, sketches of sets, special effects, out-takes, and even moving images of initial casting calls" (Besser 2001; "On Saving Sound" 2006).

A major concern with all types of digital preservation projects is obsolescence. Technical obsolescence refers to the notion that "different documents are dependent on software used to create them . . . and . . . technology used today may become obsolete tomorrow" (Bansal, Kumari, Kumar, and Singh 2005). Independent obsolescence occurs as a result of changes in licensing agreements and sponsorship. For example, while library users enjoy the convenience of accessibility with electronic records, electronic formats "give libraries no control over the preservation of materials in electronic collections. Companies that manage content determine the extent of material archived, the deletion of back files from the site, and the length of time individual issues are embargoed (held out of electronic collections to avoid competition with print versions). Aggregators purchase rights to place materials on their sites. If aggregators lose access to journals, they remove them from their collections, so material available to library patrons on Web sites today may be gone tomorrow" (Anderson 2002). The same holds true with artifacts from private or governmental Web sites and documents that can be removed or simply eliminated by the governing or sponsoring agency without notice (Block 2003; Wiggins 2001).

Offline, archivists are dealing with the looming fear of physical media deterioration in digital archives. "Even when the best of care is provided, digital media will not last indefinitely" (Hunter 2006), and even if digital media in the form of an optical disc, for example, lasts for 30 years (the physical lifetime for an optical disc under optimal storage conditions), this "life expectancy of 30 years . . . far exceeds the lifespan of hardware and software" (Byers 2003). Finally, in spite of a steady increase in digitization projects taking place in libraries, the number of staff engaged in these projects has not increased, thus placing increasing workload on a staff that in some libraries is decreasing (Kennedy 2005; Young and Kyrillidou 2005) or becoming more reliant on part-time student staff (D'Andrea and Martin 2001; Starmer 2004).

E-BOOKS AND E-JOURNALS

The digital revolution has changed the role of every member of the library staff as each department struggles to maintain a balance between print and digital resources. Librarians are faced with ubiquitous issues of cataloging, selection, costs, and access, including questions such as the extent to which old ideas about cataloging apply to new digital resources, how many and which digital resources should be added to existing collections, when and how to collaborate with other libraries on integration projects, how to measure use in meaningful ways, and how to select and implement integration tools (Ladwig and Sommese 2005; Levrault 2006; Myers 2004). Even for reference librarians, "the very meaning of reference has changed; items that in print once resided in circulating collections can be considered reference when published in digital databases" (Albanese 2004).

In terms of collection management, some colleges are using e-books to enhance their resources for growing populations of distance education students who often rely on the library's databases and other online resources for research purposes. However, e-book selection presents a unique set of problems that remain largely unanswered. No definitive protocols or policies for e-book collections have been developed at this point, in part because many librarians are still assessing the level of acceptance of this new medium. The process of selection and acquisition for e-books is especially complicated because of the "practice of 'bundling' electronic titles. Bundling makes it difficult to purchase e-book titles on an individual basis, as is possible with paper copies. Because titles must be obtained along with the service that would be used to manage their digital rights, libraries are required to follow the guidelines for purchase established by the interface provider. . . . Concurrently, libraries can only develop general collections of titles based on subject and hope for patron interest" (Myers 2004).

For students and faculty, e-books also present challenges in delivery, reliability, and usability. For example, licensing agreements with providers of e-books often prohibit single-page printing and in some cases allow an e-book to be read only online. Instructors are often resistant to e-books based on concerns about the reliability of archival access, ease of printing and saving, and the need for students to read large amounts of information directly from the computer rather than just using the computer as a delivery mechanism (Coleman 2004).

Similar challenges exist with e-journals, whose publishers and aggregators have a monopoly on the market, thus allowing them to push expensive "'big deals'—contracts in which libraries pay for a package of journals and online access to journals from a particular publisher for several years, with restrictions on early cancellation" (Mayor 2003). The increasing cost of online journals is extremely problematic for libraries. In addition to consortial agreements, which can reduce costs through volume buying (Kohl and Sanville 2006), some libraries also use "coinvestment models" where all the libraries in a particular system contribute to one contract in an amount usually proportionate to their full-time equivalent, usage, or other aspects of the library (Anderson 2006; Johns 2003). Adding to the complexity of cost is the fact that print journals cannot be totally replaced with e-journals, even when an e-journal replacement exists. User studies show that heavy use of electronic journals may actually increase total use of journals, including print resources. In addition, a user's transition from print to e-journal has been found to be strongly dependent on the subject area, discipline, quality, and relevance of the journal, with increases in print use often focused on titles that are also available in electronic format. Finally, faculty recommendations of specific journals also influence online and print use (Black 2005; Brady, McCord, and Galbraith 2006; Siebenberg, Galbraith, and Brady 2004; Tenopir 2003).

Other areas of concern related to e-journals and e-books include the library's ability to provide the e-resource in perpetuity (Stemper and Barribeau 2006) and the library's ability to create customizable Web portals that are current, highly relevant, and in full text (Letha 2006) and that provide "a single-user interface to access the entire library collection" (Brantley, Armstrong, and Lewis 2006; Ownes 2006).

ACCOUNTABILITY

Increasingly in today's world, taxpayers, policymakers, students, and their families are demanding to know the extent to which their investments in higher education are producing demonstrated educational results (Dugan and Hernon 2002). The American Council on Education indicates that transparent assessment of student learning is "needed to maintain public credibility about quality and performance in America's higher education institutions" (Business-Higher Education Forum 2004, 27), and the American Association of State Colleges and Universities (2004) "challenges each college and university to assess and publicize its own students' levels of achievement." Others point out that "legislators are reluctant to give higher education greater autonomy until the legislators [have] better measures of performance" (Immerwahr 2002, 4). And accountability is a flashpoint for higher-education legislation, as legislators ask if colleges are being held adequately accountable for their performance and whether they are being punished if they don't perform ("How Can Colleges Prove They're Doing Their Jobs?" 2004).

All six of the regional accrediting institutions clearly identify student learning outcomes assessment as a critical component of a university. The Western Association of Schools and Colleges (Accrediting Commission for Senior Colleges and Universities 2001) states that an institution must demonstrate "that its graduates consistently achieve its stated levels of attainment" (21). The Southern Association of Colleges and Schools (Commission on Colleges 2001) mandates that colleges and universities develop a Quality Enhancement Plan that "is part of an ongoing planning and evaluation process" (8). The Northwest Commission on Colleges and Universities (2002) and the North Central Association (Higher Learning Commission 2003) state that an institution's processes for assessment must be clearly defined and that expected learning outcomes for degrees must be identified. Similarly, the New England Association of Schools and Colleges (Commission on Institutions of Higher Education 2005) states that an institution must "implement and support a systematic and broad-based approach to the assessment of student learning focused on educational improvement" (12). And the Middle States Commission on Higher Education (2002) "expects institutions to assess their overall effectiveness, with primary attention given to the assessment of student learning outcomes" (21).

"We all know that libraries are wonderful entities. . . . Why does it sometimes seem that administrators and other faculty don't recognize the critical importance of our services? . . . The reason that we are often overlooked . . . is that we don't show . . . in tangible ways, how our services benefit students" (Karp 2006). In 2006, the first library assessment conference in North America was held, "with more than 200 participants from 36 states and six countries outside North America . . . representing 109 libraries, associations, library systems, and vendors" (Hiller and Kyrillidou 2006). Topics covered at the conference ranged from survey and focus group research strategies to overall assessment strategies for the entire library enterprise. And many libraries are now participating in national research projects through StatsQual, a series of library assessment tools that have been developed by the Association of Research Libraries to assess a "library's effectiveness and contributions to teaching, learning, and research" (StatsQual 2005). The *Standards for Libraries in Higher Education* (ACRL 2004) clearly identify assessment as a priority for academic libraries as they differentiate between inputs (the raw materials of library program), outputs (quantification of the quantity of work completed), and outcomes—"the ways in which library users are changed as a result of their contact with the library's resources and programs." Libraries, like all other entities in the world of higher education, are increasingly utilizing numerous assessment strategies that improve student learning outcomes, turn students into library advocates, and lead to practical applications (Deuink and Seller 2006; Powell 2006).

THE LIBRARY AS A "PLACE"

Given the increasing popularity of distance education and online library resources, academic librarians are redefining the concept of library space in order to duplicate the physical characteristics of a library in an electronic environment that encourages the types of interaction and informal conversation that occur when students are learning together in the same physical place (Mellon and Kester 2004; Nicholson 2005). Gone are the days of the seminary library that was designed as a place to "collect, access, and preserve print collections" with prime space reserved for collection and processing (Freeman 2005). "Today library space is more than [a] repository but a place for instruction, to showcase unique holdings and exhibits, and to foster student collaboration and all forms of interaction, both with information sources in all formats as well as with librarians" (Albanese 2006). Today's library builds on the Alexandrian ideal of a library as a source of access to a "universal collection" of materials through which the institution is integrated "into the community it serves . . . providing a unique cultural center that inspires, supports, and contextualizes its users' engagement with scholarship" (Demas 2005).

Important components of the modern library include flexibility and adaptability to future needs, superior or hard-to-find technology, and provision of group or individual spaces conducive to study, research, and social activities (Martin 2006). The half billion dollars spent annually on new library construction and library renovations in the United States has increased academic library use (Engel and Antell 2004; Shill and Tonner 2004) as new construction has incorporated design elements that demonstrate a paradigm shift in academic libraries "away from a teaching culture and toward a culture of learning" and away from a "poorly balanced" focus on library operations and toward a more appropriate focus on space that supports "systematic knowledge of how students learn." Design elements such as lounge seating to support the social aspects of learning and quiet formal spaces to support "particularly serious sustained study" are routinely considered in order to ensure that library spaces are "responsive to the academic and social dimensions of study in ways that allow students to control them both" (Bennett 2005). These modifications reflect the dynamic needs of students and faculty as well as the increasing efforts of libraries to compete with the comforts of home and residence halls, where many students opt to spend their study and research time and where they successfully find most if not all of the information they need.

Technology has also forced libraries to redefine the concept of space so that measurements of its use go beyond traditional counts of circulation, reserves, in-house use, and reference transactions (Carlson 2001; Martell 2005). When librarians measure library use in more inclusive ways, it has been found that the availability of online resources has actually increased the demand for physical, face-to-face interactions (Albanese 2005), thus forcing librarians to act as both "technofiles and bibliofiles" (Kohl 2004). Adding to the changing face of libraries is the dramatic change in collections and equipment that occupy a library's space. Stacks of monographs are being shipped to off-site repositories, printed government documents are being replaced by CDs and Web sites, and e-journals are replacing their print counterparts (Kohl 2006). This provides more space for architecture that supports "learning impacts rather than traditional library services" (Seaman 2006).

Next to a library's Web presence, one of the biggest shifts in the notion of the library as a place has been the advent of the information commons, also known as the instruction commons, information center, or "destination library" (Samson and Erling 2005; Sarling 2005; Warnken 2004), which takes the library's online catalog and reference services outside the library to other areas of the college campus by designating "specific locations in which electronic workstations are maintained by qualified staff for the delivery of electronic resources for research and production" (Cowgill, Beam, and Wess 2001). In addition to helping students with research questions or technology issues, an information commons promotes the reference materials and services available to users (Wong and O'Shea 2004) by offering a reminder that the physical library exists for their use. It is both a marketing device and an outreach tool for services that enable the library to provide assistance to targeted groups such as disabled or international students, those who might otherwise not take advantage of library services (Blankenship and Leffler 2006; Kuchi, Mullen, and Tama-Bartels 2004), and those who prefer to use the physical academic library for research and instructional needs (Liu and Ye Yang 2004). The information commons also provides a way to help "patrons experience a seamless environment for contemplating, planning, researching, and bringing to finished product their academic, intellectual and . . . personal work" (Bailey and Tierney 2002). These nonlibrary spaces provide increased visibility and allow librarians to establish relationships with faculty and students on *their* terms, where and when it is convenient for them, in "places such as residence halls, study halls, and student unions" (Aamot and Hiller 2004).

Librarians are using other creative ways to reach library users and nonusers by expanding the reach of the library outside its walls to remote students through the use of electronic chat rooms and groups. For example, proactive librarians post information about library resources, answer questions, or just view postings to keep informed of students' needs and habits. These "virtual" library communications can provide students with the security of knowing that the library can and will continue to support them online and on-site. In addition, the library benefits from the free promotion of in-house and online services (Mathews 2006).

CONCLUSION

"There are only three ways in which human beings learn. They learn from experience and have been doing so since the emergence of the very first human beings. They learn by interaction with people who are wiser and more knowledgeable than they—teachers, rabbis, shamans, etc.—and have been doing so since human beings first started to communicate with words. Lastly but by no means least, they learn from interaction with the human record—those aggregations of texts, images, and symbols that are the collective memory of humankind" (Gorman 2005). Always at the heart of the university, libraries and librarians will continue "to create knowledge to improve organizational effectiveness, for both themselves and their institutions" (Townley 2001), as they pursue a primary focus on teaching and education (Feret and Marcinek 1999).

REFERENCES

Aamot, G., and S. Hiller. 2004. "Library Services in Non-Library Spaces." *ARL* 237: 9. Wilson Web. Available at: http://www.vnweb.hwwilsonweb.com. Accessed September 12, 2006.

Accrediting Commission for Senior Colleges and Universities. Western Association of Schools and Colleges. 2001. *Handbook of Accreditation.* Alameda, Calif.: Accrediting Commission for Senior Colleges and Universities, Western Association of Schools and Colleges.

Albanese, A. R. 2004. "The Reference Evolution." *Library Journal* 129 (19): 10–12. Wilson Web. Available at: http://www.vnweb.hwwilsonweb.com. Accessed September 7, 2006.

Albanese, A. R. 2005. "The Best Thing a Library Can Be Is Open." *Library Journal* 130 (15): 42–4. Wilson Web. Available at: http://www.vnweb.hwwilsonweb.com. Accessed September 17, 2006.

Albanese, A. R. 2006. "Breaking Ground." *Library Journal* 131(Design Supplement): 4–7. Wilson Web. Available at: http://www.vnweb.hwwilsonweb.com. Accessed September 6, 2006.

Alamneh, D. G., S. K. Hastings, and C. N. Hartman. 2002. "A Metadata Approach to Preservation of Digital Resources: The University of North Texas Libraries' Experience." *First Monday* 7 (8). Available at: http://www.firstmonday.org/issues/issue7_8/alemneh/index.html. Accessed September 19, 2006.

American Association of State Colleges and Universities. 2004. *Our Students' Best Work: A Framework for Accountability Worthy of Our Mission.* American Association of State Colleges and Universities, September 9, 2004. Available at: http://www.aacu.org/About/statements/assessment.cfm. Accessed November 24, 2006.

American Library Association. Recruitment Press Kit. 2002. *Library Profession Faces Shortage of Librarians.* Available at: http://www.ala.org. Accessed October 29, 2006.

Anderson, D. 2006. "Allocation of Costs for Electronic Products in Academic Library Consortia." *College and Research Libraries* 67 (2): 123–35. Wilson Web. Available at: http://www.vnweb.hwwilsonweb.com. Accessed December 7, 2006.

Anderson, S. 2002. "Digital Preservation: The Future of Electronic Resources" *Alki* 18 (2): 25–26. Wilson Web. Available at: http://www.vnweb.hwwilsonweb.com. Accessed September 12, 2006.

Antell, K. 2004. "Why Do College Students Use Public Libraries? A Phenomenological Study." *Reference and User Services Quarterly* 42 (3): 227–36. Wilson Web. Available at: http://www.vnweb.hwwilsonweb.com. Accessed September 12, 2006.

Association of College and Research Libraries. 2004. *Standards for Libraries in Higher Education.* Available at: http://www.ala.org/ala/acrl/acrlstandards/standardslibraries.htm. Accessed November 24, 2006.

Bailey, R., and B. Tierney, B. 2002. "Information Commons Redux: Concept, Evolution, and Transcending the Tragedy of the Commons." *Journal of Academic Librarianship* 28 (5): 277–86. Wilson Web. Available at: http://www.vnweb.hwwilsonweb.com. Accessed July 5, 2006.

Bajjaly, S. T. 2005. "Contemporary Recruitment in Traditional Libraries." *Journal of Education for Library and Information Science* 46 (1): 53–58. Wilson Web. Available at: http://www.vnweb.hwwilsonweb.com. Accessed September 14, 2006.

Bansal, A., V. Kumari, A. Kumar, and M. Singh, M. 2005. "Securing the Future of Information: Digitization and Preservation of Documents in E-Format." *DESIDOC Bulletin of Information Technology* 25 (1): 19–26. Wilson Web. Available at: http://www.vnweb.hwwilsonweb.com. Accessed September 19, 2006.

Bell, S. J. 2005. "Creating Community Online." *American Libraries* 36 (4): 68–71. Wilson Web. Available at: http://www.vnweb.hwwilsonweb.com. Accessed September 7, 2006.

Bennett, S. 2001. "The Golden Age of Libraries." *Journal of Academic Librarianship* 27 (4): 256–59. Wilson Web. Available at: http://www.vnweb.hwwilsonweb.com. Accessed September 19, 2006.

Bennett, S. 2005. "Righting the Balance." In *Library as Place: Rethinking Roles, Rethinking Spaces,* by Council on Library and Information Resources. Available at: http://www.clir.org/PUPBS/reports/pub129/bennett.html. Accessed November 1, 2006.

Besser, H. 2001. "Digital Preservation of Moving Image Material?" *The Moving Image.* Available at: http://www.gseis.ucla.edu/~howard/papers/amia-longevity.html. Accessed November 14, 2006.

Black, Steve. 2005. "Impact of Full Text on Print Journal Use at a Liberal Arts College." *Library Resources and Technical Services* 49 (1): 19–26. Wilson Web. Available at: http://www.vnweb.hwwilsonweb.com. Accessed November 1, 2006.

Blankenship, L., and J. Leffler. 2006. "Where Are the Reference Books?" *Colorado Libraries* 32 (2): 10–13. Wilson Web. Available at: http://www.vnweb.hwwilsonweb.com. Accessed September 12, 2006.

Block, M. 2003. "Dealing with Digital." *Library Journal* 128 (12): 40–43. Wilson Web. Available at: http://www.vnweb.hwwilsonweb.com. Accessed September 20, 2006.

Bonnette, A. 2004. "Mentoring Minority Librarians Up the Career Ladder." *Library Administration and Management* 18 (3): 134–39. Wilson Web. Available at: http://www.vnweb.hwwilsonweb.com. Accessed September 12, 2006.

Bothmer, A. J., and M. J. LaCroix. 2004. "Recruitment and Retention at the Creighton University Libraries." *Nebraska Library Association Quarterly* 35 (2): 11–13. Wilson Web. Available at: http://www.vnweb.hwwilsonweb.com. Accessed September 12, 2006.

Boyd-Brynes, M. K., and M. Rosenthal. 2005. "Remote Access Revisited: Disintermediation and Its Discontents." *Journal of Academic Librarianship* 31 (3): 216–24. Wilson Web. Available at: http://www.vnweb.hwwilsonweb.com. Accessed September 12, 2006.

Brady, E. E., S. K. McCord, and B. Galbraith. 2006. "Print versus Electronic Journal Use in Three Sci/Tech Disciplines: The Cultural Shift in Process." *College and Research Libraries* 67 (4): 354–63. Wilson Web. Available at: http://www.vnweb.hwwilsonweb.com. Accessed December 7, 2006.

Brantley, S., A. Armstrong, and K. M. Lewis. 2006. "Usability Testing of a Customizable Library Web Portal." *College and Research Libraries* 67 (2): 146–63. Wilson Web. Available at: http://www.vnweb.hwwilsonweb.com. Accessed December 7, 2006.

Business-Higher Education Forum. 2004. *Public Accountability for Student Learning in Higher Education*. Washington, D.C.: American Council on Higher Education.

Byers, F. R. 2003. *Information Technology: Care and Handling of CDs and DVDs: A Guide for Librarians and Archivists*. Washington D.C.: Council on Library and Information Resources. Available at: http://www.itl.nist.gov/div895/carefordisc/CDandDVD CareandHandlingGuide.pdf. Accessed November 11, 2006.

Carlson, S. 2001. "The Deserted Library: As Students Work Online, Reading Rooms Empty Out—Leading Some Campuses to Add Starbucks." *Chronicle of Higher Education*. Wilson Web. Available at: http://www.vnweb.hwwilsonweb.com. Accessed November 1, 2006.

Cervone, F. 2005. "Library Development: A Long-Term Strategy for Library Funding." *Library Administration and Management* 79 (1): 7–15. Wilson Web. Available at: http://www.vnweb.hwwilsonweb.com. Accessed September 19, 2006.

Cervone, F., and D. Brown. 2001. "Transforming Library Services to Support Distance Learning: Strategies Used by the DePaul University Libraries." *College and Research Libraries News* 62 (2): 147–49. Wilson Web. Available at: http://www.vnweb.hwwilsonweb.com. Accessed September 19, 2006.

Chapman, S. 2001. *What Is Digital Preservation?* Available at: http://www.oclc.org. Accessed September 20, 2006.

Choi, G. 2005. "Construction of a Digital Video Library: A Socio-Technical Pilot Study on College Students' Attitudes." *Journal of Academic Librarianship* 31 (5): 469–76. Wilson Web. Available at: http://www.vnweb.hwwilsonweb.com. Accessed September 12, 2006.

Coffman, S. 2001. "Distance Education and Virtual Reference: Where Are We Headed?" *Computers in Libraries* 21 (4): 20–25. Wilson Web. Available at: http://www.vnweb. hwwilsonweb.com. Accessed September 19, 2006.

Coleman, G. 2004. "E-Books and Academics: An Ongoing Experiment." *Feliciter* 50 (4): 124–29. Wilson Web. Available at: http://www.vnweb.hwwilsonweb.com. Accessed September 12, 2006.

Commission on Colleges. Southern Association of Colleges and Schools. 2001. *Principles of Accreditation: Foundations for Quality Enhancement.* Decatur, Ga.: Commission on Colleges Southern Association of Colleges and Schools. Available at: http://www. sacscoc.org. Accessed November 5, 2006.

Commission on Institutions of Higher Education. 2005. *Standards for Accreditation.* Bedford, Mass.: Commission on Institutions of Higher Education. Available at: http://www. neasc.org/cihe.htm. Accessed November 5, 2006.

Conway, P. 1999. *The Relevance of Preservation in a Digital World* (Section 5, Leaflet 5) [Technical leaflet]. Andover, Mass.: Northeast Document Conservation Center. Available at: http://www.nedcc.org/plam3/tleaf55.htm. Accessed September 20, 2006.

Cowgill, A., J. Beam, and L. Wess. 2001." Implementing an Information Commons in a University Library." *Journal of Academic Librarianship* 27 (6): 432–39. Wilson Web. Available at: http://www.vnweb.hwwilsonweb.com. Accessed September 14, 2006.

Crawford, Walt. 2002. "Copyright Out of Whack II: Control Run Amok." *EContent* 25 (10): 42–44. Wilson Web. Available at: http://www.vnweb.hwwilsonweb.com. Accessed September 19, 2006.

Crowley, B. 2004. "Just Another Field?" *Library Journal* 129 (18): 44–46. Wilson Web. Available at: http://www.vnweb.hwwilsonweb.com. Accessed September 14, 2006.

D'Andrea, P., and K. Martin. 2001. "Careful Considerations: Planning and Managing Digitization Projects." *Collection Management* 26 (3): 15–28. Wilson Web. Available at: http://www.vnweb.hwwilsonweb.com. Accessed September 7, 2006.

Dames, K. M. 2006. "The Copyright Landscape." *Online* 20 (5): 35–38. Wilson Web. Available at: http://www.vnweb.hwwilsonweb.com. Accessed September 12, 2006.

Davis, D. 2004. *Library Retirement—What We Can Expect.* Available at: http://www.ala. org. Accessed October 29, 2006.

De Stefano, P. 2001. "Selection for Digital Conversion in Academic Libraries." *College and Research Libraries* 62 (1): 58–69. Wilson Web. Available at: http://www.vnweb. hwwilsonweb.com. Accessed September 20, 2006.

Demas, S. 2005. "From the Ashes of Alexandria: What's Happening in the College Library?" In *Library as Place: Rethinking Roles, Rethinking Space,* by Council on Library and Information Resources. Available at: http://www.clir.org/PUBS/reports/pub129/demas. html. Accessed November 28, 2006.

Deuink, A., and M. Seller. 2006. "Students as Library Advocates: The Library Student Advisory Board at Pennsylvania State-Schuykill." *College and Research Libraries News* 67 (1): 18–21. Wilson Web. Available at: http://www.vnweb.hwwilsonweb.com. Accessed September 7, 2006.

Dewey, B. I. 2005. "Leadership and University Libraries: Building Scale at the Interface of Cultures." *Journal of Library Administration* 42 (1): 41–50. Wilson Web. Available at: http://www.vnweb.hwwilsonweb.com. Accessed November 1, 2006.

Dewey, B. I. 2006. "Fund-Raising for Large Public University Libraries: Margin for Excellence." *Library Administration and Management* 20 (1): 5–12. Wilson Web. Available at: http://www.vnweb.hwwilsonweb.com. Accessed September 19, 2006.

Distance Learning Section Guidelines Committee. 2004. "Guidelines for Distance Learning Library Services." *College and Research Libraries News* 64 (10): 604–11. Wilson Web. Available at: http://www.vnweb.hwwilsonweb.com. Accessed September 7, 2006.

Dohm, A. 2000. "Gauging the Labor Effects of Retiring Baby-Boomers." *Monthly Labor Review* 123 (7): 17–25. Wilson Web. Available at: http://www.vnweb.hwwilsonweb.com. Accessed October 9, 2006.

Dugan, R. E., and P. Hernon. 2002. "Outcomes Assessment: Not Synonymous with Inputs and Outputs." *Journal of Academic Librarianship* 28 (6): 376–80. Wilson Web. Available at: http://www.vnweb.hwwilsonweb.com. Accessed September 7, 2006.

Echavarria Robinson, T. 2006. "Information Literacy: Adapting to the Media Age." *Alki* 22 (1): 10–12. Wilson Web. Available at: http://www.vnweb.hwwilsonweb.com. Accessed January 16, 2007.

Edwards, E., and W. Fisher. 2003. "Trust, Teamwork, and Tokenism: Another Perspective on Diversity in Libraries." *Library Administration & Management* 17 (1): 21–27. Wilson Web. Available at: http://www.vnweb.hwwilsonweb.com. Accessed September 7, 2006.

Electronic Frontier Foundation. 2006. *Unintended Consequences: Seven Years under the DMCA*. Available at: http://www.eff.org. Accessed November 21, 2006.

Engel, D., and K. Antell. 2004. "The Life of the Mind: A Study of Faculty Spaces in Academic Libraries." *College and Research Libraries* 65 (1): 8–26. Wilson Web. Available at: http://www.vnweb.hwwilsonweb.com. Accessed September 7, 2006.

Exner, N. 2004. An Informal Examination of Technological Skills in Library Jobs. *North Carolina Libraries* [Online] 62 (2): 84–90. Wilson Web. Available at: http://www.vnweb.hwwilsonweb.com. Accessed June 26, 2006.

Feret, B., and M. Marcinek. 1999. *The Future of the Academic Library and the Academic Librarian: A Delphi Study*. Available at: http://www.iatul.org/conference/proceedings/vol109/papers/feret.htm. Accessed December 1, 2006.

Flecker, D. 2002. "Preserving Digital Periodicals." In *Building a National Strategy for Digital Preservation: Issues in Digital Media Archiving*. Washington, D.C.: Council on Library and Information Resources and Library of Congress. Available at: http://www.clir.org/PUBS/reports/pub106/periodicals.html. Accessed December 9, 2006.

Forys, M. 2004. "The University Library's Role in Developing Future Librarian Teachers: The University of Iowa Libraries' Experience." *College and Research Libraries News* 65 (2): 67–69. Wilson Web. Available at: http://www.vnweb.hwwilsonweb.com. Accessed September 7, 2006.

Freeman, G. T. 2005. *The Library as Place: Changes in Learning Patterns, Collections, Technology, and Use*. Available at: http://www.clir.org/PUBS/reports/pub129/freeman.html. Accessed September 7, 2006.

Friedlander, A. 2002. "Summary of Findings." In *Building a National Strategy for Digital Preservation: Issues in Digital Media Archiving*. Washington, D.C.: Council on Library and Information Resources and the Library of Congress. Available at: http://www.clir.org. Accessed September 19, 2006.

Galvin, J. 2005. "Alternative Strategies for Promoting Information Literacy." *Journal for Academic Librarianship* 31 (4): 352–57. Wilson Web. Available at: http://www.vnweb.hwwilsonweb.com. Accessed November 1, 2006.

Gandhi, S. 2003. "Academic Librarians and Distance Education: Challenges and Opportunities." *Reference and User Services Quarterly* 43 (2): 138–54. Wilson Web. Available at: http://www.vnweb.hwwilsonweb.com. Accessed November 1, 2006.

Gjelten, D., and T. Fishel. 2006. "Developing Leaders and Transforming Libraries: Leadership Institutes for Librarians." *College and Research Libraries News* 67 (7): 409–12. Wilson Web. Available at: http://www.vnweb.hwwilsonweb.com. Accessed September 7, 2006.

Goldstein, P. 2006. *The Future of Higher Education: A View from CHEMA.* Council of Higher Education Management Consultants. Available at: http://www.ala.org. Accessed October 29, 2006.

Gorman, M. 2005. *The Heart of the Academy: Remarks at the Opening of the Leatherby Libraries, Chapman University, Orange, California.* Available at: http://mg.csufresno.edu/papers/Leatherby.pdf. Accessed December 9, 2006.

Griffiths, J. M., and J. Latham. 2006. *IMLS Future of the Library Workforce Study Update.* Available at: http://www.libraryworkforce.org/tiki-index.php?page = Presentations. Accessed October 29, 2006.

Hall-Ellis, S. D. 2006. "Cataloging Electronic Resources and Metadata: Employers' Expectations as Reflected in American Libraries and AutoCAT, 2000–2005." *Journal of Education for Library and Information Science* 47 (1): 38–51. Wilson Web. Available at: http://www.vnweb.hwwilsonweb.com. Accessed September 14, 2006.

Hankins, R., M. Saunders, and P. Situ. 2003. "Diversity Initiatives vs. Residency Programs: Agents of Change?" *College and Research Libraries News* 64 (5): 308–10. Wilson Web. Available at: http://www.vnweb.hwwilsonweb.com. Accessed October 30, 2006.

Hernon, P., and N. Rossiter. 2006. "Emotional Intelligence: Which Traits Are Most Prized?" *College and Research Libraries* 67 (3): 260–75. Wilson Web. Available at: http://www.vnweb.hwwilsonweb.com. Accessed November 1, 2006.

Hernon, P. E., and C. Schwartz. 2006. "Leadership: A Unique Focus." *Journal of Academic Librarianship* 32 (1): 1–2. Wilson Web. Available at: http://www.vnweb.hwwilsonweb.com. Accessed September 7, 2006.

Higher Learning Commission: A Commission of the North Central Association. 2003. *Handbook of Accreditation.* Chicago: Higher Learning Commission. Available at: http://www.ncahigherlearningcommission.org. Accessed November 24, 2006.

Hiller, S. 2004. *User Needs Assessment to Support Collection Management Decisions.* Presentation at the ALA annual meeting, Orlando, Florida, June. Available at: http://www.libqual.org/documents/admin/ALA%20Orlando%202004%20Hiller.ppt. Accessed November 24, 2006.

Hiller, S., and M. Kyrillidou. 2006. *Library Assessment Conference.* Available at: http://www.arl.org/stats/laconf/index.html. Accessed November 24, 2006.

Hisle, W. L. 2002. "Top Issues Facing Academic Libraries: A Report of the Focus on the Future Task Force." *College and Research Libraries News* 63 (10): 1–3. Wilson Web. Available at: http://www.vnweb.hwwilsonweb.com. Accessed September 14, 2006.

"How Can Colleges Prove They're Doing Their Jobs?" 2004. *The Chronicle Review.* Available at: http://chronicle.com/errors.dir/noauthorization.php3? page = /weekly/v51/i02/02b00601.htm. Accessed November 24, 2006.

Hunter, I. 2006. "Digital Archives." *PNLA Quarterly* 70 (2): 7–9. Wilson Web. Available at: http://www.vnweb.hwwilsonweb.com. Accessed September 19, 2006.

Huwe, T. K. 2006. "From Librarian to Digital Communicator: Following the Media to New Organizational Roles." *Online* 30 (5): 21–26. Wilson Web. Available at: http://www.vnweb.hwwilsonweb.com. Accessed September 12, 2006.

Immerwahr, J. 2002. *Meeting the Competition: College and University Presidents, Faculty, and State Legislators View the New Competitive Academic Arena.* Providence, R.I.: Brown University, The Futures Project.

Islam, R. L., and L. A. Murno. 2006. "From Perceptions to Connections: Informing Literacy Program Planning in Academic Libraries through Examination of High School Library Media Center Curricula." *College and Research Libraries* 67 (6): 492–514. Wilson Web. Available at: http://www.vnweb.hwwilsonweb.com. Accessed September 7, 2006.

Jackson, M. E. 2004. "Looking Ahead! The Future of Portals." *Journal of Library Administration* 43 (1/2): 205–20. Wilson Web. Available at: http://www.vnweb.hwwilsonweb.com. Accessed September 19, 2006.

Jackson, P. A. 2006. "Plagiarism Instruction Online: Assessing Undergraduate Students' Ability to Avoid Plagiarism." *College and Research Libraries* 67 (5): 418–28. Available at: http://www.vnweb.hwwilsonweb.com. Accessed September 15, 2006.

Jerrido, M., L. Cotilla, and T. M. Whitehead. 2001. "Digitizing Collections: A Meshing of Minds, Methods, and Materials." *Collection Management* 26 (3): 3–13. Wilson Web. Available at: http://www.vnweb.hwwilsonweb.com. Accessed September 12, 2006.

Johns, C. 2003. "The Economics and Management of Digital Resources in a Multi-Campus, Multi-Library University: Introduction." *Collection Management* 28 (1/2): 33–35.

Julien, H. 2005. "Education for Information Literacy Instruction: A Global Perspective." *Journal of Education for Library and Information Science* 46 (3): 210–16. Wilson Web. Available at: http://www.vnweb.hwwilsonweb.com. Accessed September 14, 2006.

Kahl, C. M., and S. C. Williams. 2006. "Accessing Digital Libraries: A Study of ARL Members' Digital Projects." *Journal of Academic Librarianship* 32 (4): 364–69. Wilson Web. Available at: http://www.vnweb.hwwilsonweb.com. Accessed September 12, 2006.

Kaliper Advisory Committee. 2000. *Educating Library and Information Professionals for a New Century: The Kaliper Report.* Chicago: Association for Library and Information Science Education. Available at: http://www.alise.org/publications/kaliper.pdf. Accessed November 11, 2006.

Karp, R. 2006. "Seeing the Library in the Broader Context on Campus: Marketing Our Services." In *It's All about Student Learning,* ed. David R. Dowell and Gerard B. McCabe, 101–22. Westport, Conn.: Libraries Unlimited.

Kennedy, M. R. 2005. "Reformatting Preservation Departments: The Effect of Digitization on Workload and Staff." *College and Research Libraries* 66 (6): 543–51. Wilson Web. Available at: http://www.vnweb.hwwilsonweb.com. Accessed September 12, 2006.

Kibbee, J. 2006. "Librarians without Borders? Virtual Reference Service to Unaffiliated Users." *Journal of Academic Librarianship* 32 (5): 467–73. Wilson Web. Available at: http://www.vnweb.hwwilsonweb.com. Accessed December 7, 2006.

Kohl, D. 2006. "Where's the Library?" *Journal of Academic Librarianship* 32 (2): 117–18. Wilson Web. Available at: http://www.vnweb.hwwilsonweb.com. Accessed November 28, 2006.

Kohl, D. F. 2004. "From the Editor . . . The Paperless Society . . . Not Quite Yet." *Journal of Academic Librarianship* 30 (3): 177–78. Wilson Web. Available at: http://www.vnweb.hwwilsonweb.com. Accessed June, 26, 2006.

Kohl, D. F., and T. Sanville. 2006. "More Bang for the Buck: Increasing the Effectiveness of Library Expenditures through Cooperation." *Library Trends* 54 (3): 394–410. Wilson Web. Available at: http://www.vnweb.hwwilsonweb.com. Accessed September 20, 2006.

Kowalczyk, B., and P. Jackson. 2006. "Where Technology and Information Literacy Meet: Interactive Web-Based Tutorials for Life-Long Learning." *LITA National Forum.* Available at: http://www.lita.org/ala/litaevents/litanationalforum2005sanjoseca/74_Jackson_Kowalczyk.ppt. Accessed June 20, 2007.

Kuchi, T., L. B. Mullen, and S. Tama-Bartels. 2004. "Librarians without Borders: Reaching Out to Students at a Campus Center." *Reference and User Services Quarterly* 43 (4): 310–17. Wilson Web. Available at: http://www.vnweb.hwwilsonweb.com. Accessed September 7, 2006.

Kyrillidou, M., and M. Young. 2006. *ARL Annual Salary Survey 2005–2006*. Washington, D.C.: Association of Research Libraries. Available at: http://www.arl.org/stats/pubpdf/sso5.pdf. Accessed November 23, 2006.

Ladwig, J. P., and A. J. Sommese. 2005. "Using Cited Half-Life to Adjust Download Statistics." *College and Research Libraries* 66 (6): 527–42. Wilson Web. Available at: http://www.vnweb.hwwilsonweb.com. Accessed September 7, 2006.

Lance, K. C. 2005. "Racial and Ethnic Diversity of U.S. Library Workers," *American Libraries* 36 (5): 41–43. Wilson Web. Available at: http://www.vnweb.hwwilsonweb.com. Accessed September 7, 2006.

Lee, J., K. A. Hayden, and D. MacMillan. 2004. *"I Wouldn't Have Asked for Help if I Had to Go to the Library": Reference Services On Site*. Available at: http://www.istl.org/04-fall/article2.html. Accessed September 12, 2006.

Lefurgy, W. 2005. "Building Preservation Partnerships: The Library of Congress National Digital Information Infrastructure and Preservation Program." *Library Trends* 54 (1): 163–72. Wilson Web. Available at: http://www.vnweb.hwwilsonweb.com. Accessed September 19, 2006.

Letarte, K. M., M. R. Turvey, D. Borneman, and D. L. Adams. 2002. "Practitioner Perspective on Cataloging Education for Entry-Level Academic Librarian." *Library Resources and Technical Services* 46 (1): 11–22. Wilson Web. Available at: http://www.vnweb.hwwilsonweb.com. Accessed September 19, 2006.

Letha, M. M. 2006. "Library Portal: A Tool for Web-Enabled Information Services." *DESIDOC Bulletin of Information Technology* 26 (5): 11–16. Wilson Web. Available at: http://www.vnweb.hwwilsonweb.com. Accessed December 7, 2006.

Levrault, B. R. 2006. *Integration in Academic Reference Departments: From Print to Digital Resources*. Available at: http://www.haworthpress.com/web/AL. Accessed September 20, 2006.

Lindstrom, J., and D. D. Shonrock. 2006. "Faculty-Librarian Collaboration to Achieve Integration of Information Literacy." *Reference and User Services Quarterly* 46 (1): 18–23. Wilson Web. Available at: http://www.vnweb.hwwilsonweb.com. Accessed September 7, 2006.

Lipinski, T. A. 2003. "The Climate of Distance Education in the 21st Century: Understanding and Surviving the Changes Brought by the TEACH (Technology, Education, and Copyright Harmonization) Act of 2002." *Journal of Academic Librarianship* 29 (6): 362–74. Wilson Web. Available at: http://www.vnweb.hwwilsonweb.com. Accessed September 28, 2006.

Lippincott, J. 2005. "Net Generation Students and Libraries." In *Educating the Net Generation*, ed. Diana G. Oblinger and James L. Oblinger, 13.1–13.15. Educause. Available at: http://www.educause.edu. Accessed November 12, 2006.

Liu, Z., and Z. Ye Yang. 2004. "Factors Influencing Distance-Education Graduate Students' Use of Information Sources: A User Study." *Journal of Academic Librarianship* 30 (1): 24–35. Wilson Web. Available at: http://www.vnweb.hwwilsonweb.com. Accessed September 14, 2006.

Lougee, W. P. 2002. *Diffuse Libraries: Emergent Roles for the Research Library in the Digital Age*. Washington, D.C.: Council on Library and Information Resources. Available at: http://www.CLIR.org. Accessed November 20, 2006.

Lubans, J. 2006. "Balaam's Ass: Toward Proactive Leadership in Libraries." *Library Administration and Management* 20 (1): 30–33. Wilson Web. Available at: http://www.vnweb. hwwilsonweb.com. Accessed November 9, 2006.

Lyman, P. 2002. "E-Books and the Challenge of Preservation." In *Building a National Strategy for Digital Preservation: Issues in Digital Media Archiving*, ed. Deanna Marcum and Laura Campbell, 38–51. Washington, D.C.: Council on Library and Information Resources and Library of Congress.

Lynch, P., and K. R. Smith. 2001. "The Changing Nature of Work in Academic Libraries." *College and Research Libraries* 62 (5): 407–20. Wilson Web. Available at: http://www. vnweb.hwwilsonweb.com. Accessed September 19, 2006.

Maness, J. 2005. "The Users Are All Here, but Where Is the Library? Distant Library Services at Career Colleges." *Colorado Libraries* 31 (3): 19–20. Wilson Web. Available at: http://www.vnweb.hwwilsonweb.com. Accessed September 7, 2006.

Mariner, V., and L. Harrison. 2004. "Florida's 'Ask a Librarian' Service: A Collaborative Success." *Florida Libraries* 47 (1): 8–9. Wilson Web. Available at: http://www.vnweb. hwwilsonweb.com. Accessed September 7, 2006.

Martell, C. 2005. "The Ubiquitous User: A Reexamination of Carlson's Deserted Library." *Portal* 5 (4): 441–53. Proquest. Available at: http://www.umi.com. Accessed November 1, 2006.

Martin, D. C. 2006. "Straight Answers from David C. Martin." *American Libraries* 37 (4): 21. Wilson Web. Available at: http://www.vnweb.hwwilsonweb.com. Accessed November 28, 2006.

Mathews, B. S. 2006. "Do You Facebook? Networking with Students Online." *College and Research Libraries News* 67 (5): 306–7. Wilson Web. Available at: http://www.vnweb. hwwilsonweb.com. Accessed September 12, 2006.

Mayer, J., and L. J. Terrill. 2005. "Academic Librarians' Attitudes about Advanced-Subject Degrees." *College and Research Libraries* 66 (1): 59–73. Wilson Web. Available at: http://www.vnweb.hwwilsonweb.com. Accessed September 7, 2006.

Mayor, S. 2003. "Libraries Face Higher Costs for Academic Journals." *British Medical Journal Online* 32 (6): 840. Available at: http://bmj.bmjjournals.com. Accessed October 18, 2006.

McCabe, D. 2005. *Center for Academic Integrity Research*. Available at: http://www.acade micintegrity.org/cai_research.asp. Accessed November 12, 2006.

Mellon, C., and D. D. Kester. 2004. "Online Library Education Programs: Implications for Rural Students." *Journal of Education for Library and Information Science* 45 (3): 210–20. Wilson Web. Available at: http://www.vnweb.hwwilsonweb.com. Accessed June 26, 2006.

Middle States Commission on Higher Education. 2002. *Characteristics of Excellence in Higher Education*. Philadelphia: Middle States Commission on Higher Education.

Mizzy, D. 2003. "When Your Campus Is Alaska." *College and Research Libraries News* 64 (5): 316–17. Wilson Web. Available at: http://www.vnweb.hwwilsonweb.com. Accessed September 7, 2006.

Myers, S. 2004. "Ebooks and the Academic Library." *Kentucky Libraries* 68 (3): 4–7. Wilson Web. Available at: http://www.vnweb.hwwilsonweb.com. Accessed September 12, 2006.

Neal, J. G. 2006. "Raised by Wolves." *Library Journal* 131 (3): 42–44. Wilson Web. Available at: http://www.vnweb.hwwilsonweb.com. Accessed September 7, 2006.

Nicholson, S. 2005. "A Framework for Technology Selection in a Web-Based Distance Education Environment: Supporting Community-Building through Richer Interaction Opportunities." *Journal of Education for Library and Information Science* 46 (3): 217–33.

Wilson Web. Available at: http://www.vnweb.hwwilsonweb.com. Accessed June 30, 2006.

Northwest Commission on Colleges and Universities. 2002. *Accreditation Standards*. Redmond, Wash.: Northwest Commission on Colleges and Universities. Available at: http://www.nwccu.org/Standards%20and%20Policies/Standard%202/Standard%20Two.htm. Accessed November 24, 2006.

O'Brien Libutti, P., and C. Zlatos. 2006. "Learning to Lead and Manage Information Literacy Instruction." *Journal of Academic Librarianship* 32 (4): 441. Wilson Web. Available at: http://www.vnweb.hwwilsonweb.com. Accessed September 7, 2006.

"On Saving Sound: Report Assesses Standards and Best Practices in Moving from Analog to Digital." 2006. *Library of Congress Information Bulletin* 65 (5): 125. Wilson Web. Available at: http://www.vnweb.hwwilsonweb.com. Accessed September 19, 2006.

Ownes, D. 2006. "Findability Enabled." *Library Journal* 131 (13): 30–32. Wilson Web. Available at: http://www.vnweb.hwwilsonweb.com. Accessed September 20, 2006.

Parker, K. 2005. "Building the Digital Library of Appalachia." *Virginia Libraries* 51 (1): 29–32. Wilson Web. Available at: http://www.vnweb.hwwilsonweb.com. Accessed September 7, 2006.

Phillips, M. E. 2005. "What Should We Preserve? The Question for Heritage Libraries in a Digital World." *Library Trends* 54 (1): 57–71. Wilson Web. Available at: http://www.vnweb.hwwilsonweb.com. Accessed September 19, 2006.

Powell, R. R. 2006. "Evaluation Research: An Overview." *Library Trends* 55 (1): 102–20. Wilson Web. Available at: http://www.vnweb.hwwilsonweb.com. Accessed September 7, 2006.

Romano, F. 2002. "E-Books and the Challenge of Preservation." In *Building a National Strategy for Digital Preservation: Issues in Digital Media Archiving*, ed. Marcum Campbell and Laura Campbell, 23–27. Washington, D.C.: Council on Library and Information Resources and Library of Congress. http://www.clir.org/PUBS/reports/pub106/ebooks.html. Accessed December 9, 2006.

Samson, S., and O. Erling. 2005. "The Academic Library as a Full-Service Information Center." *Journal of Academic Librarianship* 31 (4): 347–51. Wilson Web. Available at: http://www.vnweb.hwwilsonweb.com. Accessed September 12, 2006.

Sarling, J. 2005. "Net Connect: Denver Reengineers." *Library Journal* 12: 14. Wilson Web. Available at: http://www.vnweb.hwwilsonweb.com. Accessed June 26, 2006.

Schuler, J. A. 2003. "Distance Education, Copyrights Rights, and the New TEACH Act." *Journal of Academic Librarianship* 29 (1): 49–51. Wilson Web. Available at: http://www.vnweb.hwwilsonweb.com. Accessed September 19, 2006.

Seaman, S. 2006. "The Library as Learning Environment: Space Planning in an Academic Library." *Colorado Libraries* 32 (1): 5–7. Wilson Web. Available at: http://www.vnweb.hwwilsonweb.com. Accessed December 1, 2006.

Shill, H. B., and S. Tonner. 2004. "Does the Building Still Matter? Usage Patterns in New, Expanded, and Renovated Libraries." *College and Research Libraries* 62 (2): 123–50. Available at: http://www.ala.org. Accessed November 2, 2006.

Shincovich, A. C. 2004. "Copyright Issues and the Creation of a Digital Resource: Artists' Books Collection at the Frick Fine Arts Library, University of Pittsburgh." *Art Documentation* 23 (2): 8–13. Wilson Web. Available at: http://www.vnweb.hwwilsonweb.com. Accessed September 20, 2006.

Shirky, C. 2003. "Social Software and the Politics of Groups." *Networks, Economics, and Culture*. Available at: http://www.shirky.com/writing/group_politics.html. Accessed November 24, 2006.

Siebenberg, T. R., B. Galbraith, and E. E. Brady. 2004. "Print versus Electronic Journal Use in Three Sci/Tech Disciplines: What's Going on Here?" *College and Research Libraries* 65 (5): 427–38. Wilson Web. Available at: http://www.vnweb.hwwilsonweb.com. Accessed September 12, 2006.

Sittler, R. L. 2005. "Distance Education and Computer-Based Services: The Opportunities and Challenges for Small Academic Libraries." *Bookmobiles and Outreach Services* 8 (1): 23–35. Wilson Web. Available at: http://www.vnweb.hwwilsonweb.com. Accessed September 19, 2006.

Smith, M. 2005. "Exploring Variety in Digital Collections and the Implications for Digital Preservation." *Library Trends* 54 (1): 6–15. Wilson Web. Available at: http://www.vnweb.hwwilsonweb.com. Accessed September 19, 2006.

Springer, C. 2005. "Library Profile: The Personal and Professional Impact of the ACRL's Information Literacy Immersion Institute." *Arkansas Libraries* 62 (4): 6–8. Wilson Web. Available at: http://www.vnweb.hwwilsonweb.com. Accessed September 7, 2006.

Starmer, M. E. 2004. "Benefits of Practicum Students in Preservation: The Value of the Experience to the Department, Students, and Field." *Collection Management* 29 (2): 33–40. Available at: http://www.haworthpress.com. Accessed September 7, 2006.

StatsQual. 2005. Available at: http://www.statsqual.org. Accessed November 24, 2006.

Stemper, J., and S. Barribeau. 2006. "Perpetual Access to Electronic Journals: A Survey of One Academic Research Library's Licenses." *Library Resources and Technical Services* 50 (2): 91–109. Wilson Web. Available at: http://www.vnweb.hwwilsonweb.com. Accessed August 17, 2006.

Stephens, D., and K. Russell. 2004. "Organizational Development, Leadership, Change, and the Future of Libraries." *Library Trends* 53 (1): 238–57. Wilson Web. Available at: http://www.vnweb.hwwilsonweb.com. Accessed September 7, 2006.

Stephens, M. 2006. "The Promise of Web 2.0." *American Libraries* 37 (9): 32. Wilson Web. Available at: http://www.vnweb.hwwilsonweb.com. Accessed November 24, 2006.

Stoffle, C. J., B. Allen, D. Morden, and K. Maloney. 2003. *Portal: Libraries and the Academy* 3 (3): 363. Proquest. Available at: http://proquest.umi.com. Accessed November 13, 2006.

Tempelman-Kluit, N. 2006. "Multimedia Learning Theories and Online Instruction." *College and Research Libraries* 67 (4): 364–69. Wilson Web. Available at: http://www.vnweb.hwwilsonweb.com. Accessed December 7, 2006.

Tenopir, C. 2003. "Use and Users of Electronic Library Resources: An Overview and Analysis of Recent Research Studies." In *CLIR Executive Summary*. Available at: http://www.clir.org. Accessed November 1, 2006.

Thibodeau, K. 2002. "Overview of Technological Approaches to Digital Preservation and Challenges in Coming Years." In *Institutes for Information Science. The State of Digital Preservation: An International Perspective. Conference Proceedings*, by Council on Library and Information Resources, 1–31. Washington, D.C.: Council on Library and Information Resources. Available at: http://www.clir.org. Accessed September 20, 2006.

Thomas, J. 2004. "Digital Video, the Final Frontier." *Library Journal* [Net Connect 8–10]. Wilson Web. Available at: http://www.vnweb.hwwilsonweb.com. Accessed September 14, 2006.

Thompson, H. 2002. "The Library's Role in Distance Education: Survey Results from ACRL's 2000 Academic Library Trends and Statistics." *College and Research Libraries News* 36 (5): 338–40. Wilson Web. Available at: http://www.vnweb.hwwilsonweb.com. Accessed September 19, 2006.

Townley, C. T. 2001. "Knowledge Management and Academic Libraries." *College and Research Libraries* 62 (1): 44–55.

Trejo, N., and E. Norlin. 2001. "Recruitment and Retention Project Team: Opportunities and Outcomes." *College and Research Libraries News* 62 (5): 528–31. Wilson Web. Available at: http://www.vnweb.hwwilsonweb.com. Accessed September 14, 2006.

Turvey, M. R. 2002. "Cataloging or Knowledge Management: Perspectives of Library Educators on Cataloging Education for Entry-Level Academic Librarians." *Cataloging and Classification Quarterly* 34 (1/2): 165–87.

Tyser, D. 2006. *Copyright Licenses and Assignments. Bitlaw: A Resource on Technology Law.* Available at: http://www.bitlaw.com/copyright/license.html. Accessed November 14, 2006.

Vaughan, J. 2004. "Policies Governing Use of Computing Technology in Academic Libraries." *Information Technology and Libraries* 23 (4): 153–67. Wilson Web. Available at: http://www.vnweb.hwwilsonweb.com. Accessed September 12, 2006.

Wan, G. 2006. "Visualizations for Digital Libraries." *Information Technologies and Libraries* 25 (2): 88–94. Wilson Web. Available at: http://www.vnweb.hwwilsonweb.com. Accessed September 20, 2006.

Warnken, P. 2004. "New Technologies and Constant Change: Managing the Process." *Journal of Academic Librarianship* 30 (4): 322–27. Wilson Web. Available at: http://www.vnweb.hwwilsonweb.com. Accessed September 12, 2006.

Webb, P. 2006. "Meeting the Needs of Distance Education Students: Creating an Online-Only Library Instruction Course." *College and Research Libraries News* 67 (9): 548–50. Wilson Web. Available at: http://www.vnweb.hwwilsonweb.com. Accessed September 7, 2006.

Westbrook, L. 2006. "Virtual Reference Training: The Second Generation." *College and Research Libraries* 67 (3): 249–59. Wilson Web. Available at: http://www.vnweb.hwwilsonweb.com. Accessed December 7, 2006.

Wiggins, R. 2001. "Digital Preservation: Paradox and Promise." *Library Journal Net Connect,* 12–15. Wilson Web. Available at: http://www.vnweb.hwwilsonweb.com. Accessed September 7, 2006.

Wilder, S. 1996. "Generational Change and the Niche for Librarians." *Journal of Academic Librarianship* 22: 385–86. Wilson Web. Available at: http://www.vnweb.hwwilsonweb.com. Accessed September 7, 2006.

Winston, M. D., and T. Hoffman. 2005. "Project Management in Libraries." *Journal of Library Administration* 42 (1): 51–61. Wilson Web. Available at: http://www.vnweb.hwwilsonweb.com. Accessed November 21, 2006.

Wittenborg, K., C. Ferguson, and M. A. Keller. 2003. *Reflecting on Leadership.* Available at: http://www.clir.org. Accessed November 21, 2006.

Wong, G., D. Chan, and S. Chu. 2006. "Assessing the Enduring Impact of Library Instruction Programs." *Journal of Academic Librarianship* 32 (4): 384–95. Wilson Web. Available at: http://www.vnweb.hwwilsonweb.com. Accessed January 16, 2007.

Wong, S., and A. O'Shea. 2004. "Librarians Have Left the Building: Ask Us HERE! At Simon Fraser University." *Feliciter* 50 (3): 90–92. Wilson Web. Available at: http://www.vnweb.hwwilsonweb.com. Accessed September 12, 2006.

Yang, Z. Y. L. 2005. "Distance Education Librarians in the U.S. ARL Libraries and Library Services Provided to Their Distance Users." *Journal of Academic Librarianship* 31 (2): 92–97. Wilson Web. Available at: http://www.vnweb.hwwilsonweb.com. Accessed September 7, 2006.

Young, A. P., P. Hernon, and R. R. Powell. 2006. "Attributes of Academic Library Leadership: An Exploratory Study of Some Gen-Xers." *Journal of Academic Librarianship* 32 (5): 489–502. Wilson Web. Available at: http://www.vnweb.hwwilsonweb.com. Accessed December 7, 2006.

Young, M., and M. Kyrillidou. 2005. *ARL Preservation Statistics 2003–2004: A Compilation of Statistics from the Members of the Association of Research Libraries*. Washington, D.C.: Association of Research Libraries.

Zanish-Belcher, T., M. Christian, and C. Daly. 2001. *The Age of the Electronic Document: The Documenting Challenge of Academic Archives*. Available at: http://www.haworth press.com. Accessed September 19, 2006.

INDEX

DAVID P. BUNNELL is the director of library and media services at Griffin Technical College in Griffin, Georgia. He holds an undergraduate degree in computer science from Urbana University (Ohio), a master of arts in theological studies from United Theological Seminary (Ohio), and a master of science in library science from the University of Kentucky and is a doctoral candidate in higher education at the University of Georgia.

SUSAN M. CAMPBELL is the library director at York College of Pennsylvania. Previously, she was science librarian at Colgate University and urban documents librarian at the University of Florida. Active in the Association of College and Research Libraries, College Libraries Section, Pennsylvania Library Association, and PALCI, her expertise includes academic library buildings, information literacy, and mentoring.

EDWARD M. CORRADO is systems librarian at The College of New Jersey in Ewing, where he is responsible for the integrated library system and other library technology. Corrado has presented at various library-oriented conferences and has authored articles for issues of *Science and Technology Librarianship* and *Computers in Libraries*.

CHRISTOPHER COX is assistant director of libraries at the University of Wisconsin, Eau Claire. His work has appeared in *College and Research Libraries News* and *portal: Libraries and the Academy*. He serves as editor of *Internet Reference Services Quarterly* and is a frequent reviewer for *Choice Magazine*.

MICHAEL A. CRUMPTON is currently the assistant director for administrative services for the University Libraries at the University of North Carolina–Greensboro. He was previously director of library services at Wake Technical Community College in Raleigh, North Carolina, and served as president of the North Carolina Community College Learning Resources Association as well as an adjunct instructor at Central Carolina Community College. He obtained his MLS from the University of Kentucky. Prior to library work, Crumpton had 22 years in retail management, which included opening multiple stores.

CHRISTINE DETTLAFF manages the Learning Resources Center and Academic Technology Services at Redlands Community College in El Reno, Oklahoma. She has been director of the Learning Resources Center since 2003. Before coming to Redlands, she worked in public libraries as a children's and young adult librarian.

PATRICIA HERNAS is access and outreach librarian at Mission College in Santa Clara, California. She has worked in a variety of library settings, including K–12 schools in Washington State, internationally for the Department of Defense Dependents School System, and in special libraries for high-technology companies.

CAROL P. JOHNSON is the director of libraries, media services, and archives at the College of St. Catherine in Minnesota. She received her BA degree from

ABOUT THE EDITOR AND CONTRIBUTORS

JANET MCNEIL HURLBERT is associate dean and director of libraries services at Lycoming College, Williamsport, Pennsylvania. Her BA and MLS degrees are from the University of Denver. Prior experience includes positions at Iowa State University and Virginia Commonwealth University. She has authored book chapters and journal articles in professional and teaching journals and presented at various conferences, including the Annual Lilly Conference, Miami University.

***

AMY E. BADERTSCHER holds a BA in history from Lake Forest College and a GSLIS 1 and MS in library and information science from Simmons. She is the director of collection services at Kenyon College overseeing a joint technical services project with Denison University. Previously, she worked in a traditional corporate library and a nontraditional research group for a consulting firm.

SHEILA BECK is an assistant professor at Queensborough Community College, part of the City University of New York. She has master's degrees in education and counseling as well as an MLS. Currently, she is responsible for acquisitions and collection development and has written numerous encyclopedia articles.

BARBARA BONOUS-SMIT is assistant professor and the serials and interlibrary loan librarian at Queensborough Community College, City University of New York. Her degrees include PhD, New York University; MLS, Long Island University; and MM and BM, Boston University. An executive board member of the ACRL/NY, she is currently vice chair/chair elect of its New York City section.

Hunter College, City College of New York, her MS in library science from Drexel University, and an MA in industrial relations from the University of Minnesota.

TIMOTHY KARAS is director of library services at Mission College in Santa Clara, California. Previously, he was a faculty member at the College of San Mateo. Karas is active in the community serving as a library commissioner for the City of San Jose since 2001. Previous to working in academia, he worked as a librarian for the City of Palo Alto and Redwood City.

RASHELLE KARP is associate academic vice president, Clarion University of Pennsylvania. Dr. Karp has worked as an academic library dean, a children's librarian, and a special librarian, in addition to teaching at Clarion University in the Department of Library Science. She has published extensively in the fields of collection development, special librarianship, public librarianship, student retention, and disabilities services.

ANN M. KENNE is the head of special collections at the Shaughnessy-Frey Library, the University of St. Thomas, in Minnesota. She received both her BS in political science and her MA in library and information science from the University of Iowa.

KIRSTEN LEONARD is the electronic resources/government documents librarian at Indiana University Kokomo. Previously, she worked at Ball State University and Kettering University after receiving her MLIS from Wayne State University. She is interested in technological solutions to information management and has a background in programming and systems management.

SALLY LEVAN has taught at Gannon University, Erie, Pennsylvania, for over 30 years. She started and directed the Writing Center at Gannon as well as the Northwestern Pennsylvania Writing Project, the ESL Program, and the ESL Certificate Program. Dr. Levan holds a PhD in English from Indiana University of Pennsylvania, has presented and conducted professional development programs throughout the United States and internationally, and has published numerous articles.

EMMETT LOMBARD is electronic services librarian at Gannon University and also teaches in the Freshman Writing Program. He draws on his library background in the classroom and teaching background in the library. This arrangement has created favorable opportunities and results for both him and for Gannon.

JASON MARTIN received his BA and MLS from the University of South Florida. He is employed as a librarian at the University of Central Florida, where he is pursuing his EdD in educational leadership. He, for some reason, likes to wake up early in the morning and go running.

ELEANOR MITCHELL became director of library services at Dickinson College in August 2005. Prior to that, she was head of the Undergraduate Library at

UCLA and director of the Information Literacy Initiative there from its founding. She is coeditor of *Reference Services Review*. Mitchell has worked in libraries at Vassar College, Arizona State University, and Westchester Community College and at *Newsweek* magazine.

SUSAN NAYLOR is a graduate student in the library science master's degree program at Clarion University of Pennsylvania. She has a master's of education with a specialization in school libraries from Mansfield University of Pennsylvania and is former librarian for the New York State Office Fire Prevention and Control Training Academy.

SUSAN SWORDS STEFFEN is the director of the library at Elmhurst College in Elmhurst, Illinois. With over 30 years of experience in college libraries, she has spoken and written extensively about library innovation and has taught at the Graduate School of Library and Information Science at Dominican University as an adjunct faculty member.

ARTHUR H. STERNGOLD is an associate professor of business administration at Lycoming College. He earned a BA from Princeton University, an MBA from Northwestern University, and a PhD from Pennsylvania State University. Sterngold has written articles on plagiarism and information literacy appearing in *Change Magazine* and the *Journal of Marketing Education*. Before pursuing an academic career, he worked in advertising and government and has served as a consultant to several business and nonprofit organizations.

LARRY NASH WHITE is assistant professor and MLS program director at East Carolina University's Department of Library Science and Instructional Technology. Previously, Dr. White worked as an administrator in retail management and in public and academic libraries. He is an internationally invited speaker and presenter and consults with libraries and nonprofit organizations. Dr. White has published in the areas of performance assessment, competitive response, and financial management of libraries and was named a 2007 "Mover and Shaker" by *Library Journal*.